CHINA'S DANCE WITH THE FOREIGN DEVILS

Foreign Companies and the Industrial Development of China

DICK K. NANTO

With contributions from Andy Van Vleck

CHINA'S DANCE WITH THE FOREIGN DEVILS
Foreign Companies and the Industrial Development of China

iUniverse books may be ordered through booksellers or by contacting:

iUniverse
1663 Liberty Drive
Bloomington, IN 47403
www.iuniverse.com
1-800-Authors (1-800-288-4677)

ISBN: 978-1-4917-9731-0 (sc)
ISBN: 978-1-4917-9732-7 (e)

Library of Congress Control Number: 2016909565

Print information available on the last page.

iUniverse rev. date: 07/13/2016

To Masako, Tom and Frances Nanto

Contents

LIST OF ILLUSTRATIONS

LIST OF TABLES

PREFACE

As an economist with the Congressional Research Service, Dr. Dick K. Nanto provided economic analysis and reports to the U.S. Congress on China, Japan and the Koreas. He has published widely on U.S. economic relations with Asia and economic conditions there. He also has testified before Congressional committees on economic issues essential to U.S. national interests. His Doctoral Degree in economics and Masters in national security studies enable him to take a broad view of Chinese industrial development and the role of foreign investment there.

For much of the past two centuries, China has resented the presence of foreigners in its land. Often referred to as foreign devils, Europeans, Americans and Japanese have at various times humiliated, rescued or tried to subjugate the Chinese people. Since 1978, however, China has invited in the foreign devils, first with measured apprehension and then with restrained optimism. Over the ensuing decades, direct investment by foreign companies became a driver of change that has brought the People's Republic of China into the modern economic world. Relations between Beijing and foreign companies, including those from the Chinese diaspora in Hong Kong, Taiwan and Singapore, began as a cautious dance—at arm's length and with both sides wary of each other. The relationship gradually turned into a warm embrace, particularly at the local level, and generated heightened competition throughout the Chinese economy as companies and communities attempted to emulate the production methods and products of the foreigners. Now the PRC has become the second largest economy in the world and is using its economic wherewithal to develop a stronger and more assertive military and national champion companies of its own. Now, foreign companies—no longer feared as devils—are being squeezed by both the Chinese government and by a playing field tilted in favor of domestic Chinese competitors.

This study is intended to help anyone interested in the rise of China, in particular businesses, policymakers and students of the Chinese economy, to understand the role and experience of foreign investors and the business climate in the PRC and to shed light on the motivation behind many of Beijing's policies that affect foreign companies operating there.

This book would not have been possible without the support of many people and organizations. I greatly appreciate the Kearney Alliance and Hinrich Foundation for travel grants that enabled me to conduct research in China, Hong Kong, Taiwan and Japan. I also benefitted greatly from discussions with Merle Hinrichs and John Walsh and for their insights into business. I additionally express thanks to Taiwan's Ministry of Foreign Affairs for granting me a Taiwan Fellowship and to the National Central University for sponsoring me during a three-month stay in Taipei. I was able to travel numerous times to the PRC under the auspices of the U.S.-Asia Institute. These trips were invaluable in gaining first-hand knowledge of China during the last quarter century. I also appreciate the Congressional Research Service for hosting me as a Visiting Scholar for two years after my retirement.

This book also benefitted greatly from contributions by Andy Van Vleck and for information he acquired through his work in China, Hong Kong and Europe. I also am indebted to Dr. Thomas Lum who reviewed the manuscript and made helpful suggestions and to Michelle Harlan for editorial assistance. Finally, I am deeply indebted to my wife Masako for her patience and support as I worked on the manuscript.

All opinions are my own and should not be attributed to any of the organizations that provided support or to the Congressional Research Service, The Library of Congress or U.S. government.

ABBREVIATIONS

Alcan	Aluminium Company of Canada
AMSC	American Superconductor Corporation
AVIC	Aviation Industry Corporation of China
BIT	bilateral investment treaty
BTF	build-to-forecast
BTO	build-to-order
CATIC	China National Aero-Technology Import and Export Corporation
CCB	China Construction Bank
CDL	IBM China Development Lab
CFIUS	Committee on Foreign Investment in the United States
Chinalco	Aluminum Corporation of China
CIC	China Investment Corporation
CICC	China International Capital Corp.
CITIC	China International Trust and Investment Corporation
CNOOC	China National Offshore Oil Corporation
CNR	China Northern Railway
COFCO	China National Cereals, Oils and Foodstuffs Corporation
COMAC	Commercial Aircraft Corporation of China Ltd.
Cosco	China Ocean Shipping Company
CRL	IBM China Research Laboratory
CSR	China Southern Railway
DPP	Democratic Progressive Party

ECFA	Economic Cooperation Framework Agreement
Fab	Semiconductor fabricator
FAW	First Automotive Works Corp.
FCPA	Foreign Corrupt Practices Act
FDI	Foreign Direct Investment
FFE	foreign-funded enterprises
FIE	foreign invested enterprise
FINSA	Foreign Investment and National Security Act of 2007
FIRB	Foreign Investment Review Board
FLA	Fair Labor Association
GE	General Electric
GM	General Motors
GPA	Government Procurement Agreement
GPL	Government Procurement Law
HNTE	High/New Technology Enterprise Incentive
IC	integrated circuit
IPR	Intellectual Property Right
JV	joint venture
LCD	liquid-crystal display
LED	light-emitting diode
NDRC	National Development and Reform Commission
OECD	Organization for Economic Co-operation and Development
OPEC	Organization of the Petroleum Exporting Countries
PCT	Patent Cooperation Treaty
PLA	People's Liberation Army
PPP	purchasing power parity
PRC	People's Republic of China
R&D	Research and Development
RMB	renminbi
SAFE	State Administration of Foreign Exchange

SAIC	Shanghai Automotive Industrial Corporation
SASAC	State-Owned Assets Supervision and Administration Commission
SEZ	Special Economic Zone
Sinopec	China Petrochemical Corporation
SMIC	Semiconductor Manufacturing International Corporation
SOE	state-owned enterprise
TPPA	Trans-Pacific Partnership Agreement
TRIMS	Agreement on Trade-Related Investment Measures
TRIPS	Agreement on Trade-Related Aspects of Intellectual Property Rights
TSMC	Taiwan Semiconductor Manufacturing Corp.
UMC	United Microelectronics Corp.
VAT	value-added tax
WOFE	wholly-owned foreign enterprise

CHAPTER I.   THE NEW CHINA

In 2010, as I walked through the Beijing International Airport, I marveled at its high undulating ceiling, polished stone floors, and all the accoutrements of a first class gateway to a country. This Terminal 3, built in time for the 2008 Beijing Olympics, was the second largest on earth and in 2009 had been ranked by *Condé Nast Traveler* magazine as the World's Best Airport. The Chinese government official with me said that earlier in the year she had escorted Henry Kissinger during his visit to Beijing. When Kissinger saw the new airport, he remarked that it made JFK airport in New York City "look like shit."

This experience contrasted sharply with the dour December day in 1988 when I first arrived at the old Beijing international airport. That terminal, built when Beijing was still Peking, fit the model of socialist construction. It was dark, dingy, and had a luggage carousel so antiquated that it might have served Mao himself. When I went to claim my baggage, imagine my surprise when I saw a half dozen Santa Clauses interspersed among the drably clad Chinese leaning around the carousel waiting for their bags. The Santas with their red and white costumes, so bright and redolent of Christmas in America, seemed incongruent with their surroundings. It turned out that they were from the American Midwest and had come to the People's Republic of China (PRC) to spread some cheer and introduce the Chinese people to the spirit of giving. Little did they know that over the next quarter century, foreigners would be giving China much more than candy canes. Western and Asian companies would provide China with the keys to the kingdom—the keys to generating wealth in the 21st century.

How this happened is not easy to decipher, but the results are apparent. Just about everywhere in the PRC, the story is the same. The China of old has emerged from its convulsive past and is racing to reclaim its position as a leading country of the world. In the mid-1980s, China was a nation of unproductive state-owned industries, antiquated Soviet-based technology, grimy streets and intrusive state control. During my 1988 visit to China, on the first morning when I walked out of the hotel to greet the communist version of the Middle Kingdom, the initial sight I saw was a wagonload of coal being pulled by a horse. The coal was for the coal-burning furnaces and stoves being used to heat Beijing. The air was thick with smog, and the collar on my white shirt never stayed white for long. Our group leader warned us not to go out jogging, not to drink tap water and to avoid breathing polluted air.

At that time, U.S. dollars could not be converted into yuan, and foreign visitors had to trade their currency for Chinese foreign exchange certificates for use in approved shops such as the Friendship Stores. The boulevard passing Tiananmen Square had lanes exclusively for bicycles that were jammed with hordes of riders bundled up and braced for the cold winter winds. Beijing's leading retail establishment, Department Store No. I, had a display of coal stove implements, including a bellows, in the middle of its first floor where one would expect to find luxury cosmetics and high fashion accessories. There were virtually no neon signs. At night, the streets were dark save for rigidly placed street lamps and an occasional restaurant with a string of Christmas tree-style lights hung in front to attract potential customers. Except for a few Russian model cars and Volkswagen Santanas as well as numerous faux Western brand-name toiletries, there was little evidence of foreign products. The country had hardly been touched by the economic revolutions occurring just outside its borders that turned Japan, Taiwan and South Korea into export powerhouses. In the previous year (1987), China had exported only $35 billion in merchandise with a third of that in textiles and clothing. By contrast, South Korea had exported $47 billion, Taiwan $54 billion, and Japan $255 billion.[2]

By 1988, China was a decade into its campaign of reform and opening that was to come to a screeching halt following the 1989 Tiananmen Square incident. Deng Xiaoping was yet to take his 1992 Southern tour and to declare that "to get rich is glorious." Planning was yet to commence on building Pudong, the glitzy financial center of Shanghai, and the country was just beginning to see the benefits of foreign direct investment (FDI) and foreign invested enterprises (FIEs), particularly from Hong Kong and Taiwan. Little did Beijing realize that over the next quarter century, foreign companies would become the source of critical technology, would be instrumental in training workers to operate in the modern business world, would transfer valuable managerial skills, and would provide the gateway into global supply chains. Foreign invested enterprises would account for about half of all China's exports and a fifth of industrial assets. Without them China could not have accumulated more than $3 trillion in foreign exchange reserves nor could the country have built the modern financial and logistical infrastructure that underpins much of its entry into the world of business in the 21st century.

This is not to demean the efforts of 1.4 billion Chinese people and the ability of the government, at all levels, to create incentives and both to unleash and to guide the economic forces that lifted hundreds of millions of its people out of poverty. The rise of China cannot be attributed to a single cause but to a chain reaction ignited by the policy of reform and opening of 1978. The development process was not linear and without stumbling, nor was it without hesitantly feeling the stones while crossing the streams leading to modernization. Beijing may have allowed foreign companies to enter the market and build factories, but it was Chinese companies that emulated them and Chinese workers who toiled the long hours sewing garments, assembling consumer electronics, or gluing athletic shoes who made the factories work. Labor in China was cheap, and there seemed to be an inexhaustible supply of workers dexterous and willing to toil—often in terrible working conditions—until the orders were filled. Still, without the demand from exporters and the technology and product designs brought by foreigners, long hours of tedious labor would have brought the Chinese workers no more than the meager subsistence that existed during their Cultural Revolution.

Credit also goes to Beijing for tearing down roadblocks to progress and putting policies in place that unleashed competitive forces in the domestic economy. Beijing had and still does have an active industrial policy, as does each province, village and township. As will be shown in this study, Beijing's policies were in response to economic successes at the local level and were largely reactive not proactive. There were no genius economic planners at the top to guide the transformation of the economy but Communist Party leaders responding to pressures from below, steeped in the socialist tradition of trying to build things bigger, and who were protecting their elite positions.

By and large, at the provincial and local level, the primary policy has been to generate economic growth. At the national level, the government has attempted both to create winning companies and to rid the economy of unprofitable and inefficient enterprises. More importantly, government policy gradually allowed companies to compete freely in most markets. A China bereft of capitalism and entrepreneurship was transformed over the course of one generation to a country with highly competitive major markets and hundreds of thousands of entrepreneurs.

In the fall of 2015, a slowdown in the Chinese economy and uncertainty about how Beijing would respond triggered a drop in world stock market values. Trillions of dollars were lost in just a few days as investors feared contagion from shrinking values on Chinese stock markets and that increased competition from Chinese surplus production could be dumped on global markets. Beijing's response to the market turmoil and economic slowdown proved to be clumsy, particularly when it devalued its currency. The policies taken to stabilize its stock market and to reignite growth raised doubts about whether the Chinese economic leadership was capable of dealing with the fast-moving markets of the 21st century.

Beijing's response reflected the pattern it had followed for the previous quarter century in dealing with foreign investors. Policymakers in Beijing are caught between thinking they still stand at the top of a command economy in which heavy handed policies bring heavy handed results and recognizing that fine-tuning a primarily private sector economy based on markets requires policy expertise and deftness that goes beyond just issuing fiats. Chinese policymakers are on a long learning curve, but their interaction with foreign companies has taught them much about modern economic and financial policymaking. International businesses operating in China were not surprised at the lack of finesse in the policies announced. The actions were consistent with the way that Beijing has pursued policy paths and the way that it has treated foreign investors during its development into a modern economy.

Foreign Devils

In the sixteenth century, when European sailors first appeared off the coast of China, they were referred to as ghost men because of their light complexion. These ghost men came to be called foreign devils. At the close of the twentieth century, foreign devils in the form of foreign firms took on China and gradually became a driving force and partners in a movement that would ultimately transform the country.

China has been dancing with the foreign devils. This dance began with a wary flirtation with familiar foreigners and their companies from neighboring Hong Kong, Singapore and Taiwan. These interlopers may have been ethnic Chinese but their methods and thinking were as foreign to Beijing as those from the West. The dance then turned into a competition among industrial centers to attract world-class businesses and to emulate them and adopt their technology.

The FDI Bellwether

Foreign direct investment is a type of bellwether. The policies Beijing devised for foreign investors soon spread through the Chinese economy, and foreign business methods, products, and technology became models to be adopted by domestic enterprises and consumers. Now, Chinese investments abroad indicate how much the Chinese economy has been transformed and what the contours of future competition with Chinese companies may be. This study of FDI should help foreign investors and policymakers understand the business climate in the PRC and shine light on the motivation behind many of Beijing's economic policies.

In many ways, Beijing's dance with the foreign devils is a story without an end. China has been firmly integrated into the world economy. What was foreign is now domestic, except that Beijing seems to want the foreign technology, methods, equipment, marketing channels and managerial ability but without the foreigners themselves.

Many Chinese downplay the role of foreign investors in the making of modern China. They think that the PRC could have built its powerful economy on its own and without the help of foreigners. However, China's previous attempts to rely on its own production and indigenous exports to pay for needed imports of capital and technology resulted in disasters of monumental proportions. Even the Chinese have suppressed memories of the Great Leap Forward and Cultural Revolution. Foreign investment solved the critical constraints on China's economy.

In the 2013 United Nations survey of transnational companies, China was cited by 46 percent of the respondents as the host economy that held top priority for foreign direct investors over the near term. The United States was second with virtually the same percentage (45 percent) followed by India, Indonesia, Brazil, Germany, and Mexico.[3] In the 2014 United Nations Business Survey, global corporate executives viewed China as the best investment location worldwide. Second was the United States.[4] Another survey by the magazine *Foreign Direct Investment* found that in 2011, China easily was the top destination in the world for manufacturing projects. When destinations were ranked according to both quality and cost, China still came out first with the United States second. Germany and France scored high on quality but not on cost. In terms of cities, China was equally dominant among the top 10 city destinations for manufacturing FDI. Shanghai, Beijing, and Chongqing finished as the top three with Suzhou, Tianjin, Nanjing, and Dongguan also listed.[5]

Even though foreign companies continue to invest in the Chinese economy, conditions there are changing fast. The minimum wage has exceeded a dollar an hour in Shanghai, and workers no longer dream of becoming a millionaire by working a million hours. They are beginning to demand not only the unpaid wages that they claim to have earned by working overtime but higher wages per hour. China is moving beyond being just the workshop of the world. Also, competition in domestic markets is fierce, and industrial policy from Beijing aims at building China's own competitor companies. Through regulations, subsidies, performance requirements, withholding approvals and licenses, and government procurement, both the central and regional governments are attempting to tip the scales toward domestic Chinese enterprises.

As one American business person put it, the Chinese government will not throw a foreign company out of China, but once a domestic competitor is established, it will try to put the squeeze on the foreign company until it declares bankruptcy on its own. It is more of a subtle slow process, a death by a thousand cuts—raising taxes, forbidding foreign invested enterprises from raising prices, not renewing leases, requiring new environmental standards, providing favorable financing to a domestic competitor, requiring a joint venture to be formed and technology to be transferred, or any of a number of other methods.[6]

The problem for foreign businesses facing such a squeeze play is that there often is no recourse to the arbitrary and sometimes vindictive policies of the central and local governments in the PRC. The courts are controlled by the Communist Party, and only the largest and most egregious cases rise to a level that warrants official action by other countries. Dispute settlements and counter-measures against unfair trade practices do occur, but the dispute settlement mechanism at the World Trade Organization is slow and cumbersome. Countervailing duties on China's exports and other penalties resulting from unfair trade practice cases can be imposed, but the PRC often retaliates in kind. Official discussions and negotiations can be effective, but they usually are tedious and progress slow. Often they result in promises that may make good press but do not do much for the hard-pressed foreign-invested companies. A basic problem in resolving disputes is that foreign companies being targeted in China often are reluctant to complain because they know that the PRC government is likely to make the company pay and has a multitude of levers it can pull to make life miserable for an individual, a company, or even a country.

A senior Chinese official once confided to an American businessman the true Chinese policy toward foreign direct investment. He said, "Open the doors wide; let the foreign dogs in; milk them for all we can; close the doors and beat the crap out of them."

This attempt by Beijing to re-Sinify its economy and squeeze out foreign companies from the top down parallels what is occurring in the Chinese economy from the bottom up. There is cutthroat competition, not only from revitalized state-owned enterprises but from both private and foreign companies jockeying for position in the rapidly expanding market.

The crux of the problem lies in both China's past and its future. Lingering in the recesses of the national ethos are memories of foreign domination, victimization and unequal treatment by Western powers. And for the foreseeable future, everything depends on growth. The central government and Communist Party rely on economic growth and a rising standard of living to support their legitimacy. Provincial and local government officials depend on increased GDP in their areas to show their effectiveness as leaders and to rise in the party hierarchy. The evaluation of Party officials consists primarily of how well they can answer the following three questions:

- Did you embarrass the party?
- Did you maintain stability?
- Did you grow GDP?

In addition, both Chinese and foreign companies know that if they are not racing ahead they are being left behind. Many foreign companies also have come to rely on their China operations for growth in earnings.

Economic Giant

The Chinese economy has grown to become the second largest economy on earth. (See **Figure I.I**) Its GDP surpassed that of Japan in 2010, and it is expected to become larger than that of the United States in the 2020s even as its growth rate slows. In 2008, China surpassed the United States as the world's largest manufacturer, and despite the global recession of 2008-2009 and mounting domestic problems, China's growth rate continues to hover around the 7% per year needed for its economy to double every decade. This high rate of growth has created tremendous wealth and numerous millionaires. In 2014, the PRC had more people in the top 10 percent of global wealth holders than any other country except for the United States and Japan. It moved into third place in the rankings by overtaking France, Germany, Italy and the United Kingdom.[7]

FIGURE 1.1. GDP OF CHINA, THE UNITED STATES AND JAPAN

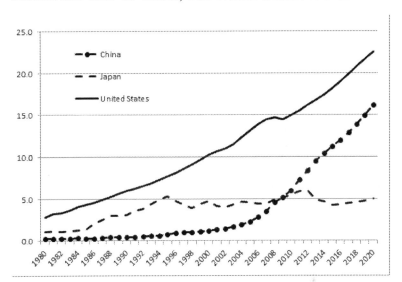

Source: International Monetary Fund, World Economic Outlook Database, April 2015.

Note: Gross Domestic Product in current U.S. dollars. (Projected beyond 2013 for China and 2014 for Japan and the United States)

This new and powerful Chinese economy provides the foundation for the re-emergence of the PRC as a world power and the flexing of its newly generated military muscle. In dealing with the PRC, whether as a business executive, military strategist, diplomat or as an interested observer, the role that foreign businesses have played in China's industrial development and their interaction with the government in Beijing provide an important piece of the puzzle that explains Chinese behavior.

How much longer can this unprecedented growth in China continue? As will be argued in this study, Chinese industrial development was initially highly dependent on foreign companies, dynamic competition, and a bureaucracy that has been compelled to act because of market pressures unleashed by the market opening. Now that the market is open and becoming more normal, the forces for change are more dispersed and coming from both international and domestic enterprises. Beijing also is attempting to shift demand from investments by companies to consumption by households.

Now the question before Beijing is this: has the Chinese economy progressed enough that it can go it alone? Are domestic enterprises, research centers, skilled workers, and managers able to compete in world markets on their own? Should the foreign devils be pushed out, or has integration into the world economy progressed so far that there is no turning back? By reverting to nationalist industrial policies, favoring domestic firms and trying to establish a new version of socialism with Chinese characteristics, will Beijing end up strangling the proverbial goose that laid the golden egg?

CHAPTER 2.   FOREIGN DIRECT INVESTMENT IN CHINA

In 1992, when Ross Perot was running for President of the United States, he characterized the flow of jobs to Mexico because of the North America Free Trade Agreement as a giant sucking sound to the south. Likewise, the attraction of foreign direct investment to China could be characterized as a giant noodle slurp from the east. China is pulling in investment from all quarters of the world. It is by far the largest recipient of FDI among emerging economies. In 2012, $121 billion in non-financial FDI flowed into the country. This was up slightly from the $115 billion in 2010, more than double the $41 billion in 2000 and dwarfed the $2 billion recorded in 1987.[8] Over the 1996-2004 period, FDI accounted for 10.6 percent of China's fixed capital formation. Since then, the foreign share has declined to between 3 and 4 percent as the level of investment in fixed capital coming from domestic sources has outpaced that coming from abroad.[9]

By comparison, from 2008 to 2012, the United States was the largest recipient of world FDI flows with an average of $208 billion per year. China was second with $113 billion per year, and Hong Kong was third with $75 billion. The combined amount for China and Hong Kong at $185 billion per year approached that for the United States. Since the U.S. GDP is twice as large as that of the PRC, FDI as a share of GDP is about the same in each country. In 2012, China accounted for 10 percent of total world FDI. This share of world FDI rose from about 2 percent in the early 1990s to as high as 13 percent in 1994. Since then it has varied according to the vicissitudes of conditions in the world and in the PRC. (See **Figure 2.1.**)

FIGURE 2.1. FOREIGN DIRECT INVESTMENT IN CHINA, ANNUAL TOTALS AND SHARE OF WORLD FDI

Billions of Dollars   Percent

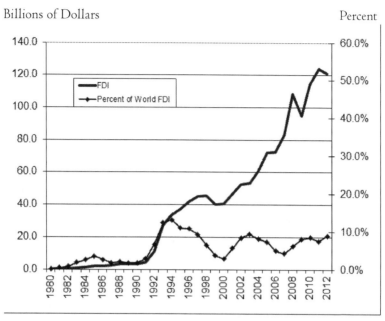

Source: United Nations Conference on Trade and Development Statistics database.

Notes: Non-financial investments not adjusted for inflation.

The Scope of FDI

In the 2003-2012 decade, an average of 1,372 greenfield FDI projects (a new physical facility in a location with no existing facilities) worth a total of $111 billion per year came into China. The 2008-09 recession caused the number of projects to fall somewhat, but foreign companies again have been building factories and other facilities from the ground up rather than acquiring existing factories in China. Over the same ten-year period, the comparable figures for the United States were an average of 1,069 greenfield projects worth a total of $52 billion each year.[10]

China is attracting FDI from virtually every country in the world. Investors hail from some 150 nations and territories, even from countries as unlikely as Angola, Belize, and Afghanistan. A problem with Chinese FDI data, however, is that considerable investment comes through offshore tax havens, such as the Virgin Islands, Cayman Islands, Samoa, Mauritius, and Barbados. In 2012, of the $111.7 billion in FDI, $7.8 billion came from the Virgin Islands, $1.9 billion from the Cayman Islands, and $1.7 billion from Samoa. The U.S.-China Business Council estimated that for 2009, Hong Kong sent $7.9 billion, Taiwan $4.7 billion, the United States $1.0 billion, and the U.K. $0.8 billion to China through these tax havens.11 Also, some investment is round tripped. It actually originates in the PRC and returns through Hong Kong or a tax haven. It is treated as foreign direct investment in order to take advantage of special incentives and protections for foreign investors.

Figure 2.2 shows PRC data on foreign capital actually utilized. One advantage of using these figures is that the PRC attempts to refine the raw FDI data to determine the actual country of origin for inflows of capital that came through the major offshore tax havens. These data are slightly lower than the totals for FDI that the PRC reported to the United Nations ($111.7 billion vs. $121.1 billion in 2012) because it is based on project approvals and does not include reinvested earnings or, presumably, round tripped PRC capital entering through the tax havens. According to these figures, of the total $111.7 billion in 2012, the largest sources of capital were Hong Kong with $71.3 billion, Japan ($7.4 billion), Singapore ($6.5 billion), Taiwan ($6.2 billion), the United States ($3.1 billion), South Korea ($3.1 billion), Germany ($1.5 billion), Netherlands ($1.1 billion), and the United Kingdom with $1.0 billion.

FIGURE 2.2. MAJOR SOURCES OF FOREIGN DIRECT INVESTMENT INTO CHINA

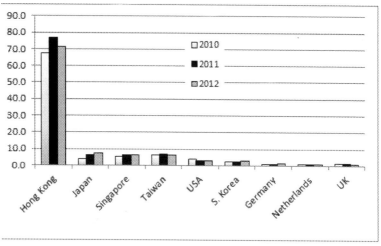

Source: Underlying data from PRC, Ministry of Commerce, "Statistics of *China's Absorption of FDI from January to December,* 2010, 2011, and 2012." **Note:** Non-financial investments. The data include investments from countries or economies entering the PRC through the Virgin Islands, Cayman Islands, Samoa, Mauritius, and Barbados.

For the PRC, the current FDI story has become one of capital flows coming mainly from the Chinese diaspora. The most foreign capital for direct investments has originated from Hong Kong, Taiwan, and Singapore. In 2012, these three sources accounted for $84.0 billion or 75 percent of the total. The next largest group of investor countries consisted of Japan and South Korea, two neighboring Asian nations with combined FDI of $10.5 billion. The United States also is a significant investor as are the leading countries of Europe.

In 2012 in the PRC, there were 56,908 foreign industrial firms with more than 300 employees and annual revenues from their principal business of more than 20 million yuan ($3.3 million). These are considered to be medium- and large-size enterprises. This total included 25,935 enterprises with investments from Hong Kong, Macao, and Taiwan. These foreign-affiliated firms represented 17 percent of the total of 343,769 such industrial firms in China.[12]

Among the 56,908 foreign-affiliated industrial firms, 34,099 (60%) were wholly-owned foreign enterprises (WOFEs), 19,965 (35%) were joint ventures (JVs), 1,681 (3%) were cooperative enterprises, and 1,163 (2%) were share-holding corporations or other enterprises with foreign funds. These medium- and large-size foreign-affiliated industrial firms had assets of $2.7 trillion in 2012 and generated profits of $221.4 billion. All foreign affiliated foreign firms employed a total of 22.15 million persons, nearly as many as the labor force of South Korea or Italy.

The Investors

The list of multinational corporations with operations in China reads like the *Who's Who* of the global business world. In 1924, China's first President, Sun Yat-sen, sent a letter to Henry Ford, inviting him to come to China and to help develop the auto industry in the country.[13] That did not happen, but Henry's great-grandson, Bill Ford, the company's Executive Chairman, has been overseeing a major expansion of the company into China. The PRC has now become the world's largest automotive producer and consumer.

China's rapid adoption of the culture of the automobile is indicative of the real Cultural Revolution that is occurring throughout the country. Just as Henry Ford's Model T became the first car for millions of Americans, so it is in China where at least two of three buyers there are getting their first set of wheels.[14] None of this would have happened without foreign investors taking a chance on investing in the PRC.

Hong Kong

In 1997, Hong Kong reverted to Chinese sovereignty but it is still counted as a foreign entity for trade and capital flows. According to the Hong Kong government, among all the foreign investment projects approved by the Chinese government, 45 percent were tied to Hong Kong interests. As of 2011, Hong Kong investors accounted for $456 billion in capital or 42 percent of all foreign utilized capital in China.[15] The geographical and cultural advantages of Hong Kong in the China market, particularly in the adjoining Guangdong Province, are obvious, but investors in Hong Kong also have been attracted by the availability of land, cheap labor, and government incentives. Early investment tended to be in manufacturing, but Hong Kong now is noted for its real estate developments. Also, before the Taiwan government allowed Taiwanese companies to invest in the Mainland, some routed their FDI through Hong Kong for political reasons.

Three types of foreign investment originate from Hong Kong. First is from investors who are actual citizens of Hong Kong. Second is from other foreign investors who establish companies in Hong Kong that also invest in the Mainland. Some foreign companies prefer to manage their investments in China from offices in Hong Kong. Hong Kong has fewer government regulations, and the long history of British influence there may make life more comfortable for Westerners. The third category consists of investors from the PRC who establish either shell companies or subsidiaries in Hong Kong in order to round trip their capital. The size of this third category is not known. Also, many PRC companies establish subsidiaries in Hong Kong that become the primary issuers of stock to sell on international bourses to raise capital for the offshore, and sometimes domestic, activities of the headquarters corporation in the PRC. If these funds are used to invest in projects in the PRC, they become part of the FDI inflow data. Later chapters in this book will examine the various incentives provided to foreign investors, including tax holidays, better protection of intellectual property, subsidies, reduced land cost and other government support that many domestic firms may not receive.

On my first visit to China in 1988, traveling from Beijing to Shanghai to Hong Kong was literally like emerging from darkness into light. Beijing then had seemed to miss the neon sign and fluorescent lighting revolution that had brightened night life in Paris, Tokyo, or New York. Darkness hung over Beijing like a curtain yet to rise. Shanghai was lit more with some billboards advertising products from state-owned enterprises that were illuminated at night. Streets were brighter, and some offices had replaced single incandescent light bulbs hanging from ceilings with banks of fluorescent lights. When I reached Hong Kong, however, the glare and glitz almost knocked me off my feet. The streets of Hong Kong looked like Japan's Ginza, the brightest shopping street in Tokyo, on steroids. (See Figure 2.3)

Figure 2.3. Hong Kong Lights

Photograph by D. Nanto

Now investors from Hong Kong have lit up streets and raised expectations for urban dwellers in China. Hong Kong has long touted itself as the gateway to the Mainland, but more than a gate, Hong Kong investors have brought the best of Hong Kong itself to urban life in the PRC. For example, Cheung Kong (Holdings) Ltd. has been instrumental in erasing the drab vestiges of Chinese communism in many locations by building modern, luxurious shopping, office, and apartment complexes. Cheung Kong is an investment holding company with 61 major property developments on the Mainland. Its founder and Chairman Li-Ka Shing even built Shantou University with $150 million of his own funds near his hometown in China. Founded in 1981, it is the only institution of higher education in the Chaoshan area in Guangdong Province. In Beijing, Cheung Kong has built Oriental Plaza, one of four major showcase projects there. It is a city-within-a-city in the heart of the capital and is one of the largest commercial complexes in Asia. Many leading multinational corporations have established offices in the Tower Offices situated a short walk from its two luxury apartment buildings and the Grand Hyatt Beijing. The Malls at Oriental Plaza cover more than 1.4 million square feet and include 1,900 indoor parking spaces for cars (and some bicycles).

Another Hong Kong investor, Ronnie C. Chan's Hang Lung Properties, has been building and managing world-class commercial complexes in key cities on the Mainland since it made its first investment in Shanghai in 1992. The company now has large retail and office complexes located in seven cities in China with two landmark properties in Shanghai: Plaza 66 and Grand Gateway 66. These properties have generated the highest tax revenues of any commercial property in the PRC. Plaza 66 has become known for its luxury retail brands and as a destination for high-end consumers and window shoppers from the countryside. Hang Lung's strategy has been to build world-class commercial complexes centered on shopping malls.

Taiwan

Taiwan's FDI into China turns out to be a special case because it is occurring under unique political and security constraints. Technically, Taiwan and China are still at war, although the rocket shells stopped falling long ago. Each side interprets the One-China principle in its own way. Both agree officially that there is but one China, but they disagree on who should rule and how unification should be decided. Despite their political differences, Taiwan and the PRC have become economically intertwined.

Official Taiwanese government policy did not allow FDI into Mainland China until 1991. As of 2013, the government had approved $133.7 billion in investments associated with 40,762 cases.[16] Unapproved investments, however, could be disguised by passing through tax havens or Hong Kong. One estimate of the actual Taiwanese FDI in China from 1979 to 2008 came to $122.3 billion.[17] In the five years since 2008, according to official PRC data, Taiwan invested an additional $51.0 billion in the Mainland. This gives a total for the 1979 to 2013 period of approximately $173.3 billion.

Mainland China is the leading destination for Taiwanese FDI. The largest investments have been in electronic components manufacturing; computers, electronic products, and optical products; and real estate. Among the Taiwanese investing companies is Hon Hai Precision with its Foxconn subsidiary that assembles Apple products. Foxconn has a million PRC workers and about 10,000 Taiwanese managers and engineers in China. UMC and Taiwan Semiconductor Manufacturing Company played important roles in the development of semiconductor fabrication in China. The Acer Group through its manufacturing subsidiary Wistron Corporation is one of many Taiwanese information technology companies to manufacture computers, particularly laptop computers in China. Chapter 7 in this book will address Taiwan's role in the Mainland's industrial development in more detail.

Singapore

Singapore's population consists mainly of ethnic Chinese, a major reason that it separated from Malaysia to become an independent city state. Much as is the case with Hong Kong, Singapore is limited in land area but abounds in managerial skills and technology. By 2012, Singapore had a total of $88.6 billion in FDI in the PRC. This investment came from both small and large firms as well as Singapore's sovereign wealth funds. Most of these investments took advantage of Singapore's skills in manufacturing and in property development. Even though Singapore's official language is English, many of its ethnic Chinese also speak Hokkien, a regional dialect from Fujian province in the PRC. This is the province from which the largest Chinese contingent in Singapore immigrated and which has been the destination of most private Singaporean FDI. In addition, Jiangsu province has been a major destination for Singaporean government-led investments.[18]

At the national level, Singapore's sovereign wealth fund, Temasek, has invested in the PRC's major financial institutions, such as China Construction Bank, Industrial and Commercial Bank of China, and the Bank of China. In 2007, Temasek and Singapore Airlines (55% owned by Temasek) sought to acquire a 24% stake in China Eastern Airlines, but it was out-maneuvered in the effort by competitor Air China.[19]

Other Countries

On a historical cost basis, in 2012, U.S. companies reported cumulative investments of $52 billion in China, of which $32 billion was in manufacturing and $3 billion in depository institutions.[20] The American Chamber of Commerce in Beijing says that it has some 2,600 members from more than 1,200 companies. Its membership list encompasses a sizeable share of the Fortune 500 corporations in the United States and includes corporate giants such as Wal-Mart, General Electric, General Motors, Bank of America, Ford Motor, and Hewlett-Packard. It also includes numerous small- and medium-sized businesses.

Japan, South Korea, and other Asian countries also have been large investors in China. Big brand-name producers such as Sony, Panasonic, Cannon, Samsung, LG, Toyota, Nissan, Honda, and Hyundai all have major operations in China. As they have moved there, their suppliers have followed. Japanese and Korean plants that once manufactured apparel and other consumer goods for multinational companies also have migrated to China.

In 2012, the PRC, Japan, and South Korea signed a Trilateral Investment Agreement. The agreement formed the first legal framework dealing with the economy among these countries and provides for the protection of intellectual property rights, prohibits unreasonable requirements of technology transfer, and enhances the level of investment protection.[21]

Japan's investors, however, continually face challenges stemming from their country's invasion and occupation of much of China during what they call the Pacific War (World War II). This is a particular problem for Japan's automakers. They are firmly entrenched in China and have manufacturing facilities in Guangdong and other areas of southern China, but in northern China war memories are still near the surface. Toyota, Nissan, and Honda must walk a tightrope hoping that there will not be another tiff over territory or flare up in diplomatic relations that will cause consumers to turn away or actively boycott their products.

European companies increasingly are sourcing and investing in China. The European Union Chamber of Commerce in China has 1,700 members in ten cities. European cars and luxury goods are popular among the rising rich not only in the Eastern urban areas but also in inland regions. Volkswagen with its locally produced Santana model was an early entrant into the Chinese market and is expanding operations there. Germany's Siemens provided technology for China's high-speed rail through a joint venture. Switzerland's ABB, a world leader in power and automation technologies, was the first to establish robotics R&D and manufacturing in China. ABB had been investing some $100 million per year in the PRC and in 2012 had 36 companies with 18,300 employees there.

Why Invest?

Why have so many foreign companies invested in a country where incomes are low, political risks are high, culture unfamiliar, and where the rule of law, court system and protection of intellectual property are still developing? Investors in China are not like George Mallory when asked why he wanted to climb Mount Everest. Companies do not go to China simply because it is there. Actually, the reason is more like the reply by the bank robber Willie Sutton when asked why he robbed banks. He allegedly retorted, "Because that's where the money is."

The reasons that companies have invested in China are complex, but essentially foreign investors go there to find a lower-cost manufacturing base; to lower transaction costs in a supply chain; to secure access to certain raw materials, skills, or suppliers; to establish a base from which to serve the Chinese market; or to reduce risk by diversifying their own production lines. In many cases, foreign companies go there because China's central or local government has enticed them with various incentives. The FDI serves the needs of both the company and the country.

Effects of FDI

As shall be shown in later chapters, foreign investment has had a disproportionate impact on the industrial development of China. More than its direct effect on production, employment, and technology transfer, its indirect effects have been instrumental in transforming thinking, economic approaches, and expectations of 1.3 billion Chinese.

The process worked through the forces of competition. First it affected China's special economic zones and other regions that attracted FDI. Incomes there rose so fast that other jurisdictions tried to emulate them. Second, FDI generated competition throughout the Chinese economy. Beijing was compelled to liberalize strictures on enterprises, such as price controls and local monopolies, as private and foreign enterprises began procuring raw materials and selling in the more open Chinese market. FDI also required efficient transportation networks and countrywide markets. The combined effect of these forces also required that commerce among provinces be liberalized and attempts at geographical autonomy and autarky be dropped.

Thomas G. Rawski, an economist, explained this process in a study of the rise of China's economy. He observed that Beijing's reform initiatives had an uneven impact on various companies and regions of the economy. The inefficient state-owned enterprises, in particular, suffered mightily. Some enterprises reacted to the resulting financial pressures by developing new products, trimming costs and raising productivity. Others pleaded for government financial assistance with claims of unfair competition. Government supervisory agencies, short of funds, often found it easier to respond with further reform initiatives than with cash. "In this way, Chinese reform created a 'virtuous cycle' that enabled myriad small reforms to cumulate into substantial institutional change. Reform expanded competition and created financial pressures that spurred some participants toward innovation, resulting in further intensification of competition. Even when financial pressures resulted in lobbying rather than innovation, the typical response involved further partial reform, which unleashed fresh rounds of competition."[22]

The most direct effect of FDI has been on foreign trade. Without FDI, China would still be struggling to pay its import bills, and the country certainly could not have built an economic war chest of more than $3 trillion in foreign exchange reserves. In 2012, moreover, foreign companies held 22 percent of the assets of all industrial enterprises that had more than 20 million yuan ($3.17 million) in revenues.

The scope, sources, effects, and rationale for FDI will be discussed in more detail in later chapters. However, in order to understand how China arrived at where it is today, one first must understand from whence China came. The philosopher Friedrich Nietzsche once said, "Everyone who has ever built anywhere a 'new heaven' first found the power thereto in his own hell." Perhaps it was the shear horror of China under Mao that gave the nation the determination to climb out of hell.

CHAPTER 3.   POST-REVOLUTION CHINA: THE FAILURE OF THE RED ECONOMY

As the world closed the door on the twentieth century, China could look forward to the twenty-first century with four valuable lessons learned through sometimes bitter experience. Those four lessons have been writ large across the face of the PRC. They were that:

- war and instability kill both people and economic progress;
- Marxist/Leninist economics fails in the most basic ways;
- open, market-based economies work well even with oppressive political regimes; and
- market capitalism creates divisions between the rich and poor but also generates the tide that lifts all ships.

Throughout the nineteenth century, China had been subjected to a series of "humiliating" treaties as the Western powers grabbed spheres of influence. It was only at the insistence of the United States which was late to join the game that the European powers agreed to an Open Door policy toward China. World War II ended the European domination, but it was costly for China as Japan invaded from the north. Between 1937 and 1945, 7.5 to 10 million Chinese were killed, and the economy was left in chaos.

During the war, the Chinese Nationalists and Communists joined forces to fight Japan, but that rapprochement did not last for long. By 1949, Mao Zedong's followers had driven the Nationalists to the island of Taiwan (Formosa) and had given birth to the People's Republic of China. During this civil war, the horrors of World War II had been extended for another four years. Another one million to two million people died in the conflict.

By 1949, the Chinese people were ready for peace and stability. But that was not to happen.

Mao accomplished one thing that had not been done in modern China—unite the country. Unfortunately for many, it was done under the banner of communism and the tutelage of the Soviet Union. In a 1949 report to the Communist Party, Mao was quoted as saying, "The Chinese revolution is great, but the road after the revolution will be longer, the work greater and more arduous."[23] Little did the Chinese people know that it would be Mao's policies that would indeed make the work greater and significantly more arduous. Over the next quarter century, millions of peasants and others out of favor at the moment were to die, perhaps a greater number than had died during World War II, and the economy was to take a great leap backwards.

With the Communist Party in power and rejected by the United States and Europe, Chairman Mao turned to Stalin's model of socialist construction, particularly during the first decade of the revolution. He engaged Soviet experts and sent Chinese specialists and students to the USSR to help in replicating what was to him at the time the authentic template of a modern socialist socio-political and economic system. Mao also was attracted by Stalin's transformation of Russia's peasant economy into a powerful industrial power capable of defeating Germany in World War II. Although Stalin initially distrusted Mao, he quickly recognized the benefits of China's inclusion in the socialist camp and evidently took a personal interest in the country's progress in building socialism. Until Deng Xiaoping's reforms in 1978, the Soviet model served as the default option after the failure of Mao's attempts to partially reject that model and to attain full communism.[24]

Land Reform and Collectivization

After Mao came to power in 1949, there was a honeymoon period when the revolutionaries celebrated the communist victory. Mao identified with China's peasant population. It was the farmers who manned his army and fed the country. One promise of the revolution was to distribute land to those who actually farmed it, to do away with the landlords. This was accomplished in an especially brutal manner. Landlords were tried for various crimes and often executed. During the first three years of Mao's rule, an estimated two million landlords and other counter-revolutionaries perished.

Mao, himself, apparently did not advocate the mass murders, but he was willing to allow excessive revolutionary fervor and unjust killings as long as his greater goals were accomplished. In 1948, in a speech at a conference of cadres (core followers of Mao), Mao stated that the aim of the land reform was to "abolish the system of feudal exploitation, which is to eliminate the feudal landlords as a class, not as individuals."[25] In practice, however, the process became an excuse for local officials and farmers to pursue old vendettas while Beijing looked the other way. Only later did Mao allow cadres to be criticized for revolutionary excesses.

The land reform was but the first step in Mao's grand plan for Soviet-style industrialization. The agricultural sector was to play a four-fold role in the nation's economic construction. The agricultural sector had to be able to produce a surplus to feed the urban sector, provide labor for the expanding industrial base, produce raw materials as inputs for industry, and become the buyer of machinery and tractors manufactured by heavy industry. In order to accomplish this, the small plots of land had to give way for mechanized farming, larger field sizes, and more irrigation and reclamation projects. Agriculture could not continue with atomized plots of land and near subsistence levels of output.

The farm surplus to be transferred to the industrial sector was to consist not only of rice and other food items to be consumed by industrial workers but also raw materials such as cotton, tobacco, hides and silk used in industries to produce clothing, cigarettes, shoes and other household items. The socialist strategy was not to allow both the agricultural grains and light industrial products to be consumed completely at home but to export part of them to generate the foreign exchange needed to buy the imported machinery and equipment for heavy industry.[26] The implication, of course, was that household consumption, particularly by peasants, had to be sacrificed to promote industrialization. Agricultural output also had to rise.

In July 1955, Mao stood before an assemblage of Party secretaries from the whole country and called for the collectivization of agriculture.

Suddenly, the land rights obtained through land reform were transferred from the farmer households to cooperatives and then to collectives. By 1956 or 1957, the peasants had lost the property rights to land and major non-labor inputs. Households, however, were able to farm discrete plots of land, so that their individual productivity was still apparent. Therefore, total factor productivity (increases in output not accounted for by increases in land, labor or capital) in agriculture continued to improve despite the ostensible breaking of the link between work and reward in a collective enterprise.[27] The peasants, however, continued to be squeezed. Grain requisitions to support industrialization kept the peasant households from enjoying any increase in production. One of the purposes of creating the agricultural cooperatives and then collectives was to make it easier for the government to requisition grain. It was more efficient to seize the harvest from thousands of collectives than from hundreds of million households.[28]

The Great Leap Forward

A major turn in Mao's attempt to industrialize China came in November 1957 when he attended the 40th anniversary celebrations of the October Revolution in Moscow. In a speech, Nikita Khrushchev boasted that the Soviet Union would overtake the United States in the output of important products within fifteen years. Later, Khrushchev expressed his confidence that within that time frame, Soviet steel output would surpass that of the world-leading United States. In 1957, the PRC was nowhere near being able to compete in the same league as the Soviet Union or United States, but Mao found that Great Britain's steel production was projected to reach 30 million tons in fifteen years. Since China's five-year plans called for 40 to 45 million tons of steel output, Mao announced immediately that within fifteen years China would overtake Britain in steel production. The number two socialist nation was to overtake the number two capitalist nation.

With such hubris, Mao in 1958 announced the Great Leap Forward, a crash program of industrialization (with an emphasis on the steel industry), provincial autonomy and mass communization of agriculture and industry. This was to be a high tide in the Chinese style of socialism and designed to be more true to Marxism and Leninism than the backsliding Soviet Union. It was intended to propel China into the club of industrialized nations.

Industrial targets under the Great Leap turned out to be wildly unrealistic, particularly for steel. Even though China managed to produce only 5.35 million tons of crude steel in 1957, Mao had the target for steel production increased to 12 million tons for 1958 and to 30 million tons by 1962. In 1958, Mao further increased the target to 30 million tons by 1959 and 60 million tons by 1962. Other targets were set that also were beyond reach. Even with a surge in imports of equipment, industries were hard pressed to meet their inflated production goals. In addition, someone had to pay for the industrial equipment and imports needed for development. Again Mao turned to the peasants to extract yet more in the form of higher grain requisitions and taxes.[29] (See **Figure 3.1**)

Figure 3.1. The Mao Model of Development

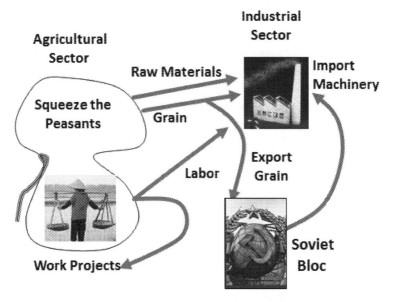

Source: Images from Dreamstime.com.

Unlike the Soviet Union that relied mainly on industrialization, China was to walk on two legs and develop both industry and agriculture at the

28

same time. Targets for agricultural output became as wildly unrealistic as those for industry. In order to meet the higher requisitions and production targets, rural collectives were merged into large People's communes each with about four to five thousand people. Ambitious cadre wielding caning sticks were convinced that they could beat and torture higher yields from the long-suffering peasants. Private plots were abolished, and as much as 40 percent of the homes in the countryside were destroyed to make room for communal mess halls, to create fertilizer, to relocate villages or just to punish their occupants.[30] Families could not even decide on their own how to ration the dwindling supplies of food. Communal canteens first became places of excess consumption then a device to administer starvation. The link between work and reward was severed, but the link between not working enough and the punishment that followed was clear. Peasants also were not allowed to leave the communes because their labor was needed not only in the fields but in small-scale industries and in constructing large public works projects.

Each commune was to be self-sufficient to reduce demands on the transportation system. So-called backyard steel furnaces proliferated, but with little knowledge of steelmaking in the general population, quality was poor and output often was increased by melting down existing metal products. Kitchen utensils, farm implements and anything else containing iron often was thrown into the furnaces. These crude attempts at industrialization resulted in a huge waste of labor and resources, and the resulting lumps of pig iron produced were virtually unusable.

During the 1958-62 years of the Great Leap Forward, an additional 30 million to 45 million people died, mostly from malnutrition but also from torture and killings. In the party, those deemed insufficiently supportive of the radical policies were attacked and censored. Communes were caught in a downward spiral. Peasants had to toil more on less and less food. Production plummeted. Apprised of the situation, Mao turned a blind eye. In a meeting in Shanghai in April 1959, Mao reportedly said that when people die, it is better to have half of them starve to death, so that the other half can eat their fill.[31]

On the urban industrial side of the Great Leap, thousands of new industrial projects were begun. The number of state employees in these industries doubled and further increased the need to procure food for their rations. Much of the equipment for the new factories was ordered from the Soviet bloc. Eventually the import bill came due and was laid on the backs of the peasants. Chinese farmers ended up eating grass, while East Germans learned to eat rice. By 1961, the failure of the Great Leap Forward became obvious, and by 1962 the misguided experiment ended.

Most modern Chinese would probably prefer to forget the excesses of the Great Leap Forward, but it played an important negative role in China's modern industrial development. It contributed to the huge gap between the actual and potential output of China that the reformers nearly two decades later could exploit.

The privation of the Great Leap Forward also seems to have played into the consumerism and desire to put rice on the table among rural workers.[32] Much in the same way that the Great Depression motivated a generation of Americans to work hard and to save, millions of migrant laborers from the countryside have today flooded into the Eastern coastal region of China to seek work and a higher standard of living. This process is occurring despite the *hukou* system of household registration that started during the Great Leap Forward to ensure that peasants did not escape from the communes. The *hukou* system means that China's 650 million people from the countryside do not qualify for the same services as urban residents if they migrate to the cities. This includes health care, education, food rations (important in the past), and access to local government jobs.[33] The government in Beijing is now grappling with this issue.

In addition, the huge increases in state employees working in state-owned enterprises under what was considered to be an iron rice bowl of permanent employment continues to be a challenge. The Great Leap Forward also increased the numbers of state and local officials whose position gave them inordinate power over those beneath them. During the Great Leap famine, the cadre who wielded the ladle in the canteen determined whether you lived or died. If the cadre dipped the ladle deep into the pot and scooped out a rich mix of meat and vegetables, you lived. If they skimmed the top with the ladle, you got a weak vegetable tea, and you died.[34] The ubiquitous presence of Party cadre, even in private enterprises in China, today hearkens back to the monitoring system created during the Great Leap Forward.

Mao's emphasis on provincial and regional autonomy partly explains why China has had as many as 51 major automobile producers and numerous manufacturing enterprises that are too small, too regionally focused and essentially bankrupt. Each was designed to serve a particular geographical area, and many are unable to compete in a modern integrated economy without government subsidies. One of the challenges for China's industrial policy has been to decide which enterprises to save, which to merge, and which to shut down.

The chagrin that Mao and other Chinese leaders felt at the relative economic backwardness of China still plays into Chinese economic nationalism today. Mao's shame that China at the beginning of the Great Leap Forward did not even produce as much steel as tiny Denmark is echoed today in policies to build national champion companies and to foster more indigenous innovation. Mao's economic nationalism also can be seen currently as Chinese leaders seek to reclaim China's position, not held since the time of Marco Polo, as the center kingdom and leading economy of the world.

The Cultural Revolution

After the failure of the Great Leap Forward, Beijing's policies began to moderate, and agriculture production recovered enough to stem more massive starvation. Mao retreated from public life for a year, and three of his top men, Liu Shaoqui, Zhou Enlai, and Deng Xiaoping oversaw the economic reconstruction of the country. Mao, however, was not about to see his country go the way of the Soviet Union and backslide into capitalism. He also was concerned that elite engineers, scientists, educators and business managers were creating a new class of people who knew little of the rigors of peasant life. Mao's drive for egalitarianism and socialism true to Marx and Lenin again captured his mind. He recruited a team of party loyalists who set out to purge the country of its recidivist tendencies. His army, this time, was to be idealistic students yet untainted by the allure of markets and consumer capitalism.

In September 1965, Lin Biao, the Minister of Defense urged students in schools and colleges to be true to the principles of the revolution and to openly criticize the revisionist liberals in the Communist Party. In 1966, Mao made a splash when he reappeared in public life by swimming in the Yangtze River. The message was clear. The 72-year old Mao was ready to resume leadership of China. In August of that year, Mao launched the Cultural Revolution when he called for Red Guards to challenge party officials for being too bourgeoisie and for their lack of revolutionary zeal. Schools were closed so students could join the Red Guard movement.

The country erupted into chaos. Anyone associated with Liu Shaoqui, the party's vice-chairman, was a target. Liu, himself, was sent to prison where he was tortured and eventually died. Deng Xiaoping, the party's secretary general, was sent to the countryside to work as a machinist, a trade he learned while working in a Renault plant as a student in France.[35] Economists, teachers, and anyone deemed to have developed a superior attitude was branded an enemy of the people and subjected to re-education, sent to the countryside to work, or simply killed. Even the Foreign Ministry and high officials there were targeted.[36] Some former landlords who survived the land reform were brutally murdered.[37] Families were torn apart as children were sent to the countryside under the slogan, "The farther from Father and Mother, the nearer to Chairman Mao."[38] Red Guard units sometimes fought with each other as they vied for leadership. They burned the British Embassy and even scraped gold off the huge bronze water cauldrons and defaced other treasures in the Forbidden City in Beijing. (See **Figure 3.2**) Antique dealers in Hong Kong and elsewhere had a heyday as the Red Guard sought to erase any vestiges of pre-communist culture. Mao had called on students to destroy the so-called Four Olds: old culture, old customs, old ideas, and old habits. Unfortunately, many Red Guards added a fifth old to the list: old people.

FIGURE 3.2. SCRAPE MARKS ON A GOLD-PLATED WATER CALDRON IN THE FORBIDDEN CITY

Photograph by D. Nanto

In one village of about 2,500 people, a 16-year old member of the Red Guard was forced to publicly denounce his father's wife and the woman who had raised him as a son. She knelt in front of a crowd day after day as he screamed at her for being a capitalist and accused her of harboring a petty-bourgeois sensibility. Her crime was to have taken in extra money as a seamstress. In that village, an estimated two tons of books were burned, nine temples ransacked, hundreds of carvings destroyed, dozens of people seriously injured, and ten people so traumatized by their beatings that they shortly afterwards committed suicide.[39]

I have long been friends with a Chinese diplomat who was a young student during the Cultural Revolution. His well-educated parents became targets, and he was sent to a commune to labor with his hands. He toiled all the day long in the fields and at night retreated to a hut where he slept alongside other tainted youth. He rarely saw his parents. Determined to pass the entrance examinations for college, he would read in the dim light of the hut while under his blanket. Later after being accepted into a prestigious university, he was sometimes accused of having unfair advantage in passing the entrance examination because he came from elite parents.

The greatest excesses of the Cultural Revolution ebbed after two years in 1968 when Liu Shaoqui resigned from the Communist Party, but the chaos continued more than eight years until Mao died in 1976 and the Gang of Four supporters of Mao (including his wife) were silenced.

The Chinese government says little about the Cultural Revolution but has estimated that 100 million Chinese, more than 10 percent of the country's population, suffered unjustly during the movement.[40] The government has not released figures on how many were killed, but the median estimate by outsiders is about a million people.[41] For China, in 1977, another nightmare had ended.

During the Cultural Revolution some Red Guards suggested changing stoplights so that the red light meant go. This was indicative of the way the entire country operated. Factories and schools said they wanted people both red (loyal to the Communist Party) and skilled, but in reality they just meant red. However, being red and being well read were entirely different. Educators complained that their students were unable to do their studies. One student submitted a blank piece of paper for his entrance exam for a university. He said that he was too busy working in the countryside to study.

Some Chinese enterprises flourished during this time, particularly large industrial complexes, such as the Anshan Iron and Steel Company and the Daqing Oilfield Company. Between 1965 and 1976, the acreage under irrigation also rose from 33 to 45 million hectares.[42] However, industrial development as a whole suffered as the political imperative took priority over actual working skills, and interpersonal trust and cooperation were destroyed. The risk hung over the head of every person that he or she could be reported and accused of being a capitalist roader. Working conditions also became hostile as workers were encouraged to publicly criticize each other and their managers. Guilt was often by association rather than action. The primary form of evidence was confession, often extracted brutally. Family support for workers was disrupted. A huge mismatch of talent and jobs developed as skilled and well-educated personnel were sent to the countryside to perform menial labor. Mao-inspired egalitarianism reigned supreme even at the sacrifice of efficiency and a logical allocation of scarce resources. The time was ripe for a change.

Chapter 4. Post-Mao China: Reform and Opening

The PRC's post-Mao industrial development began with what the Chinese refer to as a revolution in thought. According to a Chinese government retrospective report on the 30 years of industrial development, this thought revolution included two key concepts necessary to move from a planned to a market economy:

- in order to escape from poverty, people have to depend on themselves; and
- for individuals and enterprises to strive for income, profit, and wealth is not only proper and rational, but it is reasonable behavior that benefits society as a whole.[43]

These concepts echo those in Adam Smith's *Wealth of Nations* written in 1776 in which he shows that by the individual maximizing his or her own well-being, the well-being of society is also maximized. But the concepts also harken back to pre-revolution China when markets were relatively unconstrained. If the people had not followed Mao's injunction to destroy the Four Olds (old culture, old customs, old ideas, and old habits), they might have recalled that back in the Han dynasty (206 B.C. to 220 A.D.), a Chinese historian Sima Qian wrote that there must be farmers to produce food, artisans to make things, and merchants to circulate them. There is no need for government orders, each will play his part, doing his best to get what he desires. When all work willingly at their trade, just as water flows downhill, things will appear and people will produce them without being asked.[44]

The Revolution Begins

The PRC's economic revolution began when Deng Xiaoping won out over Hua Guofeng, Mao's selected successor, for leadership of the Chinese Communist Party. Deng had been rehabilitated after his stint during the Cultural Revolution working in the countryside. With Deng, a new era began in China, less dramatic than the Great Leap Forward or the Cultural Revolution, but certainly with greater impact and longevity. This new era is simply called the period of Reform and Opening. Deng would be to China's economic revolution what Mao was to its political revolution.

After the excesses of the Cultural Revolution, China was ready to go in a different direction. If putting socialism and politics first was superior to market economics, why were Japan, South Korea, Taiwan, Singapore and Hong Kong growing so much faster than the PRC? In 1978, annual per capita income in China was $190 or about 50 cents per day and far below the poverty level of $1 per day used as a general indicator of a minimum subsistence level at that time. Some rural families still were surviving the hunger season by eating tree leaves, bark, and wild plants. By contrast, the level of annual per capita income in Hong Kong was $3,930, in Singapore was $3,390, in Taiwan $1,453, in South Korea $1,240, and in Japan $7,220.[45] Worse still for the Chinese Communist Party, it had lost the public's trust in its moral and political leadership. Disillusionment with the Party increased dramatically not only within the wider population but among its members as well. The Party leaders had to reassure the people of their legitimacy to govern.[46]

The economic problems of China at that time were no different from those that Mao had faced. First was to feed the people. China's population was rapidly approaching a billion—one in four people on earth—and 89 percent of those people were in agriculture. Despite the collectivization and efforts to raise farm productivity, grain output since 1952 was rising at only about a half percent per year and was barely keeping abreast of population growth. Following the debacle with backyard steel furnaces during the Great Leap Forward, however, the communes did develop some local industries under the campaign for five small industries (metal making, machine-building, cement, chemical fertilizers and energy [coal or small hydroelectricity]).[47]

Still, in 1978 the situation in the countryside was so dire that in the village of Xiaogang in Anhui province, 18 farmer peasants risked their lives by signing a secret agreement (a contract) that divided the existing commune-owned farmland into plots for each family to cultivate. Production in the village jumped six fold the first year. Local officials allowed the experiment to continue and permitted the households to keep the surplus as long as the required grain deliveries to the state were met.[48]

This farm contract experiment eventually became the model for the de-collectivization of agriculture. The genius of Deng was not his forward-looking thinking but his willingness to be pragmatic in determining policy, to follow the facts and see what actually worked rather than relying on ideology. In 1979 the party formalized the contract responsibility system in agriculture. Soon the commune system was gone, and the perverse incentives and excessive control by local cadre over all aspects of farm life ebbed. Farmers were allowed to invest in fertilizer and machinery using their own income rather than rely on the state which was more interested in investing in the industrial sector. Villages and townships could continue commune businesses or start new ones.

Prior to 1978, limited foreign direct investment had been allowed, but China was suspicious of foreign capital. The country had tried to gain technology by importing foreign equipment and even a number of industrial plants and to reverse engineer them to find their technological secrets. This process, however, was slow and had only limited success even after the opening of China for Americans following President Richard M. Nixon's visit to Beijing in 1972. Japan also normalized relations with China in 1972 as did the European Community in 1975.

A significant result of the normalization process was that Chinese officials could travel to Western and neighboring countries to observe life there. In 1977 and 1978, delegation after delegation of Chinese officials visited foreign countries on inspection tours. This generated a sense of urgency among leaders that they needed to change policy and quickly. Even Deng Liqun, a highly conservative figure in the Party, after a trip to Japan in October 1978, remarked that in the 1950s, China had a standard of living comparable to that of Japan, but in the 1970s China had vastly lagged behind Japan. When Deng Xiaoping visited Japan, he dined with

Japanese business executives, rode the high speed railway and toured Nissan automobile and Matsushita (Panasonic) factories. Beijing became fully aware that the quarter century of isolation from the Western world had put it far behind its neighboring nations not to mention the United States and Europe. This relative backwardness raised severe security risks.

Meanwhile, in the southeastern corner of China in Guangdong and Fujian provinces, far from the emperor's eyes, a change in the industrial structure analogous to the de-collectivization of agriculture was occurring. In 1977, the huge gap between incomes in Hong Kong and neighboring Guangdong province was well known to the Chinese. At that time, the average wage in Hong Kong was 20 to 30 times higher than the wages across the border. This created a dual push and pull effect. Hong Kong manufacturers were eager to establish factories in Guangdong, while people in Guangdong were anxious to try to replicate Hong Kong's economic success. In October 1977, Guangdong officials asked permission to build what would become Shenzhen and Zhuhai as export zones to Hong Kong and Macau. Even before permission had been given by China's central government to set up special economic zones (SEZs), Hong Kong investors had contracted 100 merchandise assembly projects with the Guangdong government, and in January 1979 the Shekou Industrial Export Zone (in Shenzhen) was established.

In June 1979, Beijing announced the official policy establishing the SEZs.[49] The SEZs are a geographical region that has economic and other laws that are more free-market-oriented than the PRC's national laws. They typically included special tax incentives, fewer import restrictions, and a limited free-trade zone with no customs duties for inputs incorporated into products exported. In 1980, three SEZs were initially allowed in Shenzhen, Zhuhai, and Shantou in Guangdong province. Later that year, a fourth was established in Xiamen in Fujian province. These SEZs were to be the first enclaves of foreign direct investment that were to alter the entire economic landscape of China.

Reform and Opening—the Deng Model

For the Party leaders in Beijing, the village experiment in de-collectivization combined with the eventual success of the special economic zones started a two-pronged process that ultimately would transform the country. On the political side was a process of diffusion[50] and the conversion in the mindset, first of local officials in Guangdong and Fujian provinces and then of leaders in Beijing, that markets were compatible with socialism and that opening the country to controlled foreign investment would not threaten the Party and its doctrine.

Why did Deng Xiaoping allow the dreaded foreigners into China? As it turned out, the foreign devils that were so instrumental in the political process that changed the thinking of the Party leaders were not so foreign after all. They were primarily ethnic Chinese who had left the country and become industrialists and property developers in Hong Kong, Macau, Taiwan, Singapore, Thailand and Indonesia. In particular, Hong Kong business leaders with their Cantonese heritage could communicate well with officials in neighboring Guangdong province.

These former compatriots were different from the visages of foreign devils off the coasts of China. They were more like homing pigeons who were returning to their original nesting ground. These homing pigeons, however, carried with them all the accoutrements of capitalism. They might as well have been foreign devils because their capitalist ways were totally alien to the domestic Chinese at that time.

Deng Xiaoping and the other leaders of this Chinese industrial revolution had to weigh the risks that loosening the Party's hold on the economy could put them and their supporters on a slippery slide leading to oblivion. They could reform themselves out of power or worse yet be killed. In the volatile atmosphere engendered during the Cultural Revolution, their decisions were a matter of life and death. Deng's first, and always paramount, goal was to maintain the Party's monopoly in politics. The economic system could be liberalized but not the political system. Mao had relied on continuous revolution to keep the Party in control, but in reality, the excesses of the Cultural Revolution had undermined the Party's legitimacy and moral authority. The Party had to regain its grip on politics while loosening its control over the economy.

On the economic side, reform and opening began a process that would cause a chain reaction ignited by the greater efficiency, higher technology, and desirable consumer goods brought in by foreign direct investors.

Deng Xiaoping understood well that China's industries lacked modern equipment, up-to-date technology and workers who were highly motivated. Mao's emphasis on socialist egalitarianism had stifled any desire by both enterprises and workers to excel. To try to get ahead raised the risk of being accused of being a capitalist roader and censured. For enterprises, excess production and profits accrued to the state, not to the managers or workers. Even private enterprises were controlled indirectly by the state through allocations of raw materials and controls on prices. This time, the leaders in Beijing had to make it official that economic development had priority over politics. The change was given official sanction in 1978 in a strategic decision made by the Third Plenum of the Eleventh Central Committee of the Chinese Communist Party. It decided to transfer its focus from politics, or class struggle, to economic construction, or socialist modernization.[51]

The way to accomplish the industrial transformation was obvious. China had to duplicate the experience of Hong Kong, Taiwan, South Korea and Japan but to carry it out in a way that maintained the primacy of the Party. How did these economies develop? They accomplished it through a process of importing technology, substituting domestic production for imports, and by promoting exports. In each of these cases, the United States opened its huge market to their exports and often countenanced their trade and investment protectionism because of overriding security and diplomatic concerns.[52] Foreign direct investment was allowed but, particularly in Japan and South Korea, strictly controlled. Those two governments often required joint ventures, and foreign companies, themselves, frequently sought out local partners who were more familiar with government procedures and could better understand the business landscape and idiosyncrasies of the market. In Japan's case, the Ministry of International Trade and Industry went so far as to scrutinize and often modify the conditions of private contracts to import machinery or technology in order to tip the balance more in favor of the Japanese company involved.

The objective of modernization and industrial development was clear, but the question was how to do it. What model should they follow? Beijing had studied the possibilities and came up with three basic choices. The first was to modify what Mao had tried to accomplish and to emulate countries of the Soviet bloc such as Yugoslavia. This socialist model would have entailed supporting state-owned enterprises and importing more technology but paying for it by generating savings domestically. The second choice was to follow the model of Japan, South Korea, France, and Germany: import technology, borrow to pay for it, allow limited foreign direct investment and rely on exports to generate foreign exchange. The third choice was to adopt the model of Hong Kong, Macau, and Taiwan: rely on controlled foreign direct investment, exploit low-cost labor to export goods, develop special economic zones, and decentralize government decision making. The economic policy makers in Beijing preferred the first two choices. In discussions with France, Germany, and Japan, China had been assured that loans and technology transfers would be available. They considered the third choice with economic liberalization too much of a break from Chinese communist dogma and experience. Also, their analysis of option three was based primarily on the Hong Kong experience. To them Hong Kong was too small to serve as a model for the rest of China.[53]

Because China was a completely socialist country, Beijing also had to alter some fundamental institutions and practices that had been instituted during the Mao era. The government had to address issues that are basic to any economy, issues that Japan, South Korea, Taiwan, or Germany did not have to deal with during their periods of rapid economic growth. For example, how much should labor be paid? Under Marxism or any economic system, workers contribute according to their ability, but should they be paid according to their ability, need, or productivity? Or, should they just be paid the same as other workers? Should they hold their position for life or can they be fired at any time? Should individuals be allowed to hold capital and receive a return for it? Should farmers be allowed to move to cities and still have rights to food, schooling and government jobs? Should loans from state-owned banks to state-owned enterprises be repaid? Or are such loans merely transfers within the state system and not real financial obligations? Should the people be allowed to start private enterprises, particularly if they compete with state-owned enterprises? For China, the resolution of each of these issues was not a simple task, especially with the socialist underpinnings of the political economic system, and some are still not completely resolved. How each was addressed bore directly on the how the economy developed, the speed at which it grew, and the basic well-being of the Chinese people.

In reality, China did not choose one economic model to the exclusion of the others. Instead, events led the decisions. The key policy was not to block any of the options and let each of the processes operate as the opportunities arose. The overriding decision for Deng was not which model to follow but whether to go ahead with reform and opening. Many of the intense policy debates in Beijing were with hard line party officials who still were seeing apparitions of foreign devils lurking offshore and who sought to maintain their Party positions through loyalty to Marxist doctrine and Mao's teachings.

As shown in **Figure 4.1**, the essential Deng model was quite different from that of Mao. The agricultural sector was liberalized and free to generate a surplus that could be sold to the industrial sector. Labor also flowed from the countryside to the cities. The needed technology, machinery, and managerial skills were provided primarily by foreign businesses through FDI. Exports went through the supply chain structure already existing among foreign businesses. As global sourcing moved to China, any company could join the competitive fray and try to sell into international markets. The resulting increase in exports and favorable balance of trade generated foreign exchange that went into the central government's reserves and helped pay for imports. Businesses also paid taxes or, in the case of state-owned enterprises, shared profits with the central government. The Chinese Communist Party also benefitted from revenues received and positions for Party members provided by companies, particularly state-owned enterprises. Even foreign-funded enterprises have slots reserved for communist party cadre.

FIGURE 4.1. THE DENG MODEL OF DEVELOPMENT

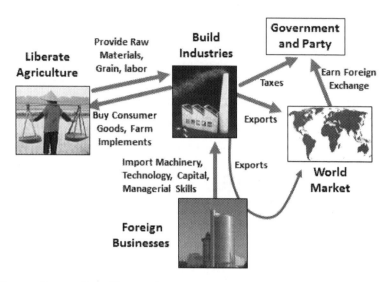

Source: Images from Dreamstime.com.

Throughout the reform period, Deng had to defend his policies against critics within the Party. In a speech in 1982, he said, "In carrying out our modernization program, we must proceed from Chinese realities. Both in revolution and in construction, we should also learn from foreign countries and draw on their experience, but mechanical application of foreign experience and copying of foreign models will get us nowhere.... We must integrate the universal truth of Marxism with the concrete realities of China, blaze a path of our own and build a socialism with Chinese characteristics...."[54]

As soon as China began to open its doors to outside investment, loans, and technology, the operations of markets and physics took over. The second law of thermodynamics states that if one system is in isolation from its environment, energy will flow between the environment and the isolated system. For example, if a cold object is brought into a warm room, heat will flow naturally from the room into the object without any work being required. Likewise, in markets, when an isolated market is opened, entrepreneurs will seek to take advantage of gaps in factor costs and product prices in order to generate profits.

However, unlike physics, the process with markets is much more complicated and requires considerable work, policy changes and trial and error. Also, in physics, each transfer of energy is a win-lose situation. The energy gained by the isolated object is lost by the other. In markets, transactions are intended to be win-win for the actors involved. Each side has to have some prospect of gain or the transaction will not occur. For policy makers, the question with markets is whether transactions that are beneficial to individual companies or local jurisdictions also are beneficial to the country as a whole or, in China's case, to the ruling Communist Party. A win-win transaction at the local level may be a win-lose proposition at the national level. As will be discussed in this study, Beijing is continually grappling with this dilemma and devising policies aimed at ensuring that what is good for the various enterprises and provinces also is good for the Party and government in Beijing.

Figure 4.2. A Deng Xiaoping Billboard Overlooking a Construction Site.

Photograph by D. Nanto

Special Economic Zones

The special economic zones (SEZs) were like huge rocks thrown into a pond that created waves that expanded outward until they reached even the deep recesses along the shore. SEZs differ from the export processing zones or free trade zones that exist in other countries in that they encompassed a wide geographical area and included liberalized self-government that was given considerable latitude in promoting economic development. Immediately after opening, the SEZs attracted foreign direct investment, particularly from Hong Kong, Macau, and indirectly from Taiwan. FDI which began as a trickle quickly became a steadily increasing flow. In 1981, the four SEZs accounted for half of the total of $265 million of FDI inflow into China. By the end of 1985, the realized FDI in the four zones had reached $1.17 billion and was rising fast.

Almost overnight, Shenzhen grew from a sleepy fishing village to a bustling economic center. Located directly across the border from Hong Kong, Shenzhen was the first experiment in Deng Xiaoping's open door policy. It had special tax rates and liberalized trading and investment rules. It recorded growth rates of 58 percent per year from 1980 to 1984 as it also attracted investment from within China. Shenzhen was such a draw for workers seeking jobs that the city had to be fenced off and an entry checkpoint established. No one could enter the city without permission or a specific purpose.

When I visited Shenzhen in 1997, the population had grown to more than 3.5 million (2.5 million of whom were non-permanent residents). Since 1980, its domestic production had grown at a rate of 35% per year. Glistening 60-story buildings etched out a modern skyline. In 1996 its stock market had greater turnover than that of Hong Kong, and it had temporarily bypassed Shanghai and Beijing in retail sales. Officials in Shenzhen explained that foreign investment was being attracted to Shenzhen because of its open trading environment, low tax rates, proximity to Hong Kong and strong infrastructure support. According to the Municipal Foreign Investment Office, in the previous 18 years, the city had approved 18,000 joint ventures with foreign companies. Over $10 billion had been invested by American companies such as IBM, Compaq Computers, DuPont Chemicals and Wal-Mart. The city was allowed to approve foreign investments with value of less than $30 million without referring the application to the provincial or national authorities. The city offices provided a one-stop chop shop (stamps of approval could be obtained in one office). Disapprovals averaged less than 5 percent and usually occurred because of environmental considerations or because of restrictions imposed by Beijing. Even Chinese state-owned enterprises had invested in Shenzhen.

The SEZ experiment was so successful that the word quickly spread to other cities. They too sought similar designations. In 1984, the government established 14 more open coastal cities, and then in 1985 opened cities in the Pearl River Delta, the Yangtze River Delta, and the Min Delta in Fujian Province. In 1988, at the time Hainan Island became a province (instead of a special administrative zone under Guangdong Province), the government designated the island as a fifth special economic zone. The Tiananmen Square incident in 1989 caused foreign investors to question the stability of the country and the ability of the central government to maintain order, but FDI continued to flow in at about $3.4 billion per year. In 1990, the Pudong New District in Shanghai was established, and by 1992, more cities in the border areas and all capitals in the provinces and autonomous regions were opened.[55]

In parallel with the SEZ model of reform and opening to FDI, China also was pursuing the Japan/South Korean model. It was borrowing heavily to finance imports of equipment and technology. The $2.2 billion in bank loans outstanding at the end of 1983 had increased to $6.6 billion by the end of 1985. More than 70 percent of the loans in 1985 had a maturity of one year or less. At that time, China's banks had obligations of $3.5 billion and the government had $2.2 billion outstanding. Only $1.4 billion in loans outstanding had a maturity of two years or more—the type of loans for development envisaged under the Japan/South Korea model.[56] This meant that China still had a dire need for hard currency to pay its debts.

International Trade

On the international trade side, the sudden increase in imports dropped China's trade balance deep into deficit. From an export surplus of $3.8 billion in 1977, the trade account plunged to a deficit of $2.01 billion in 1979. After recording a surplus in 1982 and 1983, the balance sank to an alarming deficit of $14.90 billion in 1985. There was little prospect that FDI and bank borrowing alone could finance such a large trade bill. This raised concerns in Beijing. What was good for individual enterprises and local jurisdictions was creating a potential disaster at the national level.

The creation of the SEZs and free trade zones meant that China's main means of restraining imports into these zones were weakened severely. It could no longer rely primarily on high customs duties and restrictions on access to foreign exchange to control imports (and protect domestic industries from foreign competition). Companies came to China to take advantage of low labor rates, but they still had to import machinery, pay salaries to foreign managers and engineers, and import parts and components. Even with relatively labor-intensive items, such as clothing and apparel, the sewing machines, special fabrics, and fasteners often had to be imported. In many industries, domestic sources of parts and components that met global standards were simply not available. Foreign invested enterprises could import to meet these needs without paying China's high import tariffs, since FDI agreements usually included a waiver of import duties on equipment needed to establish the foreign invested enterprise.

It was during this period of time that Beijing began to impose performance requirements on foreign invested enterprises. Foreign companies in SEZs were required either to export all their output or at least to balance their import requirements with exports. China's economic model began to resemble those in Japan, Taiwan and South Korea. A major component had to be an export strategy. The performance requirements for FDI in Beijing's new international trade policy helped China move its trade balance from deficit to surplus. The 1993 trade deficit of $12.2 billion was to be the last. The balance turned to a surplus in 1994, and the surplus continued to rise to peak at $298 billion in 2008 before the global recession caused it to subside to a low of $155 billion in 2011, recover somewhat to $224 billion in 2012 and reach a new high of $370 billion in 2014. (See **Figure 4.3**)

FIGURE 4.3. CHINA'S MERCHANDISE EXPORTS, IMPORTS AND TRADE BALANCE, 1977-2014

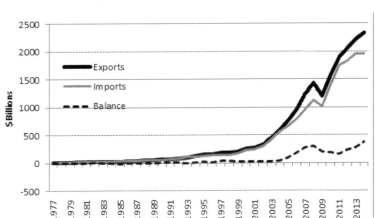

Source: Data from PRC, Ministry of Commerce through China Data Online.

It is said that success has many fathers but failure is an orphan. In the case of PRC trade, the huge trade surplus has many causes, but the utter failure of China to balance its trade, let alone generate surplus, during the turmoil of the Great Leap Forward and Cultural Revolution can be laid directly at the feet of Mao Zedong. When I visited the Mao Memorial Hall in Tiananmen Square, uniformed guards whisked me by the crystal casket enclosing the visible body of Mao still preserved. After emerging from the hall, one of my colleagues remarked that what we saw was a real peasant under glass. The infusion of market capitalism that has transformed the PRC is probably enough to make that peasant turn over in his crypt. On the other hand, given the difficulty under Mao to pay for imports, the roughly $200 to $300 billion that China earns each year from its surplus in trade could be enough to make that peasant break a broad smile if not fly the crystal crypt.

What Mao could not grasp was that the PRC could never earn enough in trade if it relied primarily upon its agricultural sector and outdated industries for exports. There never could be enough rice, silk, and Chinese handicrafts to export in order to finance needed imports of machinery and technology and still feed its people.

During the years of China's turmoil, moreover, the world had changed. Global companies served global consumers with tastes that were rapidly converging on global standards. Businesses strived for global best practices, and the idea that supervisors could beat and intimidate workers into raising productivity had long before become passé. In this new world economy, only companies with knowledge of global markets and that had the requisite managerial skills and manufacturing capabilities could produce the goods in global demand. And only those companies that were integrated into global supply chains could sell their products into global markets and hope to compete successfully. For China in 1978, only foreign firms could meet those requirements.

The export performance of foreign firms was the key to the reversal in China's trade balance. In 1985, foreign-funded enterprises exported only $0.3 billion or about 1 percent of China's total exports. By 2006, these exports had surged to $564 billion, or 58 percent of the total and in 2011 had risen further to $995 billion, but the share fell to 49 percent of total exports as domestic Chinese firms increased their share of export products. **Figure 4.4** shows the importance of foreign-funded enterprises (FFE) exports for the first decade of the 21ˢᵗ century. Clearly for China, exports from FFEs were critical to the country's economic success. Without the FFEs, China would have had neither an export growth strategy nor most exports at all. [57]

FIGURE 4.4. TOTAL AND FOREIGN FUNDED ENTERPRISE EXPORTS FROM CHINA

Billions of U.S. Dollars

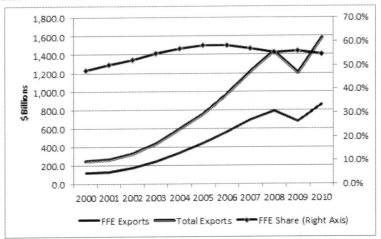

Source: Data from *China Statistical Yearbook*, various years.

Foreign Investment Revitalized

By periods, the initial phase of foreign investment reform lasted from 1979 to 1985 when the legal and institutional framework for FDI was gradually established and the first four SEZs were created. The period from 1986 to 1991 was a continuous development stage in which the government promulgated some laws and regulations, such as the "Law on Enterprises Operated Exclusively with Foreign Capital." The laws eliminated time restrictions on the establishment of joint ventures, provided some assurances against nationalization, and allowed foreign partners to become chairs of joint venture boards. The government also opened additional geographical areas to FDI.

In early 1992, the reform movement faced strong opposition following the Tiananmen Square incident. In 1989, this brutal crackdown quelled demonstrations centered on Tiananmen Square that were led primarily by students. The grievances being protested initially were economic—high inflation and lack of jobs—but the issues soon evolved into demands for more reforms, including political reforms and freedom of the press. After seven weeks of what leaders feared might turn into another Cultural Revolution or outright rebellion, Deng Xiaoping and other leaders ordered the military to squash the demonstrations. On June 4, 1989, the tanks rolled into Tiananmen Square clearing the streets using live fire. The tanks hesitated only when they came into range of Western television cameras. With hundreds or more dead in the aftermath, Western governments imposed additional sanctions on China, and foreign investors paused to reassess how much risk the political turmoil had engendered.

When I visited Beijing a year after the Tiananmen incident, flags waved in the breeze around the square, and security was relatively low. The stone steps on one monument still were unrepaired after being broken by the tread of a tank. In a conversation with a government official, I was told that there were two factors not highlighted in the Western press coverage of the incident. The first was that China had a well-armed military prepared to fight a war and a police force that was not accustomed to dealing with civil disturbances. The military knew only how to use lethal force, and the police had no riot equipment or gear. The police were not trained in riot control. There was nothing in between shooting to kill and standing by. The second factor was that as long as the demonstrators were students, the government was confident that it could handle the situation and that no second Cultural Revolution would occur. However, workers from Shanghai and other cities began to join the demonstrations. When factories shut down so workers could join the protests, Beijing knew it was in real trouble. The demonstrations had to end. Beijing could not stand by any longer for fear that someone would begin calling out, "Workers of the world, unite!"

In the eyes of government officials, the critical issue in the crackdown was stability. The pro-democracy movement had caused such instability that it threatened economic progress. The country needed a stable internal and external environment to achieve its goals for development. What became clear in my conversations with officials, however, was that what had occurred in Eastern Europe weighed heavily in their decision to use brutal force to stop the movement. They were keenly aware of how anti-Communist movements had swept through Poland, Hungary, East Germany, Czechoslovakia and particularly Romania. There was no way that they were going to allow something similar to the ousting of Romania's Communist Party leader Nicolae Ceauşescu to occur in China. They were particularly concerned that Romania's military had switched sides and joined the anti-Ceauşescu forces. A communist ruler knows he is in trouble when the guns on the turrets of the tanks surrounding his palace switch from pointing outward at the revolutionaries to pointing inward toward him. That was not going to happen in Beijing.

The military force that Deng ordered to be used to quell the student demonstrations provided live ammunition to the critics of reforms. They charged that market reforms had gone too far, too fast, and had helped to fuel political unrest. At that time Deng was officially retired but still was China's paramount leader. He faced fierce internal criticism from hardliners who blamed his reform and opening policies for weakening the Party's hold on power. Many observers wondered whether the country's experiment with markets would come to an end.[58]

Much like Mao's swim in the Yangtze River, the ailing Deng needed a dramatic and strong response to his critics. It came in 1992 when he took a surprise tour to southern China that began in the Shenzhen Special Economic Zone. He visited and praised the enterprises of Shenzhen and the Pearl River Delta, many of them affiliated with foreign investors. The news media showed pictures of him before shiny new buildings and modern factories. During this trip, Deng declared that to get rich is glorious. This Southern Tour, as it came to be known, helped to stifle critics and served to unleash a new wave of foreign investment in Guangdong province. Theretofore, most of the foreign investors had been from Hong Kong who relocated their light manufacturing plants to Shenzhen. After Deng's tour, new forms of investment came in from multinationals and Taiwanese firms whose factories produced shoes, garments, furniture, plastics, and electronic components for multinational buyers.[59] This was assisted by a decision by the government of Taiwan to legalize Taiwanese investment in the Mainland.

Deng's Southern Tour commenced a period of high growth in FDI flows. From 1992 to 2001, average FDI inflows increased to more than $40 billion per year.[60] The surge in FDI into China, however, did not occur in isolation. It coincided with similar trends worldwide. The second half of the 1990s saw an unprecedented increase in the world outflow of foreign capital—a more than six fold increase from an annual average of $225 billion during 1990-95 to $1,492 billion in 2000. According to the *World Investment Report* by the United Nations Conference on Trade and Development, there were three forces at work—all related to globalization. First, many governments liberalized capital flows into their national economies. This allowed foreign investment to enter more freely. The process was further accelerated by the privatization of government-owned enterprises in both developed and developing countries. Second, increasing costs of production and various technological developments induced enterprises to spread their operations and risks internationally. Concurrently, the cost of transportation and communications fell, thereby enabling firms to locate their production processes in different parts of the world and to supply products, parts, and accessories from long distances. Finally, increasing competition forced enterprises to enter new markets at an early stage and to transfer some production there to nationalize the product and to reduce production costs.

These forces also were at work for firms considering how to deal with the new China. Large manufacturers everywhere in the world had to come up with a China strategy. Regardless of whether they were or were not investing in manufacturing or sourcing products in the PRC, China was becoming the so-called bull in the China shop. Every major company found that their operations were affected either by imports from China, by competing firms locating to China, by parts of their supply chain moving to China or the prospect that if they did not have a plan for selling in the China market they could lose over a billion potential new customers.

The competitive pressure on companies was also pushing hard on the government in Beijing to liberalize its policies toward foreign investment. In 1991, China granted more preferential tax treatment for wholly foreign-owned businesses and contractual ventures and also for foreign companies that invested in selected economic zones or in projects encouraged by the state (such as energy, communications, and transportation). In 2000 and 2001, China revised significantly its laws on foreign-owned enterprises and joint ventures. It eased export performance and domestic content requirements, attempted to make the legal framework more transparent, and assured that foreign-investment-related enterprises would not be nationalized except under special circumstances.

Entry into the World Trade Organization

The next period in China's FDI history began in 2001 when China joined the World Trade Organization (WTO). The post-WTO membership period in FDI activity begins from 2002 and continues to the present. This is a time of China's integration into the global marketplace. In its 2002 FDI Confidence Index survey of top corporate decision-makers, A.T. Kearney (a business consulting firm) found that confidence in China was booming. For the first time since the survey began, China surpassed the United States to become the destination most likely to attract investment. The survey found that more than any other country, investors held a more positive outlook toward China, with 46 percent more optimistic about the Chinese market at that time than in the previous year. The investors also were expected to commit more first-time investments to China than to any other country.[61]

China's entry into the WTO required that it lower tariffs and other barriers to investment and trade. China's accession agreement covered eight areas, ranging from agriculture to intellectual property rights and contained nearly 700 individual commitments. Most of the commitments dealt with the PRC's trade regime, but others touched on foreign investment and access to the Chinese market. The agreement confirmed China's general obligations to adhere to World Trade Organization principles of nondiscrimination in the treatment of foreign and domestic enterprises. It also provided for access to a broad range of market sectors that were of key importance to foreign investors. The service sector openings included insurance, banking, distribution, telecommunications and professional services. Membership in the WTO also required the PRC to adhere to more than 20 existing multilateral WTO agreements, including the Agreement on Trade-Related Aspects of Intellectual Property Rights, the Agreement on Trade-Related Investment Measures and the Agreement on Subsidies and Countervailing Measures.[62]

With membership in the World Trade Organization, the PRC became a full-fledged member of the international community. It had inherited its seat on the Security Council of the United Nations, but it had earned its membership in the WTO.

Accession to the WTO did bring to an end the perennial debates in the U.S. Congress on whether or not to extend most-favored-nation status (permanent normal trade relations status) to the PRC. These debates had brought subtle threats of retaliation by the PRC government against U.S. companies and great uncertainty among foreign investors in China. In these debates, the international business community tended to side with the PRC and tried to calm the rhetoric coming mainly from Capitol Hill. They too wanted to ensure that most-favored-nation status for China would be extended so that U.S. tariffs would not revert back to the high levels that existed in pre-World War II days. Many of the international businesses also were shipping products made in China, or procured by their Chinese operations, to the United States. After WTO accession, Members of Congress still had ways to debate policies toward the PRC and even to vilify China, but issues gravitated more toward security considerations or particular cases involving a company from the PRC. The threat of a major breach in the bilateral economic relationship and the risk of major retaliation aimed at U.S. investors retreated into the background.

Even though entry into the World Trade Organization required the PRC to open its industries to foreign businesses, Beijing was allowed to protect certain important or strategic sectors of its economy from foreign control in the name of national security. Because of this provision, PRC's approval system for foreign investment divides sectors of the economy into four categories: (1) prohibited, (2) restricted, (3) permitted and (4) encouraged. This system, governed by China's *Foreign Investment Catalogue*, assumes that approval for domestic projects will be granted automatically as long as such projects do not require government financing and as long as they fall into the permitted and encouraged categories. The catalog allows for some flexibility, since companies in the permitted category are considered to be encouraged if they export 100% of their output. Similarly, enterprises in the restricted category may be upgraded to be permitted if their exports account for at least 70% of their output.[63]

Under the WTO's dispute settlement mechanism, countries could file complaints and legally take retaliatory action against China for violations of WTO rules. Membership in the WTO also provided for more transparency with respect to barriers to trade and investment and more official reporting of economic conditions throughout the country. These provisions promised to be of great assistance to foreign investors. Questions remain, however, on how thoroughly Beijing abides by the rules and whether stripping away barriers to trade and investment is like digging through shale. Taking away an official layer merely exposes multiple layers underneath, and some jolting process, such as hydraulic fracking, is needed to release the benefits trapped beneath.

As will be discussed later in this book, despite its accession to the WTO, the PRC government is still able to maintain considerable control over foreign investors through its licensing and other processes. Virtually every activity by businesses requires a license, and like that which occurs in other bureaucracies, license applications can inexplicitly be pushed to the bottom of the pile. The application also can become like a slight of hand trick—now you see it, now you don't.

The FDI Solution to Mao's Problem

The inflow of foreign direct investment and the forces it unleashed in the PRC economy provided a solution to the economic constraints faced by China under Mao. In general, FDI has two primary effects. The first is the direct effect on capital formation, employment, production, exports and national income. The foreign invested enterprise uses imported equipment, hires local labor, produces for export and perhaps also for local consumption and pays wages that generally are higher than those in domestic companies. Without foreign investment or the emulation of products of foreign investors, there would be few products made in China that could be sold on international markets.

Perhaps more important are the indirect effects of FDI on technological progress, in generating competition, and in the demonstration effect. These effects are more difficult to quantify. Technology often is embedded in machines and in the manufacturing process. The products of the foreign-invested enterprises often spawn a host of competing products ranging from outright copies that compete with the foreign brand name to cheaper domestic versions which are a better match for the wallets of local consumers. The foreign-invested enterprise ultimately becomes a conduit for information about the outside world, and company managers may bring a higher standard of living into the community that locals seek to emulate.

From the previous chapters summarizing China's attempts to modernize and industrialize following the 1949 revolution, it is apparent that FDI contributed to solving several basic economic problems of the Maoist economy.[64] The major cause of the starvation in the countryside during the Great Leap Forward and food shortages during the Cultural Revolution was not the lack of agricultural production. The peasants starved because the industrial sector needed capital and resources to develop, and these resources had to be taken from somewhere. Other than agriculture, there was no other source of surplus capital and production. With FDI and reforms, capital and resources could come from abroad without placing additional burdens on the farmers or borrowing excessively from foreign sources. FDI may not have raised production of agricultural goods, but it reduced the need to requisition harvests from the farmers.

The second problem that FDI solved was that the industries needed technological upgrading and modern equipment. Since reverse engineering went only so far, the technology and equipment had to be imported. However, even importing modern production machinery might not resolve the problem completely, since engineers would have to be brought in to train workers on how to operate and repair the machinery. These foreign hires also required payments in foreign exchange. The increased need for imports also generated a deficit in trade and a shortage of foreign exchange. FDI helped to resolve this problem since foreign firms usually paid for the equipment with their own funds, and in the case of joint ventures, the Chinese side only needed to provide the land and labor and to navigate the local and national approval process. Since about half of Chinese exports have originated from foreign invested enterprises, without them, China would not have had the foreign exchange to pay for needed imports.

In order to appreciate the difference that foreign invested enterprises have made in China's access to foreign exchange, one only has to go back to Deng's trip to a special session of the United Nations in 1974. This was the first time a modern leader of China had visited the United States. Before departing for New York, the government reportedly scoured the banks in

Beijing for foreign exchange to pay for the trip. They could scrape together only $38,000, barely enough to pay for the hotels, food, and transportation for the entourage.[65]

Compare that to the situation after reform and opening. As shown in **Figure 4.5**, in 1980, the PRC's foreign exchange reserves stood at -$1.3 billion. By 1990, the reserves had risen to $11.1 billion, and then to $165.6 billion in 2000, before rising to $2,847.3 billion in 2010 and to $3,311.6 billion in 2012. This $3.4 trillion in foreign exchange reserves is an incredible amount considering that China's GDP as recently as 2007 also was $3.4 trillion.

FIGURE 4.5. CHINA'S FOREIGN EXCHANGE RESERVES

Billions of U.S. Dollars

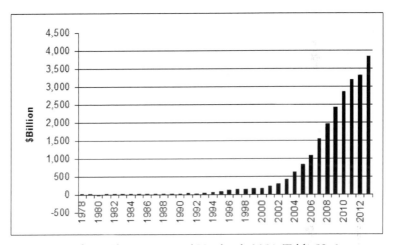

Source: Data from China Statistical Yearbook 2014, Table 19-6.

The third problem that FDI solved was that China's default economic model was that of the Soviet Union and Marxism. China first tried to emulate the Soviet Union and then to surpass it by being more true to the doctrines of Marx. FDI was the key to changing the thought process of Party leaders and convincing them that markets were an integral part of socialism. This change in thinking led to their breaking down the institutional barriers to China's adoption of market-based principles.

Even those Chinese leaders critical of FDI have been compelled to recognize its influence. Some claim that FDI has had a negative effect on China's economic growth because domestic firms have been unable to compete with foreign branded and designed goods. Many of these domestic firms have had to close or have survived as zombie companies meeting payrolls through state or local subsidies. Competition in the Chinese marketplace, however, is intense not only between foreign and domestic firms but also among domestic enterprises. Over time, even without foreign competition and imports, the more inefficient zombie enterprises would have had to close because of domestic competition and because local governments cannot continue to subsidize their operations forever. In fact, Beijing often has a hand in consolidating firms in an industry with too many uncompetitive small enterprises that require local subsidies to survive.

Others criticize FDI for creating income gaps between the rural poor and the rising urban middle class and *nouveau riche*. They also point to regional income disparities between the inland provinces and those with FDI and foreign influence on the eastern coastal regions. However, when an economy grows at rates exceeding 10% per year for a quarter century, some people and some companies will rise faster than others. In China, the tide of development has lifted all boats as hundreds of millions of people have been pulled out of poverty. The root cause of rural discontent, however, is likely to be less the income gap but the overt discrimination against rural residents that began during the Great Leap Forward and continues today with the *hukou* registration system and also confiscation of farmland by local governments.[66] Some of the income gap, moreover, is due to corruption by local officials. Foreign enterprises are not the problem. In some cases, they are helping to solve it. The economic planners in Beijing recognize that the way to raise rural and inland income is not to halt inflows of foreign capital but to encourage foreign investors to locate factories where incomes are lower and labor is plentiful. The current emphasis and incentives for FDI are directed toward having it flow into areas away from the east coast to the western and interior regions and on servicing the domestic market rather than just exporting. Chengdu and Chongqing, cities inland from the eastern coast, are becoming centers for new FDI.

The larger issue with respect to FDI is the current attempt by China to retake its position as the central economy of the world. It is creating national champion companies that can compete on a global scale and is gradually making it harder for foreign companies to compete in the Chinese domestic market. Beijing would like nothing better than to make the twenty-first century the Chinese century. This attempt by Beijing to re-Sinify its economy may not bring Chinese industrialization to a halt, but it may bring unintended consequences.

Now the question before Beijing is this: has the Chinese economy progressed enough that it can go it alone? Are domestic enterprises, research centers, skilled workers, and managers able to compete in world markets without foreign input? Or has integration into the world economy progressed so far that there is no turning back? Should Beijing back off and let the markets decide who the winners and losers are? By reverting to nationalist industrial policies and trying to establish a new version of socialism with Chinese characteristics, will Beijing end up strangling itself?

In the following chapters, we examine the actual FDI experience in China in more detail—first from Hong Kong and Taiwan, then from the United States, Japan, South Korea, and Europe. We then look at Chinese industrial policy and how Beijing is pursuing its goal to become a dominant economy and force in the world, and finally we examine Chinese outward direct investment and how Chinese companies are going global.

Chapter 5. FDI and the Special Economic Zones

Foreign direct investment has pervaded almost every corner of China. From formerly being excluded by a xenophobic and anti-capitalist leadership, FDI now is actively courted by pro-capitalist officials at all levels of government. According to data reported to the United Nations Conference on Trade and Development, annual FDI inflows that began as a trickle in 1980 from neighboring areas in Hong Kong, Macao, and Taiwan, reached $40 billion per year in 1996, surpassed $100 billion in 2008, and reached $124 billion in 2011 before ebbing to $121 billion in 2012. The accumulation of realized FDI reached $400 billion in 2005, passed $800 billion in 2008, and exceeded $1 trillion in 2010. (See **Figure 5.1**.)

Data Cautions

Data on FDI, which are notoriously difficult to compute for any country, are even more problematic for the PRC. In addition to the general problems that affect the reliability of statistics in China, two major problems arise to distort data. The first is that the individual provinces and other reporting units may under- or over-report totals depending on the policy *de jure*. If some activity is encouraged and Party officials are judged on how fast it is growing in their jurisdictions, they may overstate the actual numbers. For example, for 2010, the total FDI reported by the provinces in China was $173.4 billion, not the $115 billion reported as the total FDI for the nation.[67]

FIGURE 5.1. ANNUAL AND ACCUMULATED AMOUNTS OF FOREIGN DIRECT INVESTMENT IN CHINA

Billions of U.S. Dollars

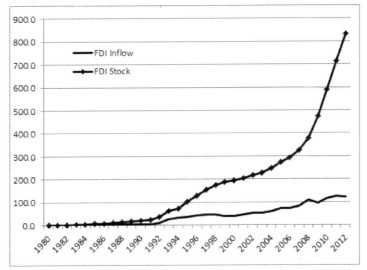

Source: Data from United Nations Conference on Trade and Development, UNCTADStats database.

The second problem with China's FDI data is that advanced industrialized countries report FDI to the United Nations on a net basis. The data on gross direct investment based on registrations and approvals are adjusted for capital flows between the parent companies and their foreign invested affiliates. If, for example, a U.S. parent company repatriates capital from a subsidiary in China, this capital flowing back from China is subtracted from investment capital going to China. Likewise, if the subsidiary retains profits that are then invested into its China operations, those profits count as FDI. These intra-company capital flows are added to the raw FDI numbers to give a net inflow number for direct investments. For China, a difference between its domestic data on foreign direct investment reported as foreign capital utilized and the data it reported to the United Nations as FDI appears after 2004. The higher U.N. numbers presumably include reinvested profits by foreign subsidiaries in China. By 2012, the

U.N. total for FDI capital stock in China at $1,353.9 billion is $11.4 billion higher than the *China Statistical Yearbook* total of $1,276.1 billion.[68] Since 2004, the PRC government apparently has been reporting the net inflow number for FDI in accord with international practice.

Investment Incentives

FDI in China was much more than a marriage of convenience. Companies were pushed to go to China by rising costs and the operation of global supply chains. They also were pulled to China by attractive incentives provided both by Beijing and by local governments. For most of the period of reform and opening, China provided special tax incentives to foreign companies to invest there and in special economic zones (SEZs) in particular. The major tax incentives were:

- The corporate income tax on foreign invested enterprises located in special economic zones, state new- and high-technology industrial zones or economic and technological development zones was levied at the rate of 15 percent instead of the 33 percent on other enterprises with foreign investment.

- Production enterprises with foreign investment were exempt from income tax for the first two years from the year they became profitable and were allowed a 50 percent reduction for the following three years.

- Income tax on enterprises with foreign investment located in mid-west China that were engaged in projects encouraged by the government were levied at a reduced rate of 15 percent for a period of another three years following the expiration of the five-year period of tax exemption and reduction.

- Enterprises with foreign investment that adopted advanced technology were exempt from income tax for the first two years and allowed a 50 percent reduction for the following six years.

- In addition to the two-year tax exemption and three-year tax reduction treatment, foreign-invested enterprises producing for export were allowed to reduce their income tax rate by 50 percent as long as their annual exports accounted for 70 percent or more of their sales volume.[69]

Each SEZ also has been able to provide additional benefits and incentives. SEZ governments also have more freedom in negotiating and entering into trade contracts. They may provide partial exemptions to the value-added tax and more liberal rules on foreign currency trade. Free trade zones also have simplified customs procedures including fee exemptions for stored and transit goods. Imports entering the zone from outside China are exempt from both customs duties and value-added taxes. Goods which are eventually imported into China from the free trade zone, however, are subject to a 17 percent value-added tax and customs duties.

The incentives for FDI often are quite lucrative. For example, in October 2010, Intel began manufacturing wafers at its first Asian fabrication plant for semiconductors located in Dalian in the Bohai Sea Economic Rim area. This entailed an investment of $3 to $5 billion. Intel said that the incentives by the Chinese government to locate the new plant there could increase the profits of the plant by $100 million a year.[70]

The effect of investment incentives on the eventual location of greenfield plants can be illustrated by a case of a cross-strait tug-of-war for investment. In 2003, Taiwan's Hon Hai Precision Industries (Foxconn) planned to set up a new global operations headquarters together with an R&D center in Taipei County in Taiwan. The company became so frustrated in its negotiations with local authorities that it considered reducing or even withdrawing its plan. As it turned out, Hon Hai had a competitive offer from the Shanghai City government to locate there. In addition to the usual tax incentives, Shanghai offered a large tract of land with roads and other infrastructure including optical cable as well as water, power and gas utilities free of cost. Shanghai also offered a golf-course improvement beside the proposed Hon Hai facility. In contrast, Taipei County could only offer tax advantages.[71]

There is little doubt that China has become an attractive location for FDI. In addition to ranking number one in various surveys of investment climate, the size and growth rate of the Chinese domestic market provides a draw that companies can ignore only at their peril. One American company that supplies equipment for airports and is locating production to China stated that the cost savings were not that significant but China was expected to build over a dozen new airports.[72] They had to be closer to the action and qualify as domestic production if certain Buy China provisions were imposed.

Clustering

FDI in China exhibits four distinct patterns. The first is the clustering effect, created partly by the opening of special economic zones and regions with explicit incentives for FDI to locate there.[73] The second is the westward movement of investment away from the densely populated and relatively high wage regions on the east coast and in Beijing toward the interior and less densely populated areas of the country. The third is a gradual progression from labor-intensive manufacturing primarily for export toward manufacturing to sell in the domestic Chinese market. The fourth is a progression up the value chain from low-end manufacturing toward services and research and development. In this section, the focus is on clustering. The remaining three distinct patterns are addressed in the context of discussions on the foreign investment record and government industrial policy.

When the period of reform and opening began, Chen Yun, one of China's top economic planners, postulated his bird in a cage thesis in a December 1980 speech. He emphasized that the enlivening of the economy through markets should not overstep central planning. For Chen, the relationship between the two is like a bird in a cage. The bird is the market mechanism, and the cage is central planning (and control). The bird should not be held so tightly that it dies; it needs some room to fly but only within the cage. Without the confines of the cage, it will fly away (spread uncontrollably).[74] In order to enliven the economy, central planning should control markets. Markets should not dictate central planning. At this time, Chen also compared the reform process to crossing the river by feeling the rocks underneath, and he emphasized the go-slow approach. He clashed with Deng Xiaoping who wanted faster growth and reform, and he was eventually sidelined, but the concept of the bird in a cage continued.

By attempting to keep FDI and the market mechanism confined within the cage of special economic zones, China serendipitously created two beneficial effects. The first has been the clustering effect well known and practiced in global manufacturing circles. The second is a competitive effect as each special economic zone competed with others to attract industry. This competition among SEZs has helped to improve the business environment not only in the zones that are competing with each other but in other parts of China as well.

Foreign production in the SEZs also created a strong demonstration effect. International companies and their employees brought world-class, brand-name products into the economy that consumers could buy and domestic companies could emulate. Even products made strictly for export somehow made it into the local economy. The secret extra shift at factories, shipments that fell off the truck or C-grade production items that should have been destroyed fed black markets in the local economy. Deliberate copying of foreign products, particularly consumer goods, also has been rampant, so much so that some have argued that the *faux* products serve as free advertisement for the genuine product. As incomes have risen, so has demand for the real thing. In many cases, Chinese companies have been able to adapt the foreign product to Chinese tastes and conditions and also make improvements. Today, China's markets are some of the most competitive in the world. For consumers, stores carry not only the Western brand-name items but popular items from Japan, South Korea, Taiwan, and other neighbors in Asia. There also is a proliferation of domestic brand-name products. This competition is brutal, but it has brought a higher level of consumption to Chinese households.

As popularized by Harvard professor Michael Porter, the clustering concept posits that creativity and productivity are enhanced when a set of companies producing both inputs for and outputs of a particular type of product locate within a geographical region. He has stated that "in a global economy—which boasts rapid transportation, high-speed communication, and accessible markets—one would expect location to diminish in importance. But the opposite is true. The enduring competitive advantages in a global economy are often heavily local, arising from concentrations of highly specialized skills and knowledge, institutions, rivals, related businesses, and sophisticated customers."[75] An industrial cluster is formed when a critical mass of companies locate in a particular geological space. This space can be a country, state, region, or even a city.

Some of the well-known industrial clusters in the world include Silicon Valley in California for computers and information technology; Detroit, Cologne and Nagoya for automobiles; Hollywood for motion pictures; Paris, London, and New York for fashion; Digital Media City in Korea for information technology; and the leather footwear and ski equipment clusters in Italy. In China, the Pearl River Delta (which includes Guangzhou, Shenzhen, Zhuhai, and Dongguan) attracted a cluster of firms centered on low-cost manufacturing of electronic equipment, toys, furniture, and apparel. The Yangtze River Delta (which includes Shanghai, Suzhou, and Kunshan) also has become a cluster of firms specializing in finance, heavy industry, research and electronic equipment, particularly notebook computers.

The key benefits of clustering are not just access to inputs needed for manufacturing and lower costs of production but the impact on innovation and productivity. In a globalized world, inputs as bulky as iron ore or coal can be shipped from distant places overseas, but hiring skilled engineers who have worked for best-practice competitors, meeting in coffee shops or tea houses to discuss ideas, or designing a component with just the right characteristics that fits precisely into a product becomes less difficult as the concentration of potential actors in a geographical space is increased.

Clustering also takes advantage of lean manufacturing as pioneered by Toyota Motors. Toyota's just-in-time production system relies heavily on suppliers that both innovate on their own and deliver components and parts just as they are needed on the production line. This reduces the need for warehousing parts, allows defects to be eliminated more quickly, and promotes efficiency and increased productivity. It was said in the 1980s that while Japanese industry relied on just-in-time, American industry relied on just-in-case; that is, stocks of spare parts were kept just in case there was a logistical delay or strike.

Hong Kong investors understood well the concept of manufacturing clusters and infrastructure. Hong Kong's geographical space is so small that by necessity suppliers and buyers had to cluster and highways and ports had to be in place to handle the manufacturing inputs and production to be exported. In addition to manufacturing, Hong Kong investors also were instrumental in property development and in infrastructure construction in the SEZs.

In the 1980s, the SEZ of Dongguan became China's leading center for the manufacture of computers and computer parts. The industrial chain in Dongguan became so complete that the city was able to supply 95 percent of all the component parts needed to assemble a desktop computer. It became the purchasing center for the world's top computer companies including IBM, Compaq, and Hewlett Packard. The city was so important to the global computer industry, that an IBM vice-president once made the hyperbolic remark that a traffic jam on the Dongguan-Shenzhen expressway could be enough to cause worldwide fluctuations in computer prices.[76]

In the SEZs and other special regions in China, as large manufacturing plants, particularly from Taiwan, Japan, and South Korea, moved there, their suppliers followed. This was the *guanxi* (relationship) effect. Suppliers moved with their buyers based on long-standing relations in their home economies. For the large manufacturers, these existing suppliers were trusted, their products proven and transactions could be accomplished without extensive legal work and documentation. The resulting mini-clusters amounted to business supply chains that had a history of being linked together elsewhere.

For a true cluster to develop, however, a region needs more than one vertically linked supply chain. It needs to be able to attract a variety of businesses associated with a particular industrial sector. For example, the business cluster might have a plant assembling laptop computers that has attracted investments by the associated suppliers of parts, components and shipping services, but it also needs makers of similar products, such as cameras, navigational devices, or telecommunication gear in order to benefit from both the economies gained by proximity and the cross-fertilization of ideas so vital to progress in high-technology industries.

A 2011 World Bank study of China's rapid development concluded that "the special economic zones and industrial clusters have made crucial contributions to China's economic success. Foremost, the special economic zones (especially the first several) successfully tested the market economy and new institutions and became role models for the rest of the country to follow."[77]

Competition for FDI

As the Chinese economy has developed, intense competition has emerged among industrial areas to capture clusters of firms. This new competition is driven mainly by local governments whose first responsibility it is to create a high quality business environment and then to recruit businesses to locate there. Among the requirements that depend on local government are, first, basic utilities, such as safe drinking water and a reliable electrical and natural gas supply. Second, there must be a modern and efficient transportation infrastructure so firms can use advanced logistical methods. Third, there must be access to both well-educated people and to skilled labor. Fourth, there must be personal safety, an effective police force and freedom from extortion and other crimes. Fifth, there must be cooperative and transparent government. If regulatory red tape is onerous, businesses must devote time to endless dialog with government and spend considerable resources on entertainment of local and central government officials. Sixth, there must be a court or arbitration system that can resolve disputes quickly and fairly.[78]

Table 5.1 shows the amounts of foreign direct investment actually realized (as opposed to contracted) by the top ten provinces or metropolitan areas during 1990, 2000, and 2010 with cumulative amounts over that 20-year period. From 1990 to 2010, and also in prior years, Guangdong Province was the top recipient of FDI with $270.18 billion. Jiangsu Province was second with $228.37 billion, and Shanghai was third with $113.55 billion. Other provinces ranked high were Shandong, Liaoning, Zhejiang, and Fujian. All these jurisdictions are located on China's east coast. Those provinces to China's west and interior, such as Tibet, Ningxia, Gansu, and Xinjiang ranked lowest in FDI received.

TABLE 5.1. TOP TEN PROVINCES AND METROPOLITAN AREAS FOR FOREIGN DIRECT INVESTMENT

Billion U.S. Dollars

Province or Metropolitan Area	2010	2000	1990	Cumulative 1990-2010
Guangdong (Includes Guangzhou, Shenzhen, Dongguan, and Zuhai)	20.26	11.28	1.46	270.18
Jiangsu (Includes Suzhou, Nanjing, and Changzhou)	28.50	6.43	0.14	228.37
Shanghai (Includes Pudong)	11.12	3.16	0.18	113.55
Shandong (Includes Qingdao and Yantai)	9.17	2.97	0.15	107.43
Liaoning (Includes Shengyang and Dalian)	20.75	2.04	0.25	100.33
Zhejiang (Includes Hangzhou and Ningbo)	11.00	1.61	0.05	89.86
Fujian (Includes Fuzhou and Xiamen)	5.80	3.43	0.29	88.09
Tianjin (Includes Taijin Aeronautic Industrial Zone)	10.85	1.17	0.08	64.28
Beijing	6.36	1.68	0.28	58.22
Hubei	4.05	0.94	0.03	32.99

Source: Underlying data for FDI actually realized from various Chinese national and provincial statistical yearbooks accessed through China Data Online.

The amounts for the three sample years show how much FDI has increased over the period, even though the data are not adjusted for inflation. In 1990, except for Guangdong's $1.5 billion, most provinces received less than $300 million. After Guangdong, Fujian ($290 million), directly across from Taiwan, and Beijing ($280 million) had received the most FDI. In 2000, Guangdong continued to lead significantly with $11.28 billion received, but considerable amounts also were received by Jiangsu ($6.43

billion), Fujian ($3.43 billion), and Shanghai ($3.16 billion). In 2010, the FDI received by Jiangsu ($28.50 billion) and Liaoning ($20.75 billion) in the Bo Hai Sea area on the northern coast exceeded that received by Guangdong ($20.26 billion). As will be discussed below, this reflects rising wage rates, lower incentives for investors, and the central government's emphasis on spreading FDI to western and northern regions of the country. Although the amounts of FDI for Beijing are smaller than those in other leading areas, they are significant because they tend to be in offices, services, and research and development.

Table 5.2 shows other provinces with rising amounts of FDI. In 2010, FDI received in the central provinces of Sichuan ($7.01 billion), Chongqing ($6.34 billion), and Henan ($6.2 billion) exceeded that received by coastal Fujian ($5.80 billion).

TABLE 5.2. OTHER PROVINCES WITH RISING FOREIGN DIRECT INVESTMENT ACTUALLY REALIZED

Billion U.S. Dollars

Area	2010	2000	1990	Cumulative 1990-2010
Hunan	5.18	0.68	0.01	32.46
Hebei	3.83	0.68	0.04	30.63
Jiangxi	5.10	0.23	0.01	29.75
Henan	6.25	0.56	0.01	29.21
Sichuan (includes Chengdu)	7.01	0.44	0.01	23.72
Anhui	5.01	0.32	0.01	23.26
Chongqing	6.34	0.24	0.00	20.43

Source: Underlying data from various Chinese national and provincial statistical yearbooks accessed through China Data Online.

CHAPTER 6.   TWO INVESTMENT CLUSTERS

Guangdong and Shenzhen Investment Clusters

As noted in previous chapters, the clustered FDI development in China began with investment mainly from Hong Kong. Businesses from Hong Kong were the first back into China after the tumultuous years of the Cultural Revolution. At that time, most companies from Western countries and other Asian neighbors were reluctant to step into China's great unknown. Suspicions lingered about whether property would be appropriated by the government, whether stability in the country would last, whether profits, if any, could be repatriated, and whether communist egalitarian labor could be trained to work in market-based enterprises. For many Hong Kong entrepreneurs, however, the prospective benefits of being able to take advantage of low-cost labor and ample land directly across the border overshadowed the potential risks of operating in the much too communist China.

In 1979, Yuan Geng, who had been born in Guangdong, proposed establishing the Shekou Industrial Export Zone in Shenzhen to the Guangdong government and the Ministry of Transportation in Beijing. Later in 1979, business leaders in Hong Kong suggested that the Shekou zone be expanded to include property development and tourism. They proposed the name "special economic zone" be applied to reflect this broader scope. The SEZs were approved by the National People's Congress in August 1980 and included special provisions for overseas Chinese to transfer equipment for investments without paying customs duties.[79]

At first, Hong Kong businesses relocated their production of low-end, labor intensive products, such as toys, shoes, and consumer electronics, across the border to Shenzhen and other locations in Guangdong province. Production from these factories would be shipped back into Hong Kong for export to markets all over the world. Some referred to this as store in front, factory in the back, meaning that things were made in neighboring China but sold through Hong Kong.

As an SEZ, Shenzhen's city government was given considerable latitude in attracting investments and in building the city. Almost everyone in Shenzhen came from somewhere else, so the city was less hampered by the need for *guanxi* (business and political connections) to get things done. By the time Deng Xiaoping visited Shenzhen in 1992, the rustic fishing village had grown to 2.6 million people. Hong Kong still dominated in FDI in Shenzhen with $2.26 billion invested from 1986 to 1992. However, Japan with $776 million, Taiwan with $187 million, and the United States with $161 million invested were overcoming initial misgivings and, in the case of Taiwan, government restraints.[80]

Shenzhen and the surrounding Guangdong province benefited from the 1984 Sino-British Joint Declaration that opened the way in 1997 for Hong Kong to revert back to Chinese sovereignty. Beijing recognized that the income gap between Hong Kong and nearby regions in China would make it difficult to keep Chinese citizens from attempting to emigrate to Hong Kong once it reverted back to the PRC. They addressed this problem partly by promoting rapid economic growth in the border region to narrow the gap in incomes and standards of living.

Despite the growth throughout Guangdong province, the development of Shenzhen made it an attractive city for migrants. Shenzhen, much like Hong Kong, had to be fenced off from the rest of China. It has maintained 17 checkpoints through which 198 million people and 16 million vehicles crossed in 2010.[81] Since Shenzhen is a customs zone, the checkpoints also are used to control unauthorized transfers of raw materials and other goods from this free-trade zone to the rest of the PRC.

When I passed through one of the Shenzhen checkpoints in 1997, security was less stringent than that at the crossing point into Hong Kong. Our driver had to show some paperwork, and we proceeded without much delay. At the Hong Kong checkpoint, the process was equally efficient, but I noticed some guards lying on the ground looking at the road as vehicles passed by. I was told that they were looking at mirrors that allowed them to check for undocumented workers riding under the trucks.

A sure sign that markets were returning to China occurred in 1990 when Shenzhen established the Shenzhen Stock Exchange. This bourse was to mirror the stock exchange in Hong Kong and relied heavily on advice and training from officials of the Hong Kong Stock Exchange. At first, investors in southern China did not know anything about investing in stocks, and foreigners could buy shares only of specific Chinese companies.

While in Shenzen, I met with a government official who said that not too long after the stock exchange was established, it was struggling to attract investors. An order came down from Beijing that government officials in Shenzhen were to buy stocks on the exchange. Being good Party members, the officials withdrew funds from their savings accounts and bought shares in Chinese companies. Eventually, values on the stock market soared. This official said that he gained enough on his investments that he bought a vacation villa up the coast from Shenzhen. The office in Beijing that had originally issued the order was so chagrined that Party members had made so much money from this quintessential capitalist institution that it ordered the officials to give the money back that they had made. No one did, except perhaps the official in Beijing who had issued the order. In 2012, there were 1,427 companies listed on the Shenzhen Stock Exchange with a combined market value of more than $1 trillion.

By 2010, Shenzhen with its population of 10.3 million had grown larger than New York City. Among the numerous foreign companies operating there were many of the large multinational corporations, such as Taiwan's Foxconn that assembles electronic products for companies such as Apple and Dell. Shenzhen also has attracted domestic Chinese companies. Huawei (electronics, information technology) started as a marketing agent for Hong Kong. It established its electronics business in Shenzhen after becoming frustrated with the bureaucratic process in Beijing.[82] BYD (batteries, electric cars) and Shenzhen Hasee Computer Co. also are headquartered in the SEZ. CSG Holding, China's largest architectural glass manufacturer, and Vanke, China's largest property developer, also are resident there. With labor costs rising, the SEZ is now moving from assembly plants to services, particularly financial services and logistics, cultural industries, Internet-based industries and research and development.

A typical experience might be that of the Compaq Computer Company. According to plant managers on a visit I made in 1997, Compaq had operated an assembly plant in Shenzhen since 1994 that made personal computers, power supplies, and chassis. It had achieved the highest level of quality of all the company's overseas plants. As an enticement to locate in Shenzhen, the company was offered two years of tax exemption, a tax rate of 7.5 percent after the first profits and continuing for three years after which the rate was to go to 33 percent, the usual Chinese rate. The basic monthly wage in the plant was 600 yuan ($69) with a 200 yuan bonus. Workers also received free food, lodging and other allowances.

Shenzhen has served as a link between the Chinese Mainland and Hong Kong and a transport hub in coastal southern China. More than just a manufacturing center, Shenzhen has also become a bridge to the rest of the Pearl River Delta. Shenzhen facilitated the expansion of manufacturing out of Hong Kong and its dispersion throughout the Pearl River Delta. Shenzhen has risen as a major shipping competitor to Hong Kong. The ports of Shenzhen rank right behind those in Hong Kong as the fourth largest in the world with actual throughput of 22.5 million 20-foot equivalent container units in 2010.[83] Sino-foreign joint ventures developed the port with investments of more than $20 billion.

Shenzhen also has led in policy developments, such as the duty free import of raw materials used in processing as long as they are incorporated into products for export. This aspect of export processing zones so common elsewhere in the world was not understood well in China in 1978 when Shenzhen forged some initial agreements for processing products from Hong Kong. Eventually this small step, once it became a feature of other special economic zones, became a key factor in attracting huge amounts of foreign investment in manufacturing plants in other such zones throughout China.[84]

Beyond Shenzhen lies the rest of the Pearl River Delta Economic Zone that is centered on Guangzhou in Guangdong province. The zone includes Zhuhai and Dongguan, also SEZs. From the beginning of reform, Guangdong province as a whole was given greater freedom to pursue economic reforms. During the initial ten years of reform, the internationalization of the Chinese economy occurred primarily in the Pearl River Delta. In 1988 Guangdong was designated a comprehensive economic reform area.

The province of Guangdong has become the home to more than 90,000 foreign-invested enterprises, nearly a quarter of all such enterprises in China. These enterprises account for half of Guangdong's exports and industrial output. Maersk Line, the global shipper, has its largest global office in Guangdong, and Suzuki Motors and Intel have moved parts of sensitive departments such as R&D there. Major investors in the province come from Hong Kong, Taiwan, Japan, South Korea, Singapore, and the United States, but domestic enterprises equally drive the growth of the economy.[85] Labor intensive, export oriented enterprises, such as furniture making, also gathered to Guangdong. (See **Figure 6.1**)

FIGURE 6.1. WHOLESALE FURNITURE MART IN GUANGDONG

Photograph by D. Nanto

Shenzhen and the wider Pearl River Delta are a prime example of the bird that flew from the cage. Foreign direct investment created counter forces of competition that came not only from other enterprises but from governments elsewhere in the country that sought to emulate the Pearl River Delta experience. Beijing was compelled to continuously expand the bird cage until markets spread to most of the Chinese economy. Beijing still refers to China's modern economy as socialism with Chinese characteristics, but in reality it has become a form of market-based socialism. Most economic decisions are made on the basis of market conditions, but aspects of socialism continue as evidenced by the emphasis on five-year plans, on state-owned enterprises, and on heavy government regulation.

The Suzhou and Kunshan Cluster

The government in the special economic zone of Suzhou and one of its jurisdictions, the Kunshan Economic Technological Development Zone, in the Yangtze River Delta in Jiangsu Province near Shanghai is a good example of competition among SEZs for industrial clusters. Suzhou traditionally was an agricultural region situated in the downstream of the Yangtze River Drainage Basin. With a history of more than 2,500 years it is known for being a Paradise on Earth because of its natural beauty, classical gardens, bridges, and waters. Now Suzhou is a booming center for electronics production. Suzhou and in particular Kunshan city have built an industrial cluster producing notebook (laptop) computers. Suzhou has strived to complete a full house of notebook computer producers, suppliers, and supporting infrastructure and has succeeded in becoming the largest notebook computer production center in the world. Nine of the top ten Taiwanese notebook vendors have transplanted over 90 percent of their production lines to Suzhou with many concentrated in Kunshan. In 2005, Suzhou produced over 15 million sets of notebook computers, accounting for nearly 40 percent of the global total.

The movement to Kunshan began in 1993 when Hon Hai Precision Industries came in not only with its flagship subsidiary Foxconn but with a dozen other companies in which it had invested. These were the early Hon Hai companies that mainly produced the connectors, cases, and components for electrical equipment. Over the next twelve years, other Taiwanese companies also established facilities in Kunshan. Among them were MiTAC Technology (GPS, pocket PC, mobile phones, laptops), Entery Industrial (computer peripheries), Jowle Technology (connectors),

Twinhead (laptops), Clevo Computer (laptops), Advantech Company (industrial computers), Compal Electronics (monitors, laptops, TVs), Wistron InComm (laptops and PCs), Altec Company (digital cameras) and Coretronic (monitors, projectors, optical components).

Compal Electronics alone brought nearly 300 chain suppliers with it when it located two laptop production plants in Kunshan. U.S., Japanese, South Korean, and European firms also have made sizable investments in Suzhou. Two notable examples are Japan's Fujitsu and Europe's Nokia. Kunshan also has been attracting other types of foreign investments. In 2012, Taiwan's leading food manufacturing company, the President Enterprises Corporation, announced that it would spend $100 million to build a second factory in Kunshan.[86]

The density of the transplanted supplier chains in Kunshan has become so high that all the components and parts for producing a laptop computer could be gathered in an hour or two within a 40-mile area.[87] This close geographical spacing has become increasingly important as the information technology business model has changed from build-to-forecast (BTF) to build-to-order (BTO). Rather than producing according to forecasts, companies build as orders come in. This model reduces waste by eliminating the need to stockpile output, but it requires increasingly quick reaction times in production and shipping and works best in closely packed and streamlined production networks.[88]

Kunshan made it as easy as possible for the Taiwanese companies to settle there. It established industrial parks and high-technology centers similar to those in Taipei. Through a process called strategic coupling, Kunshan sought to replicate the industrial parks and special export zones in Taiwan. Kunshan's political leaders made six visits to Taiwan's Nantze Export Processing Zone (a combination export processing zone and industrial park) and Hsinchu Science Park (Taiwan's Silicon Valley with more than 400 information technology manufacturers). While in Taiwan, they learned about the operation of information technology manufacturing, including the legal system and related regulations, tax policy, and the structure of the administrative organizations. Kunshan officials specifically targeted what they called the "anchor tenants" that would attract secondary suppliers. They especially sought those companies at the final assembly level of the global IT supply network.

At one point, Kunshan's ex-Vice-Mayor Zhu Fengquan actually disassembled a notebook computer in order to understand the organization of the IT production chain. He determined which firms among the 800 or so parts and component producers had not invested in Kunshan and developed a strategy to attract the leading ones to the city.[89]

Figure 6.2 shows shipments of notebook computers by the leading brands in the 2009-2011 period. HP (U.S.) and Acer (Taiwan) were the two top brands with 25 million to 40 million units shipped. They were followed by Dell (U.S.) and Lenovo (China) with 20 million to 25 million units shipped. A common perception among American consumers is that U.S. companies have moved their production of computers to China. What actually has occurred in the notebook computer sector is that U.S. companies source their products almost completely from China. The notebooks, themselves, are made primarily by Taiwanese companies located there, particularly in Kunshan.

FIGURE 6.2. TOP NOTEBOOK COMPUTER BRAND SHIPMENTS

Million Units

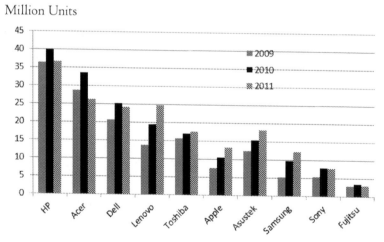

Source: Data from DIGITIMES.

Most of the firms that were attracted to Suzhou already had located production facilities in the Pearl River Delta. These companies built facilities in Suzhou in addition to, rather than in place of, their existing facilities in the south.[90] However, the computer makers MiTAC and Acer relocated their Mainland-based production there from Guangdong and the Pearl River Delta primarily because of the better business environment and infrastructure planning in Suzhou and Kunshan as the industry shifted toward the build-to-order business model.[91]

The experience of Suzhou in attracting investment and forming an industrial cluster of manufacturers is being emulated throughout China. Every province is seeking new FDI and industry, but it is becoming more and more difficult to develop complete industrial clusters as occurred in Guangdong and Jiangsu provinces. Still, as foreign investment is dispersed into other parts of the country, the economy as a whole is being upgraded.

CHAPTER 7. TAIWANESE INVESTMENTS AND SECURITY CONCERNS

For Taiwan, the political relationship with Mainland China is quite different from that of Hong Kong. Unlike Taiwan, sovereignty over Hong Kong reverted to the PRC in 1997. There are political differences but no threat of war between Hong Kong and Beijing. Even during the Great Cultural Revolution, when Red Guards began to move toward Hong Kong, Mao told them to back off.

For Beijing, however, the communist revolution cannot be complete without the return of Taiwan. After Chiang Kai-shek retreated to the island in 1949, there has been both hope and revulsion, depending which side one is on, about the prospect of being reunited under a one-China policy. Beijing sees only a renegade island that needs to be rejoined with the Mainland and become part of the PRC. Taipei also would hope for reunification but has a fading dream of bringing the Mainland back to its previous status as the Republic of China. Beijing offers a "one country, two systems" solution. Many in Taiwan seek recognition of the status quo: "two countries, two systems." If reunited with the Mainland, Taiwan ostensibly would do so only if the political system there were democratic and free.

The active shelling of each other across the Taiwan Strait with live ammunition ceased in 1958. The shelling on alternate days with leaflets stopped in 1979 when the United States and the PRC normalized relations. However, China's buildup of missiles pointed toward Taiwan, and Taiwan's purchases of military equipment from abroad have kept the stalemate anything but stale.

One of the reminders of the cross-strait contention is the huge red slogan signs erected on the coastlines facing each other. The sign on the Xiamen side in Fujian province says, "One Country, Two Systems," On Taiwan's Kinmen Island less than three miles across the water from Xiamen the sign says "Three Principles of the People Unite China." (See **Figures 7.1 and 7.2**) On a 2005 visit to Kinmen Island, I was told that one time a typhoon knocked over the Kinmen Island sign. With so much reconstruction required elsewhere, it went unrepaired for a while. Finally, the government of Xiamen sent a request to Kinmen to please repair the sign because it was a favorite tourist attraction for sightseeing boats from Xiamen. Indeed, as our boat neared the Kinmen Island sign, it passed by a heavily festooned boat loaded with tourists from Xiamen.

FIGURE 7.1. THE XIAMEN RED SIGN POINTED TOWARD TAIWAN "ONE COUNTRY TWO SYSTEMS"

Photograph by Dick Nanto

FIGURE 7.2 KINMEN ISLAND SIGN "THREE PRINCIPLES OF THE PEOPLE UNITE CHINA"

Photograph by D. Nanto

Fujian province had been the home of many of the Chinese who migrated to Taiwan in earlier centuries and found refuge there in 1949. It was natural, therefore, for many businesses in Taiwan to invest in Fujian province, one of the first of the four SEZs to be designated when reform and opening began. It too quickly grew from a fishing and agricultural island into a center for industry and commerce.

Taiwan's Policy Dilemmas

For Taiwan, investments and trade with the Mainland pose several dilemmas. While these policy issues amount to a somewhat existential challenge for Taiwan, they also apply to nations, particularly the United States, Japan and South Korea, with companies that are investing in the PRC. The dilemmas can be summarized as follows:

- **The security dilemma.** Is investment in and trade with the PRC undermining the security of Taiwan?
- **The economic dilemma.** Is investment in the PRC causing Taiwan's economy to hollow out (lose key manufacturing facilities) and to lose needed jobs?
- **The technology dilemma.** Is providing the PRC with high-technology knowledge, skills, or equipment contributing to the growth of a formidable competitor and military power?
- **The democratic and social dilemma.** Is the overwhelmingly large size of the Chinese market and the great number of Taiwanese operating there causing political attitudes to shift toward those more favorable to accommodation with the Mainland?

For Taiwan, the question of security hovers behind all relations with the Mainland. For many, the issue strikes at the heart of Taiwan's existence. Will Taiwan continue as a *de facto* independent state, or will it be absorbed into the Mainland under a framework similar to that of Hong Kong? China's concern is that Taiwan over time will "inch toward independence," while Taiwan's concern is that the economic integration of the two economies will, in the short term, lead to a hollowing out of the Taiwanese economy and, over the long term, lead to a loss of political autonomy as well. Beijing has indicated that it, indeed, is using the economic embrace of Taiwan (both luring Taiwanese companies to the PRC and fostering Taiwan's economic dependence on the Mainland) to promote political integration, to raise popular pressure on the government of Taiwan and "to lead to the unification with the motherland."[92]

Taiwan's policy through most of the post-1949 period has been to restrict economic relations with the Mainland, although this policy has been eased in steps as the rapidly developing cross-strait economic ties and potential investment opportunities pulled government policy along. For security reasons, Taiwan has maintained restrictions on its companies that invest in high technology production in the Mainland. The government's rationale includes both national security and economic security considerations. With respect to national security, Taiwan seeks to prevent dual-use products (civilian-use products with military applications) and economic production in general from contributing to Chinese military power. In terms of economic security, Taiwan has attempted to maintain its competitive edge at home and to keep its economy vibrant as production has moved to the PRC. Taiwan also has sought to use its restrictions on investments as bargaining power to compel Beijing to negotiate and to establish a national identity for Taiwan; that is, for Beijing to view Taiwan as a nation and diplomatic counterpart instead of as a province over which it should have sovereignty.[93]

Unlike the Berlin Wall, however, the government-imposed wall separating Taiwan from the Mainland economy has been more like a breaker along the seashore than a levee. The breaker diminishes the force of the large waves, but ultimately the water goes around the barrier to calmer seas on the other side. By 1990, the degree of dependence of Taiwanese exports to the Mainland market had surpassed the warning line of 10 percent established by Taiwan's Ministry of Economic Affairs. Exports continued to rise, despite the added cost of transshipment through Hong Kong or Macau where the cargo was either off-loaded onto trains or transferred to a ship bound for a Mainland port. This added considerably to the cost of Taiwan's exports to the PRC. It also raised production costs for Taiwanese factories that had located to the Mainland and required parts and components from their home base. It was estimated by the mid-1990s, that from one-third to two-thirds of all goods exported from Taiwan to the PRC were being shipped to Taiwan-invested enterprises.[94] This economic factor added to the pressure on Taipei to loosen restrictions on direct travel and shipping to the Mainland.

Even after 1991, when Taiwan gave official approval to cross-strait investments, the government in Taipei issued strict regulations to govern the activity. However, it rarely enforced them. The law stipulated that all investment activities on the Mainland had to be approved in advance and all investment activities conducted previously had to be registered within six months. Violators were to be fined up to NT$3 million (U.S. $120,000).[95] Until the end of 1993, however, Taiwan's Ministry of Economic Affairs had not punished any businesses for illegal investments in China.[96] Between 1993 and 2004, Taiwan reported that about $11 billion in previously unregistered investments had been approved and added to the government's list of official cross-strait investments.

By the year 2000, Taiwanese business leaders in both traditional and high-technology industries joined in pressuring their government to loosen the restrictions on investments in the PRC. Small- and medium-sized businesses could circumvent the strictures simply by using shell investment companies in Hong Kong or the Virgin Islands or other offshore tax havens, but if larger companies invested in Mainland manufacturing plants, their presence there would be too obvious for Taipei to ignore. The businesses asserted that the go slow, be patient policy and the existing bans on direct trade, shipping, travel, and postal services were hurting their ability to compete in global markets. In 1997, the president of Formosa Plastics, a company that was investing heavily in the Mainland but was having one project blocked, said of Taiwan's restrictions on investment, "I want to say something to Lee Teng-hui (the President of Taiwan). We are an egg trying to hit a rock. How can we win?"[97] In addition, Taiwan (using the name Chinese Taipei) and the People's Republic of China were both preparing for entry into the World Trade Organization (which became effective on January 1, 2002). Under WTO rules and accession commitments, trade restrictions between them would have to be lowered.

In 2002, the Democratic Progressive Party's Chen Shui-bian administration, under pressure from the business community, relaxed some of its restrictions on cross-strait economic relations. Called the principle of positive opening, effective management, this was a compromise between the industrial and business side of the pro-independence Democratic Progressive Party (DPP) and the farmers who sought protection from China's agricultural exports. The business interests wanted more access to the Mainland market while the farmers feared a flood of imports of food from across the Taiwan Strait. The compromise had been recommended by the 2001 Economic Development Advisory Conference established by President Chen.

The new policy was to open but keep some restrictions on relations with the Mainland (i.e., to manage economic relations). Under this new policy, Taipei increased the scope of products allowed to be imported from China from 2,000 to nearly 5,000 items. The government also allowed banks to establish representative offices (not branches) on the Mainland thereby making direct remittances across the Strait possible. The policy also increased the range of investments allowed, including production of high-technology consumer items such as notebook computers, mobile phones, and DVD players.

The approval process for investments in the Mainland also was simplified. Applications were divided into a general category that required approval on a case-by-case basis, and a prohibited category. The prohibited investments included those in the service sector, high-tech sectors, state-designated strategic and defense-related industries, agriculture receiving research and development subsidies from the Beijing government, and infrastructure projects such as power generation and water supply.

Taipei also raised the ceiling for the amount to be invested from $50 million to $80 million per project. Investments exceeding $80 million required a special review process. Applications for investments of less than $20 million would be automatically approved if no decision had been made by the regulatory authorities within one month.[98] The DPP government also opened the three mini-links with the Mainland from the two offshore islands of Quemoy (Kinmen) and Matsu primarily for Taiwanese with roots in those islands. This unilateral Taiwanese policy allowed for people and goods to go directly from the two islands to harbors in Xiamen in Fujian province. In essence, this legalized the smuggling of goods across the waterway by Taiwanese fishing boats that already had been occurring.

When I visited Kinmen Island in 2006, I expected to see the remains of fortifications and a small island economy with a smattering of tourist facilities. Instead, Kinmen was a bustling transshipment port with an airport that was bursting at the seams with travelers. Our host explained that island residents could fly from Taipei to the airport and then travel directly by ship from Kinmen to Xiamen in the PRC because of the mini-link that had been established. Obviously, the definition of a resident had been broadly interpreted. These people did not have to go through Hong Kong to get to China. It saved a lot of time and expense.

The next day our group of Americans toured the island and saw the forts and tunnels dug through solid rock where Taiwan's naval ships could dock without being exposed to incoming shells. Our plan was to stay the night and return to Taipei in the morning. However, a typhoon was approaching, and it was likely that the airport would be closed for a few days after it hit. Instead of going to the hotel, we returned to the airport and learned what might be a side benefit of friendly relations between the United States and Taiwan. Even though the returning flight that evening was booked solid, the airline bumped enough passengers with reservations to allow us to board. As we took our place in the line, we felt a tinge of guilt and hoped those whose seats we took would get out the next morning. We were relieved when our plane took off and later approached the main island and we saw the lights of Taipei 101, the Taipei World Trade Center, once the tallest building in the world.

Cross-strait ties were further liberalized in 2005 when the two sides agreed to allow direct cross-strait airline flights during the lunar New Year period. Under Taiwan's Ma Ying-Jeou's administration, cross-strait relations turned from confrontation to cooperation. His position was of One China, respective interpretations. This opened the door to a series of agreements on everything from trade and travel to law enforcement and customs cooperation.[99] In 2008, direct flights were allowed throughout the year, and direct shipping by air and sea also was authorized.

In 2013, Taiwan exported $81.8 billion in merchandise to the PRC. That made China Taiwan's top export destination with 27 percent of Taiwan's global exports. Taiwan's surplus in merchandise trade with the Mainland in 2012 at $40 billion was larger than its overall trade surplus of $30 billion.[100] Without trade with the PRC, Taiwan likely would be running a trade deficit instead of a surplus.

This dependence on trade with the Mainland continues to be a concern to policymakers in Taipei. In 2006, I visited Taiwan's Chung-Hua Institution for Economic Research. I was told by a member of the research team that if Taiwan became overly dependent on the PRC, then trade and investment would become too concentrated. All of Taiwan's eggs would be in one basket. She also noted that Beijing's influence over business is greater and exercised more bluntly than in a democratic state.[101]

Four Waves of Investment

Taiwan's investment in China has occurred in four phases or waves. The mainstays of the first wave that began in the late 1980s were small- and medium-sized firms in labor-intensive, cost-oriented, traditional sectors, such as garments, shoemaking, and food-processing, as well as firms in the mid- and downstream production chain of the petrochemical industry. This was in the early period of reform when the preferential policies to attract foreign investment were concentrated mainly in the southeast coastal regions. Taiwanese investment at this time was primarily in Fujian and Guangdong provinces.

The second wave in the mid-1990s was spearheaded primarily by upstream, often large-scale, firms such as plastics. These companies were testing the limits of the government's go slow, no haste policy.

The third wave, beginning in the late 1990s, was led by the high-technology sector. Firms in the information technology sector, notably those producing computer peripherals, assembling computers, programming and semiconductors joined the rush to the Mainland. In addition, large firms in traditional sectors undertook or expanded production there.[102] New investments in this third wave primarily moved north to the Yangtze River Delta area in locations such as Suzhou and Shanghai.

The fourth wave of investment beginning in the 21st century has become more dispersed with moves to northeast China and central and western regions to locations such as Dalian, Chengdu, and Chongqing.[103] This pattern of Taiwanese investment also has paralleled a general pattern of investments by companies from Japan, South Korea, the United States, and Europe.

More than 80,000 Taiwanese firms have invested in the PRC. As of December 2013, Taiwan's government had officially approved $133.7 billion in investments in the Mainland, while the government in Beijing reported $59.1 billion worth of investments from Taiwan.[104] More than a million Taiwanese business men and women are resident in the PRC. In 2013, 5.2 million Taiwanese visited the Mainland, and 2.8 million Mainland Chinese visited Taiwan.

Many Taiwanese families have lived in China for so long that their children have become acculturated to life on the Mainland. Other than returning to Taiwan for holidays, their entire lives have been spent there. Thousands of Taiwanese have married local Chinese. In the 1990s, I asked a Taiwanese government official why so many Taiwanese men have taken Chinese brides. He replied that a Taiwanese man can get a higher quality wife in China given his attributes (or lack thereof) than he can in Taiwan! **Figure 7.3** shows Taiwanese investment in the Mainland by year since 1991. The amounts have not been adjusted for inflation, but they show the steady increase in both the amounts invested and in the average amount per case.[105] The annual amounts were about $1 billion to $2 billion from 1993 to 1999. They reached $2.6 billion in 2000, $7.6 billion in 2006, and $14.6 billion in 2010. In recent years, while the number of cases has decreased to fewer than 1,000 per year, the average amount per case has risen to around $15 million from less than $4 million prior to 2005.

FIGURE 7.3. TAIWAN'S YEARLY INVESTMENTS IN MAINLAND CHINA

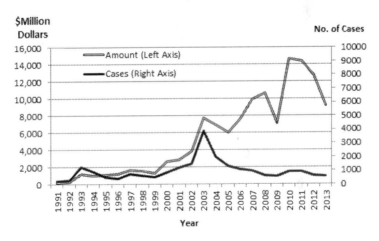

Source: Data from Taiwan's Mainland Affairs Council. PRC data differ considerably.

Geographical Location

By geographical location, Taiwanese investment has been concentrated in five areas on the Mainland (see **Table 7.1**). The greatest number of investments has been in Guangdong Province where 12,316 cases had been approved over the 1991-2010 period. These figures include retroactive and lagged approvals. By value, however, Jiangsu Province (Suzhou and Kunshan), where information technology industry firms are clustered, has received the largest amount with $33.4 billion. Guangdong Province with $22.0 billion is second. Shanghai with $14.1 billion is third, and Fujian Province with $6.7 billion is fourth.

TABLE 7.1. TAIWANESE INVESTMENT IN MAINLAND CHINA BY AREA, 1991-2010

Area	Cases	Amount ($Millions)	Share of Total Amount (Percent)
Jiangsu Province	6,164	33,382.31	34.3
Guangdong Province	12,316	22,041.95	22.6
Shanghai	5,365	14,144.9	14.5
Fujian Province	5,383	6,743.9	6.9
Zhejiang Province	2,024	6,434.0	6.6
Shandong Province	969	1,936.9	2.0
Tianjin Municipality	910	1,849.2	1.9
Beijing	1,181	1,682.4	1.7
Chongqing	209	1,281.4	1.3
Others	4164	7,823.9	8.0

Source: Republic of China, Ministry of Economic Affairs.

Restrictions on Semiconductor Technology

Taipei has tried to keep Taiwan's most advanced technology at home to keep the domestic economy vibrant and growing. This is Taiwan's technology dilemma. Should Taipei keep its companies from using the latest technology to manufacture in the PRC? Should Taipei allow its companies to transfer technology to PRC companies, especially state-owned enterprises, which would make them more competitive in global markets and who also may supply products to the People's Liberation Army?

The most visible of the restrictions on high-technology investments by Taiwanese firms in the Mainland have been in semiconductor fabrication. In order to keep companies from moving their highest levels of fabrication technology to the PRC, the Taipei government restricted the wafer size allowed to be produced in Taiwan-affiliated fabrication plants there. These restrictions on cross-strait semiconductor investment were relaxed somewhat in 2002 by the DPP's Chen Shui-bian administration. Under this policy, three Taiwanese firms were allowed to establish silicon-wafer foundries in Mainland China, but the level of technology was limited to that required to manufacture 8-inch wafers or less. In addition, for each 8-inch fabrication plant on the Mainland, each Taiwanese company was required to launch a new investment project to produce the higher-technology, 12-inch wafers at home. Taiwanese semiconductor companies also were not allowed to invest in cutting-edge micro-circuit technology in the PRC.

Taiwan's industry, however, learned ways to get around Taipei's restrictions. There were suspicious links between Taiwan's second-largest foundry, United Microelectronics Corp. (UMC), and a $1.2 billion fabrication plant in the Suzhou Industrial Park called HeJian Technology for which construction had begun before the investment ban was lifted. HeJian advertised itself as a "first class foundry service enterprise with abundant foreign capital and ... state-of-the-art integrated circuit technologies." It began production from its first 8-inch fabrication plant in 2003 with monthly capacity of 60,000 wafers.[106] Taiwan's regulators had investigated the plant, but HeJian would not disclose its sources of financing. The plant officially was owned by a British Virgin Islands holding company, Invest League Holdings Ltd., whose ultimate ownership was unknown. UMC conceded that HeJian was run by former managers of their company but denied involvement in the venture.[107]

It appears that that United Microelectronics had made a strategic decision to circumvent the intent and probably the letter of Taiwan's laws by assisting HeJian under the condition that UMC would be compensated later. In 2005, United Microelectronics received 15 percent of HeJian shares worth $110 million as compensation for what they called administrative consulting, but what outside observers felt must have been compensation for technology assistance. Some UMC shareholders protested that the $110 million was too small an amount. They thought UMC should receive half of the shares of HeJian.[108] By 2005, HeJian was producing semiconductors with 0.15-micron feature size despite the prohibition by the Taiwanese government of investments in Mainland production of less than 0.25 microns. In 2010, United Microelectronics sought permission to acquire the remaining 85 percent of HeJian, but Taipei denied it ostensibly because that would have exceeded the three-company limit for Taiwanese fabrication plants on the Mainland. In 2012, however, UMC did receive approval to increase its ownership share to about 85 percent in the holding company of HeJian.[109]

Taiwan's top semiconductor foundry, Taiwan Semiconductor Manufacturing Corp. (TSMC), officially waited until the ban was lifted to build an 8-inch fabrication plant in Shanghai. It has kept most of its production at home in its ten domestic fabrication plants. It also, however, has a plant in Singapore and one in the United States in Washington State. In 2004, when it built the $898 million Shanghai plant, TSMC installed fabrication equipment from Taiwan that was six or seven years out of date in accord with Taipei's policy at that time. By 2010, however, Taipei had approved the use of 0.13-micron process technology to make chips at TSMC's eight-inch wafer plant in Shanghai. This was an upgrade from 0.18-micron technology and was considered necessary to keep up with competitors.[110]

TSMC, however, has had an indirect and somewhat tenuous relationship with Mainland China's Semiconductor Manufacturing International Corporation (SMIC), the top domestic semiconductor fabricating company in the PRC. Richard Chang, who founded SMIC in 2000, is a Taiwanese-American who previously had worked for TSMC. The company was incorporated in the Cayman Islands. One research article refers to SMIC as a Taiwanese company registered as an American company to skirt restrictions by Taipei.[111] When SMIC was first established, a TSMC engineer was prosecuted for illegally transferring technology to it. When SMIC went public in 2004, it listed among its major shareholders

Shanghai Industrial Holdings, Ltd. (owned by the Shanghai municipal government) with 12 percent, Motorola with 11.4 percent, and 15 directors and executive officers together holding 50.1 percent.11[2]

SMIC quickly became a darling of Beijing's industrial planners and a formidable competitor to TSMC. In 2006, TSMC filed several lawsuits in the United States accusing its Chinese rival of causing more than a billion dollars in damages through theft of intellectual property. These lawsuits were settled in 2009 with a $200 million judgment in TSMC's favor. At the same time, TSMC announced that it would take a 7.2 percent stake in SMIC, with a warrant for an additional 2.8 percent of the shares.11[3]

Economic Cooperation Framework Agreement

In June 2010, Taiwan and China took a significant step in opening economic relations between them. They signed an Economic Cooperation Framework Agreement (ECFA) under which the two sides agreed to gradually reduce tariffs and other barriers to trade and investment, to provide investment protection, and to facilitate trade and industry cooperation. The agreement also included an early harvest list of tariff concessions by China covering 539 Taiwanese products including machinery, petrochemical raw materials, certain agricultural products, and textiles. It also paved the way for greater Taiwanese investments in financial services by further opening China's banking, insurance, securities, and hospital operations to Taiwanese firms.11[4] The agreement also allowed Chinese investment in Taiwan and for greater flows of tourists.

Some view the ECFA as the foundation of a type of common market that encompasses both economies and would include Hong Kong and Macau. For example, Fujian province has rebranded itself as the Economic Zone on the West Coast of the Taiwan Straits. This is to promote the idea that Fujian and Taiwan make up one large economic zone. Xiamen serves as the center of the west coast part of the zone given its SEZ status and location facing the offshore Taiwanese islands. Instead of trading artillery shells, the commercial exchanges and tourist trade are thriving. For discussing production in information and computer technology industries, the *Digital Times*, a high-technology newspaper in Taiwan, often refers to the industries dominated by Taiwanese firms with subsidiaries in the Mainland as Greater China or "Chiwan."

Foxconn's Operations on the Mainland

Taiwan's electronic equipment manufacturers in Mainland China are moving up the value chain from manufacturing equipment according to buyer specifications to becoming original design manufacturers. They not only manufacture but they design products which are eventually branded by another company. Even Apple Computer relies heavily on Foxconn, a subsidiary of Hon Hai Precision Industries of Taiwan, to transform its software and ideas into a usable product. Foxconn does more than just assemble products according to given specifications. For the iPhone, for example, Apple came to Foxconn with the software and a certain design idea. Since Foxconn engineers knew production and hardware, they said that Apple's design was not workable. The phone would be damaged by heat. If the phone became too hot, it would quit working after about an hour of use. The design had to be changed. Foxconn communicated back and forth with Apple engineers in Cupertino, California, on a better design. The difference in time zones facilitated making the necessary adjustments. A design proposal could be sent from Taiwan in the afternoon, and a reply could be back by the next morning. In the end, Foxconn came up with a workable phone.11[5] Some have referred to Terry Guo as the father of the iPhone, since the company he chairs, Hon Hai/Foxconn, played such an important role in its development.

Even with Foxconn's input into product specifications, on occasion Apple designers imposed requirements nearly impossible to meet. When the iPhone 4 was nearing production, both companies discovered that the metal frame was so specialized that it could only be made by an expensive, low-volume machine usually reserved for prototypes. Most manufacturers possessed only one such machine. Apple's designers insisted that the metal frame be used, so Foxconn ordered more than 1,000 of the $20,000 machines from Japan's Fanuc Ltd.11[6]

Foxconn also has played an important role in helping to train China's labor force. With a payroll of a million employees in the PRC, Foxconn is continually recruiting new people. Their human resources departments must hire 20,000 to 30,000 people each month. In their assembly plants, the goal for the lowest education level for line workers is a five-year high school degree. The course work also must include classes on working and skill development. Those recruited for office jobs are college graduates from Chinese educational institutions. Foxconn has established relationships with 400 colleges in China. The company has cooperative programs and provides scholarships. The colleges queue up their graduates for company interviews. Each year, Foxconn hires about 10,000 graduates from these colleges. In China, there also are special technical schools that are a source of recruits.

A major challenge for Foxconn is holding on to its skilled employees. Other companies are continually poaching on their workforce. Foxconn in China is similar to General Electric or Microsoft in the United States. It is a trainer of skilled managers and workers. Competitor companies often offer to double the salaries of Foxconn people if they will go to work for them. Huawei, in particular, regularly tries to lure employees from Foxconn. If a person is working at Foxconn and applies for a job at Huawei, he usually will be hired. Huawei is number one in China's domestic IT industry. It is learning from Foxconn. Huawei too has relatively high salaries, continuous improvement and is rising quickly.

Despite the large number of local hires, Foxconn factories are still managed primarily by some 10,000 Taiwanese expatriates. The ratio of Taiwanese to locals is about 1 to 100. The major roles in the company are being covered by Taiwanese, but some local Chinese are promoted to high levels. However, the local hires tend to be in departments of human resources, general affairs and security. For major production lines, Taiwanese engineers and other expats do the management.11[7]

In 2011 and 2012 Foxconn plants came under international scrutiny because of alleged poor working conditions and about a dozen suicides by their workers. The issue made headlines because the plants in question assemble the popular Apple iPads, iPods and iPhones. Some foreign investigative reporters also claimed to have found underage workers, unpaid overtime, workers being called back to the assembly line at midnight to begin making a new product and other alleged abuses. Apple responded by requesting an audit by the Fair Labor Association (FLA) which first visited the Foxconn plant in Shenzhen.11[8] The FLA logged some 3,000 man-hours in three Foxconn's factories and did find some noncompliance with its Worker Code of Conduct and the Chinese government's labor law. Both Apple and Foxconn agreed to remedial measures and to periodic future inspections.11[9]

With respect to wages paid, the FLA found that wages were paid on time and were above the applicable legal rates. The legal minimum wage in Shenzhen was RMB1500 ($245) per month, while the starting wage at Foxconn was RMB1800 ($295) and would rise to RMB 2200 ($360) per month after a probation period. Overtime was paid separately.

When I interviewed a Foxconn manager, he stated that the alleged abuses were against the company policy but that some managers tended to be overzealous in assuring that orders were met. He said that if a worker puts in overtime, the company must pay for it. Some managers may not pay for overtime because they claim the workers did not do a good job during normal hours. But that is actually not allowed. The Chinese New Year always is a problem if an order comes in from abroad. Chinese take a week off for the New Year holiday and go home to be with family. But if an order comes in, it has to be filled, even if it is the New Year. The company rule is 1.5 times normal pay for overtime, double pay for weekends, and triple pay for holidays.

As for suicides, the Foxconn manager said that they tended to occur during the winter when there is less sunshine and things are dark. He said that the company psychiatrists tell them that those who commit suicide seem to have a genetic tendency to do so. When they get depressed, particularly during the winter, they rationalize suicide and jump from the high-rise dormitories. The factory managers dread this time of the year. Each day they hope and pray that nothing like that will happen in their business units. Foxconn has established care and counseling centers staffed with Taiwanese and Chinese doctors and installed hot lines in the dorms and factories. Anyone can dial 8888 and get connected directly to the care center and to a suicide specialist. The company also put up railings and fences on the top of buildings and strung more than three million square meters of nets all around windows to catch any who attempt suicide. Some of those who committed suicide apparently hoped their families could cash in on insurance policies the company has for its workers.

Foxconn/Hon Hai Precision epitomizes the relentless drive for production efficiency and cost savings by Taiwanese manufacturers. Hon Hai's CEO, Terry Guo, is constantly working. He often will continue meetings with his managers on the Mainland in a specially equipped vehicle while driving him back to the airport to fly to Taipei. If the business of the meeting is not complete, the session will be extended to the airplane flight. His top China managers carry their passports with them when he is visiting—just in case they end up unexpectedly in Taoyuan Airport in Taipei.

Effects on the Chinese Economy

Investments from Taiwan have made a significant impact on the industrial development of China. One study examined Taiwan's contribution to the economic development of the PRC over the 30-year period from 1988 to 2008 and concluded that the contributions were immense. The estimated $122.3 billion in Taiwanese direct investment from 1979 to 2008 accounted for 14.3 percent of all FDI over that period. Between 1980 and 2008, Taiwan's business accounted for 10 percent of Mainland China's total international trade and 9.5 percent of its exports. At the end of 2008, Taiwan's enterprises on the Mainland employed 14.4 million workers or 1.9 percent of the total labor force. From 1992 to 2007, Taiwan's businesses contributed an estimated $87.8 billion in tax payments to the PRC. This accounted for 2.7 percent of China's fiscal revenues over that period.[20]

In addition to the direct effects on production, labor, and government revenues, FDI from Taiwan has helped to train the PRC's labor force. Chinese who have worked in Taiwanese companies have carried their skills to domestic enterprises. In contrast to the long tradition of the iron rice bowl for China's state-owned enterprises, the younger generation of workers in foreign enterprises is mobile. They often will quit one job and move to another for just a moderate increase in pay.

Dick K. Nanto

The Dilemmas Writ Large

In many respects, the dilemmas faced by Taiwan are indicative of those faced by countries and economies throughout the world. As will be discussed later in this book, the security dilemma is particularly acute for countries such as Australia and the United States. For Australia, the question is whether to allow the PRC, with its enormous appetite for energy and raw materials, to acquire old-line Australian industrial corporations or to take over or develop operations to extract Australian natural resources. Will the economic grip of the great Chinese dragon be a warm embrace or an economic squeeze play?

For the United States, the security dilemma dovetails with the technology dilemma. Both revolve around the intentions and potential threat of the People's Liberation Army (PLA). How will technology and factories being transferred to the PRC affect the Chinese military? Will investments by Chinese companies in the American economy provide access to technology by the PLA or provide a strategic vantage point for activities such as spying, be it cyberspying through the U.S. communications system or merely using telescopes to observe U.S. testing of unmanned drones? This dilemma has reached a new urgency among U.S. military planners because in their war games over the past two decades, the side representing the PLA has consistently beaten the U.S. Pacific Command in regional battle scenarios. For policymakers in the U.S. defense establishment, therefore, the PRC may have moved from being an economic competitor to a direct military threat. They seem to be adopting the view that the PRC's missile, submarine, and space satellite programs that ostensibly were aimed at preventing Taiwan from declaring independence also may have the capability to go "beyond Taiwan" and deny U.S. forces access to East Asia.[2]

The economic dilemma and the concomitant debate over hollowing out occur in any economy that has seen its manufacturing move to the PRC. When manufacturing plants close, jobs are lost, and workers who previously tightened bolts on an assembly line now are expected to flip burgers or become computer programmers. For the United States, Detroit is the archetypal example of what can happen when both imports and "runaway factories" leave a city holding an empty economic bag. The city, having had to declare bankruptcy, appears to be but a hollow of its former self. Its population has dropped from 1.8 million in 1950 to 701,475 in 2012. Some critics accuse U.S. automakers of being un-American for building assembly plants in the PRC.I[22] The problem in the debate over hollowing out is that job losses are local and not necessarily compensated by job gains elsewhere, particularly if those gains are in a different region of the country or abroad. Sales of Buicks in China or increased runs in the GM assembly plant in Texas provide little comfort to a laid-off autoworker in Detroit.

When GM started manufacturing in China, it was totally dependent on parts manufactured in the United States. GM put pressure on its suppliers to invest in their own subsidiaries and move production to the PRC. The hollowing out of Detroit is partly the story of suppliers chasing assembly plants in China. However, the lifespan of a foreign supplier in the PRC is limited by its ability to compete with local producers. Eventually, local companies learn the technology needed to make the product and are able to compete head to head with the foreign subsidiaries. Within three to five years, Chinese suppliers usually are able to undercut the prices of foreign supply companies. At some point, the Chinese suppliers reach the scale of manufacturing that enables them to export to the United States and to Europe.I[23] A competitive death spiral may then begin for those competing with imports from the PRC.

The democratic and social dilemma is less a challenge for Western nations than it is for Taiwan. A significant percentage of Taiwan's population either lives on the Mainland or has close ties to people there. A future generation of Taiwanese may be willing to make the trade-off between the gains and losses from being reunited under some configuration with the Mainland. These Taiwanese may be largely indifferent about whether they are ruled from Beijing or Taipei as long as they are able to work, travel freely, and live out their dreams.

Unlike expatriates from Taiwan, however, Westerners seem unlikely to become Sinicized and grow to favor the PRC over their home countries. In policy debates in Washington, not only is the emperor far away but also lives in a strange land. Still, lawmakers are sometimes taken aback at how firmly the business community with investments in China tends to oppose any measure that might disturb peaceful and stable relations with the PRC. Moreover, U.S. businesses in the PRC have seen the Chinese become more like Americans than Americans become more like Chinese.

In fact, Beijing makes it tough for foreigners to even live in China. A European acquaintance who is married to a Chinese woman and who lives in the PRC remarked that of the approximately 600,000 foreigners living in the PRC, less than 6,000 have the equivalent of a green card (allowing for permanent residence). His first application for a green card was refused because of lack of support by a state-owned enterprise that he once criticized for attempting to squeeze out an American competitor company. He thinks his second application may be approved since he is married to a Chinese woman, has paid taxes in China for eleven years, and has no criminal record. He also has a secure retirement income in addition to his work for a Chinese company and for a Chinese university. Still, he has found it extremely difficult to obtain a driver's license as well as a credit card from a local bank. He describes the barrier confronting him as a foreign devil as the Great Cultural Wall of China.[24]

CHAPTER 8. NON-ETHNIC CHINESE AND SECTORAL INVESTMENT IN THE PRC

Hong Kong and Taiwanese investors paved the way and did much of the hard lifting in changing the policies of local governments and the central authorities in order that investments from the United States, Europe, Japan, Singapore, South Korea, and other countries could enter China. These non-ethnic Chinese investors (except those from Singapore) have been the real foreign devils that have been allowed to enter the Chinese economy but with mixed emotions on both sides.

This chapter first provides data on the size of FDI from other countries and regions of the world other than from Hong Kong and Taiwan. It then briefly examines investment in selected sectors including footwear, finance, transportation equipment, computers and electronic equipment, chemicals and retail.

U.S. Investments

Direct investments in the PRC by American entities range from those by large multinational corporations to small consulting and representative offices. There are more than 3,700 companies and individuals with membership in the American Chamber of Commerce in Shanghai. These investments have been made in a large variety of industries. There are working committees covering 23 industrial sectors operating within the American Chamber in Shanghai.[25] The list of U.S. corporations in the PRC includes large multinationals such as Federal Express, DuPont, Coca-Cola, Apple Computer, Avon, GE, AT&T, International Paper, Eaton, GAP,

Navistar, Allergan and Caterpillar as well as large U.S. financial firms, accounting houses, and other service providers.[26]

The Singer Manufacturing Company, maker of the Singer sewing machine, was one of just four American companies to set up shop in China in the nineteenth century. In 1883, the company opened its first Chinese office on Foocho (Fuzhou) Road in Shanghai. After the turn of the twentieth century, as Western fashion became more popular, Singer's machines came to be an essential item in Chinese households. Lacking access to Paris boutiques, Chinese women could cut patterns from fashion magazines or order them through the mail and sew the latest fashionable clothing for themselves.[27]

According to both U.S. and Chinese data, cumulative U.S. FDI in China has been estimated to be $50 to $60 billion. As indicated previously, however, there are discrepancies between the U.S. and Chinese data sets. These differences likely arise from the accuracy, methods, and timing of FDI statistics on each side.[28] The PRC has used figures for FDI actually utilized in its statistical yearbooks. These amounts are derived from the investment approval process. The United States uses company reporting to determine net outflows of FDI—an amount that accounts for repatriated profits or disinvestments and for retained earnings in the foreign invested enterprise. The largest discrepancies in the two data sets tend to occur during and following periods of recession in the United States, such as in 2001-02 and in 2018-12, when U.S. companies are more likely to tap their investments in China for cash. In 2009, for instance, during the global financial crisis, U.S. FDI was a net negative $4 billion because U.S. companies pulled money out of China to bolster the finances of parent companies. General Motors, for example, in 2009 sold 1 percent of its holdings in the joint venture, GM-SAIC Motor Co., to its Shanghai partner. According to Chinese data, however, in 2009, U.S. investments worth $2.55 billion were realized (from previously contracted invested amounts).

Both sets of data, however, indicate that until the 2008-09 global financial crisis, U.S. FDI in China had been increasing. According to Chinese figures, in 1990, the flow of American FDI into China was only about $0.5 billion; by 2002, it peaked at $5.4 billion; and then leveled off to about $3 billion per year. Since U.S. data are net, they fluctuate more. U.S. figures show an increase from a few hundred million per year in the early 1990s to $3 billion in 1999 and then falling during the recessionary years of 2001 and 2002. U.S. investment into China then surged to $24 billion in 2008 before the global financial crisis caused a negative $4.1 billion in 2009 and then recovered to $10 billion in 2010 before falling for the next two years.[29] (See Table 8.1)

U.S. companies invest all over the world, and most foreign investment by industrialized countries tends to go to other industrialized nations. China has not been the primary location for U.S. investment. It was not until 2006 that China accounted for more than 1 percent of worldwide U.S. FDI. In 1982, China ranked in 51st place among the major recipients of U.S. FDI. By 1990, it had climbed to 45th place just below India, and by 2000, China had jumped to the 21st position to be in the same neighborhood as Argentina and Venezuela. In 2010, China had climbed further to 15th place just below India and above Spain. In 2012, the PRC remained in 15th place below Belgium and just ahead of Hong Kong. The $51 billion American companies had invested in China in 2012 was less than half that invested in Japan, Singapore, or Germany. It was less than a tenth of that invested in the top destinations, the Netherlands and the United Kingdom.

European Investments

In 1975, the European Community and the PRC agreed to establish diplomatic ties. Upon his return, Christopher Soames, who had negotiated the agreement with Chinese Prime Minister Zhou Enlai, told the European Parliament that the relationship would be of considerable significance. That turned out to be a vast understatement.[30] The original foreign devils off the coast of China were primarily traders from Europe. Now those ghosts have returned, not only to trade but to invest in the Far Eastern country they once called Cheena.

TABLE 8.1. U.S. DIRECT INVESTMENT IN CHINA, 1990-2012

Billion U.S. Dollars

Year	U.S. Foreign Direct Investment Utilized (Chinese Data)		U.S. Direct Investment in China (U.S. Data)	
	Annual Inflow	Cumulative Since 1990	Net Annual Amount	Net Cumulative Amount
1990	0.45	0.45	-0.08	0.35
1995	3.08	8.91	0.21	2.76
1996	3.44	12.35	1.08	3.85
1997	3.24	15.59	1.30	5.15
1998	3.90	19.49	1.20	6.35
1999	4.22	23.71	3.05	9.40
2000	4.38	28.09	1.74	11.14
2001	4.86	32.95	0.94	12.08
2002	5.42	38.37	-1.51	10.57
2003	4.19	42.56	0.69	11.26
2004	3.94	46.5	6.36	17.62
2005	3.06	49.56	1.40	19.02
2006	2.86	52.42	7.44	26.46
2007	2.62	55.04	3.25	29.71
2008	2.94	57.98	24.22	53.93
2009	2.55	60.53	0.14	54.07
2010	3.02	63.55	4.93	59.00
2011	2.37	65.92	-3.69	55.30
2012	3.13	69.05	-3.94	51.36

Sources: PRC, Ministry of Commerce, news releases. *China Statistical Yearbook.* U.S. Bureau of Economic Analysis.

Note: The net cumulative amount is the U.S. direct investment position or stock.

In 2012, the 27 countries of the European Union reported net cumulative direct investments of $79.9 billion in the PRC. (See **Table 8.2**) More than half of this investment occurred between 2004 and 2012. The stock of investments by the EU-27 was more than that by the United States ($51.4 billion) but less than that invested by Japan alone ($100.6 billion). Net direct investment flows into China from the EU-27 were around $4 billion per year from 2001 to 2004 and were at around $5 billion from 2005 until the European debt crisis in 2012 when they dropped to $2.5 billion.

TABLE **8.2**. EUROPEAN FOREIGN DIRECT INVESTMENT STOCK IN CHINA

Million U.S. Dollars

Year	EU27	France	Germany	Italy	Netherlands	Sweden	United Kingdom
2001	30,232	4,968	7,066	2,052	3,766	711	9,800
2002	33,943	5,543	7,994	2,229	4,338	810	10,696
2003	37,873	6,147	8,851	2,546	5,063	930	11,438
2004	42,112	6,804	9,909	2,827	5,874	1,051	12,231
2005	47,305	7,419	11,439	3,148	6,918	1,163	13,196
2006	52,630	7,802	13,418	3,498	7,759	1,367	13,922
2007	56,584	8,271	14,176	3,854	8,399	1,496	14,781
2008	61,579	8,859	15,076	4,347	9,261	1,635	15,695
2009	66,647	9,512	16,293	4,699	10,002	1,962	16,374
2010	72,132	10,750	17,182	5,095	10,917	2,123	17,084
2011	77,332	11,519	18,311	5,483	11,678	2,298	17,666
2012	79,927	11,519	19,762	5,483	12,822	2,298	17,666

Source: UNCTAD FDI/TNC database

Investments by Japan, South Korea, and Singapore

By country, the largest European investors in the PRC in 2012 were Germany with $19.8 billion in FDI stock and the United Kingdom with $17.7 billion. Other major investors were the Netherlands with $12.8

billion and France with $11.5 billion. During 2012, as Europe retrenched, Germany and the Netherlands were the only European countries with new direct investments in China.

As for non-European Union countries in Europe, Sweden with FDI stock of $2.3 billion in 2012 was the largest investor. Both Finland and Switzerland reported about $0.8 billion in FDI stock in China.

Japan, South Korea, and Singapore also have been major investors in China. As shown in **Table 8.3**, direct investments from Japan ranged around $6 billion to 7 billion from 2006 to 2010 but then nearly doubled to $12.6 billion in 2011 and $13.5 billion in 2012. South Korea's investments in the PRC declined from $3.3 billion to $1.0 billion in 2009 following the outbreak of the global financial crisis in 2008. The investment flows recovered somewhat to $2.9 billion by 2012, but they still were below the level they were in 2007.

TABLE 8.3. FDI FLOWS BY JAPAN, SOUTH KOREA AND SINGAPORE INTO THE PRC

Billion U.S. Dollars

Year	Japan	S. Korea	Singapore
2006	6.2	2.1	6.3
2007	6.2	11.5	6.7
2008	6.5	5.8	14.2
2009	6.9	3.5	6.1
2010	7.2	5.4	8.6
2011	12.6	5.7	12.9
2012	13.5	5.4	6.0
Cumulative Position	100.6	49.4	91.2

Sources: Statistics Bureau of Japan, Korea Statistical Information Service, Singapore Department of Statistics

Of these three countries, Singapore has been investing the most. Levels of FDI flows into China have generally been rising from $6.3 billion in 2006 to $12.9 billion in 2011 with a surge in 2008 to $14.2 billion.

Chinese in Singapore played an important role in opening the PRC to early foreign direct investment in a similar manner to that done by ethnic Chinese from Hong Kong and Taiwan.

In terms of cumulative direct investments, as of 2012, South Korea had invested $49.4 billion in the PRC, almost as much as the U.S. net investment position there. Both Japan ($100.6 billion) and Singapore ($91.2 billion) had invested roughly twice as much in the PRC as had South Korea.

Investments by Emerging Market and Other Countries

Investments in the PRC from emerging market and other countries are relatively small but steady. As shown in **Table 8.4**, in 2011 and 2012, FDI flows from the first three countries comprising the BRICS (Brazil, Russia, India, China and South Africa) have not been large. Those from Brazil, Russia and India for the two years ranged between $30 million and $60 million per year with more coming from Brazil and India than from Russia. Investments from Australia and Malaysia were running at a much higher rate at around $300 million per year, while those from Brunei, the Philippines, United Arab Emirates, and New Zealand amounted to $70 million to $255 million per year.

Investments by Sectors

Foreign direct investment in the PRC has occurred across the industrial spectrum (except in sensitive sectors where FDI is prohibited). **Figure 8.1** shows investments in China by U.S., Japanese and European companies and illustrates the variety of sectors receiving foreign investments.

TABLE 8.4. FOREIGN DIRECT INVESTMENT INTO THE PRC FROM EMERGING MARKETS AND OTHER COUNTRIES/ECONOMIES

Millions of U.S. Dollars

Country/Economy	2011	2012	Stock in 2012
Macao, China	680.43	505.56	10,383
Australia	309.53	337.97	n.a.
Malaysia	358.28	317.51	6,010
Brunei	255.82	151.09	n.a.
Philippines	111.85	132.21	2,892
United Arab Emirates	71.40	129.63	n.a.
New Zealand	74.22	118.9	n.a.
Brazil	43.04	57.6	n.a.
India	42.17	44.06	n.a.
Russia	31.02	29.92	n.a.

Sources: *China Statistical Yearbook* 2013, Stock from UNCTAD FDI/ TNC database

FIGURE 8.1. U.S., EU AND JAPAN'S DIRECT INVESTMENT POSITION IN CHINA BY SECTOR

Million U.S. Dollars

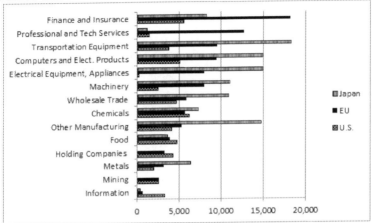

Sources: Data from Eurostat, U.S. Bureau of Economic Analysis, Japan Statistics Bureau.

Note: U.S. data are for 2011, EU for 2010 and Japan for 2012.

Since there are thousands of companies that have invested in China and all have stories to tell, in this section we will briefly examine just a few of the leading sectors for foreign capital. This includes footwear, finance, transportation equipment, computers and electronic equipment, chemicals and retail.

Footwear

Footwear makers were among the first to source products from China. The labor-intensive nature of assembling athletic shoes made it a good fit for the fledgling Chinese manufacturers. The experience of Nike has been typical. In 2008, I visited the headquarters for Nike footwear production in China. At that time, Nike had contracted with 16 factories for footwear, and the PRC was the largest source country for Nike. In the headquarters operation, there were 140 Chinese employees and 25 expatriates from all over the world. Most were from the United States, but others were from Europe and South Africa.

Nike in China began sourcing footwear in China in the 1980s. At first, Nike teamed with state-owned enterprises, but those arrangements proved to be a challenge to implement, so Nike turned to Korean and Taiwanese manufacturing companies that had moved their operations to China. They had supplied products to Nike in their home countries, so Nike was accustomed to working with them.

With respect to intellectual property rights, in 2004, Nike started a working group with Adidas aimed at counterfeit products. Rather than trying to attack small stands selling counterfeit products, they attempted to find the source of the bogus products. They worked with the public security ministry who conducted raids on warehouses and factories and confiscated counterfeit products. They found that the confiscated shoes usually had some genuine materials, but other parts were bogus. The makers worked out of factories in close proximity to real Nike factories. A worker, for example, might take some genuine shoe soles out of a Nike factory and sell them. The buyer would then combine the purloined soles with counterfeit parts to make the shoe. Nike has been working with its source factories to keep their inventory shrinkage down, especially for high-end products like the Michael Jordan shoe, but violations of intellectual property rights are an ongoing challenge for Nike. Many local areas are trying to develop as fast as possible and will often turn a blind eye to the counterfeiting of products in order to pursue economic development goals.

With respect to labor and the environment, Nike indicated that many laws and regulations had been mandated at the national level, but the authority to implement and enforce them was not well developed. At the local level, there is much autonomy and flexibility to interpret the requirements as they saw fit. The central government seemed to have a genuine desire to improve the situation, but China is a huge country.

At that time, China had a glut of unemployed workers—about 130 million—many from state-owned enterprises that had been shut down or cut production. Nike factories were able to offer good jobs to many of these workers. Nike's contracting factories employed 130,000 to 150,000 workers. In Nike's largest contracting factory, the neighboring town began with a population of 15,000 to 20,000. The town in 2008 had 100,000 people working in the Nike factory plus two other factories. The factory also had attracted supplier companies that produce chemicals, shoe components, laces, etc.

In 1992, Nike was the first sports and fitness company to adopt a code of conduct for its contracting factories in order to improve working conditions. Nike had been a target of protest groups since the company was large and visible. Nike had been working directly with the factories by training managers and workers in the code of conduct, labor laws, wages, benefits and related issues. Between 70 and 80 percent of the workers in contract factories had parents who were farmers and had agrarian backgrounds. Most did not understand their rights as laborers.

The Nike Code of Conduct requires each contractor to certify that it: (1) does not use any forced labor, (2) does not employ any person below the age of 18 to produce footwear or 16 to produce apparel, (3) pays at least the minimum wage, (4) provides legally mandated benefits, (5) complies with legally mandated work hours and compensates for overtime, (6) has written health and safety guidelines and (7) complies with applicable country environmental regulations.

In the factories, Nike started educational programs. They had surveyed the workers and found that 82 percent wanted vocational training in areas such as computers, management, stitching and in the English language. The training took two or three nights per week over nine months. Nike also ran seminars dealing with personal hygiene, health, and financial management. Most workers were 18 to 25 years old, so they need practical information. Most were women (85 percent). As the educational programs were completed, workers could be offered greater opportunities at the factories. As it turned out, 90 percent of the workers wanted to stay at the factories only two or three years at the longest. They had come for the jobs and wages which were better than those in their home communities, and many of them were saving 70 to 80 percent of their salaries to use after they returned home. With educational programs, the hope was that some workers would want to stay longer and move to higher positions in the factories.

In addition to wages, benefits for many included free housing, meals, medical care (through a clinic on site if the factory had 1,000 workers). If the plant had over 5,000 workers, there usually were two doctors, one of which was a woman. Most clinics had one bed per 1,000 workers. A doctor would be on call. Some factories allowed the local population to use the clinics. These benefits had a value of another 800 RMB ($96.62) to 1,000 RMB ($120.77) per worker. Nike workers paid 3 RMB ($0.36) per day for room and 1.25 RMB ($0.15) per day for board.

Nike had received complaints that even athletic shoes made in China were expensive. The problem was that Nike policy was to sell only A-grade products. It did not sell seconds, so Nike footwear was costly, even if it was made locally. The reason was that even locally produced shoes had materials from twelve countries in them and carried import duties of up to 125 percent.

Finance

By sector, finance and insurance has been an attractive destination for foreign investors. Depository banks, in particular, have been a leading target for both European and American investments. The pattern has taken a dual track: investments in existing Chinese banks and expansion into the PRC with representative offices and branches by global banks. The rush to invest in Chinese banks, however, reversed itself following the Global Financial Crisis in 2007-09. As quickly as foreign banks invested in China's banks, most have turned toward disinvesting. This can be attributed to three major factors. First, it has become apparent to foreign investors that Beijing has come to feel that it no longer needs the expertise of foreign banks, although their presence has become an integral part of the Chinese financial scene. China's largest banks in 2011 were more profitable than their U.S. and European competitors.[1]1 Second, new capital requirements are being imposed on international banks that discourage holding shares of Chinese banks, and third, the 2007-09 Global Financial Crisis and ensuing turmoil generated a need for capital at home by Western banks. International banks, however, still are expanding their own operations in China.

Foreign banks originally were a part of the strategy by Beijing to clean up its financial sector. Under the PRC's socialist system, the banking sector consisted primarily of state-owned banks that often acted as a conduit for state assistance to industries through local and regional banks. Many borrowers, especially state-owned enterprises, considered the loans to be subsidies that would not have to be repaid. Now those local and regional banks have been privatized and are required to make a profit despite their overhang of non-performing loans. In 2004, 13 percent of bank loans in China were non-performing, and others were in arrears in payments. Getting rid of the bad loans has been a huge task for China's domestic banks. They have been whittling away at their backlog of non-performing loans for more than a decade.

One part of the government's policy was to increase competition in the sector by allowing a limited number of well-managed foreign banks to enter the market. The government came to require that (except for the large policy banks) its banks operate without government subsidies and compelled many of them either to form joint ventures with foreign banks or list their shares on a stock exchange. Banks had to partner, become self-reliant, or perish. This has brought pressure on the banks to modernize and become self-sufficient. This strategy, along with the rapid growth in the economy, seems to be working, although hidden bad debt, particularly by local governments that have borrowed to finance infrastructure improvements, still hangs over China's banking system.

China's financial sector illustrates the dualism in the economy. Certain modern financial conveniences are rapidly being adopted but basic habits remain ingrained. Chinese households have long been known for their thrift and high savings rates. Individuals rarely appeared at loan windows, and cash was king. By 2013, however, the PRC had 4.2 billion bank cards in circulation, enough for every adult to have more than three.[32] Savings rates remain high—as much as 50 percent for households in 2013. Households save as their incomes rise rapidly and also because families face potential high costs for education, medical care, and uninsured natural disasters. With few attractive places to invest, most savings end up in banks.[33]

In 2012, there were 412 foreign bank operations in China with assets of 238 billion RMB ($38.74 billion) representing 1.82 percent of total banking assets in the country. Of these, 38 were wholly-foreign-owned banks operating 267 branches, three were joint ventures and one was a wholly-foreign-owned finance company. Another 95 were foreign bank branches. The leading foreign banks were HSBC (Hong Kong/U.K.), Standard Chartered Bank (U.K.), Citibank (U.S.), Bank of East Asia (Hong Kong) and Hang Seng Bank (Hong Kong).[34] The Hong Kong banks, along with Standard Chartered Bank, have had a large advantage in providing banking services to the more open Chinese economy because of their close cultural and geographical proximity.

Some major U.S. and European banks have been operating in China for a century or more. The modern HSBC developed from the Hong Kong and Shanghai Banking Company. For regulatory purposes, in 1991, the HSBC Group headquarters was incorporated in London, but its roots are in Hong Kong, and that is where the head of the Group is located. In 1865, shortly after being established in Hong Kong, the bank opened an office in Shanghai, the embodiment of the second half of the bank's name. In 2007, the bank formed HSBC Bank (China) to serve the PRC and also became the first international bank to establish a bank in rural China. By 2010, HSBC had nearly a hundred outlets in the PRC. It has invested more than $5 billion in PRC financial institutions, including an 8 percent stake in the Bank of Shanghai (2001), a 15.57 percent stake in Ping An Insurance Company (2002) and a 19 percent share of the Bank of Communication (2004). HSBC China offers debit cards that can link a renminbi account and up to two foreign currency accounts.[35] In what might be a sign of the times, in 2011, HSBC laid off several hundred investment bankers in London and Hong Kong while injecting 2.8 billion yuan ($437 million) into its operations in the PRC.

The U.K.'s Standard Chartered Bank entered China in 1858 and was one of the first foreign banks to do so. After the Communist victory in 1949, its Shanghai branch was permitted to remain and assist the new government by providing financial services and loans for the PRC's chemical and steel industries. After the PRC joined the World Trade Organization in 2001, Standard Chartered increased its presence in Hong Kong and Taiwan in anticipation of the day that banks would be allowed to re-enter the mainland. After the door opened in 2007, Standard Chartered simply moved some of its personnel and operations inland. The bank has 23 branches and 77 sub-branches in the PRC and focuses on loans to small- and medium-sized enterprises.

Other Western banks began investing in China in earnest as the market re-opened. Many of them also have a long history of operations there. American banks wanted to get a piece of Chinese banks because they knew the Chinese were quite capable of avoiding Wall Street to raise capital. This was a way of getting into the market.[136]

Citibank had initially established an office in Shanghai in 1902. It was the first bank to fly the red, white and blue U.S. flag there and became known as the Flower Flag Bank. Reopened in 1983, by 2013, Citi China had 13 corporate bank branches and 48 consumer bank outlets. It was the first foreign bank to be authorized to distribute domestic mutual funds and also to issue sole-branded credit cards. The bank also was the first to open a full-service outlet in a Chinese airport and a consumer outlet in the Shanghai metro subway system. The bank has played a leading role in the internationalization of China's currency, the renminbi.

In 2005, Countrywide Financial, a company that would be acquired by Bank of America, paid $3 billion to acquire 9 percent of the shares of China Construction Bank (CCB). CCB is China's largest lender to home buyers. In the aftermath of the 2008-09 global financial crisis, new capital requirements were imposed on banks. Over the 2011-13 period, Bank of America sold off its stake in the CCB for a total of about $16.3 billion, a highly lucrative return on investment.[137] The two banks, however, continue to cooperate with each other in a strategic partnership.

In 2006, Goldman Sachs bought a 4.9 percent stake in the Industrial and Commercial Bank of China for $2.58 billion. This stake, however, turned out to be a conspicuous, and at times volatile, item in Goldman's quarterly results. In 2011, it caused a full-year net loss in Asia for Goldman. It also never fulfilled its promise as a potential gateway to a much bigger share of China's investment-banking market. In 2013, Goldman completed the sale of its investment in ICBC, even though ICBC had become the world's top bank by tier 1 capital. Goldman gained $10.1 billion from that sale.[138]

J.P. Morgan and Chase Manhattan Bank have had a long history of working with clients in China. In 1911, J.P. Morgan headed a syndicate of underwriters to manage the Huguang Railway's $7.5 million bond issuance, the first public offering of Chinese railway bonds. In 1921, Equitable Eastern Banking Corp., a company that merged with Chase Bank in 1930, opened a Shanghai branch and then another in Tientsin (Tianjin). In the 1960s and 1970s, David Rockefeller, then-chairman of Chase Manhattan, frequently visited Hong Kong and opened more branch offices there. In 1973, the bank became the Bank of China's first American correspondent bank. Chase returned to the PRC in 1981 when it opened its first of two representative offices. J.P. Morgan and Chase Manhattan merged in 2000, and in 2009 the new company opened branch offices in Guangzhou and Chengdu. The bank then established the locally-incorporated JPMorgan Chase Bank (China) and, in 2013, established a Beijing-based joint venture to underwrite domestic securities.[39]

Morgan Stanley initially got burned in its foray into China. In 1995, Morgan Stanley joined with China Construction Bank and other investors to found China International Capital Corp. (CICC), the first securities joint venture in China. Morgan Stanley invested $35 million for a 34.3 percent stake in the company. Beijing wanted to build China's first investment bank, and it allowed Morgan Stanley to invest in CICC in return for sharing the needed expertise.

The venture, perhaps, stands as a warning to companies with knowhow and skills that Beijing wants domestic companies to acquire. Morgan Stanley saw the CICC as a foot-in-the-door for developing its business in China. The bank sent management talent to introduce advanced investment banking technologies and to manage the joint venture. The Chinese side, however, had another idea.[40]

In 1998, Levin Zhu, the princeling son of former Premier Zhu Rongji, joined CICC and quickly rose in the ranks. He deferred becoming CEO until 2002 after his father's term as Premier had ended. The younger Zhu's superb connections, in a country where relationship banking is the norm, proved hugely beneficial for CICC. Zhu also tended to manage by fiat. By 2000, only five years after CICC had been founded, disputes and management clashes within the joint venture ended in Morgan Stanley ceding control and withdrawing its management staff. Zhu reportedly blocked attempts by Morgan Stanley to reclaim a larger management role of the company in 2004 and 2005, and Morgan Stanley remained as only a passive investor.

In 2004, Central Huijin Investment Ltd., the investment arm of China Investment Corp., the PRC's sovereign wealth fund, acquired 43.3 percent of CICC. In essence, CICC indirectly became a state-owned enterprise and a potential national champion company. CICC soon developed into the top-ranked underwriter of share sales in the country, especially for state-owned enterprises. Zhu's influence was apparent in 2006 when CICC was abruptly included as an underwriter for the $12 billion flotation of the Industrial & Commercial Bank of China, replacing Goldman Sachs at the 11th hour.

Even though in 2006 Morgan Stanley was allowed to establish Morgan Stanley Bank International (China) and become the first foreign bank to be granted a wholly-owned banking license in China, PRC regulators kept Morgan Stanley from establishing a competing securities company because of its stake in CICC. Morgan Stanley tried unsuccessfully to sell its CICC shares in 2008 and eventually did sell them in 2010 for an estimated $1 billion. In 2011, Morgan Stanley established an RMB private equity investment firm. The company also partnered with Huaxin Securities to launch Morgan Stanley Huaxin Securities fifteen years after its failed investment in CICC.[141]

Switzerland's UBS and the Royal Bank of Scotland also have been reducing their shares of the Bank of China. UBS, however, still operates brokerage and mutual fund joint ventures with local partners and in 2012 launched UBS (China), its locally-incorporated subsidiary. This allowed UBS to conduct yuan business in key areas such as wealth management.[142] UBS Securities represented the first time that a foreign entity had been allowed to invest directly into a fully-licensed securities firm. In 2012, UBS (China) became the only foreign firm among the top ten originators in China's A-share equity market.[143]

Other banks incorporated in China include RBS China (Netherlands), Australia and New Zealand Banking Group, The Bank of East Asia (Hong Kong), the Bank of Tokyo-Mitsubishi UFJ (Japan), DBS Bank (Singapore), Hang Seng Bank (Hong Kong), Mizuho Corporate Bank (Japan), Oversea-Chinese Banking Corporation (Singapore), United Overseas Bank

(Singapore), Woori Bank (South Korea), Shinhan Bank (South Korea), Societe Generale (France) and Bank of Montreal (Canada).

According to PriceWaterhouseCoopers, foreign banks in the PRC have long endured a limited ability to innovate because of strict regulatory licensing requirements, lengthy approval processes and stringent capital requirements. Their market share remains small and just able to keep up with growth in the economy as a whole. Among the foreign banks, however, there is some optimism over the new Shanghai Pilot Free Trade Zone, established in September 2013. The provisions of the zone significantly relax offshore RMB exchange, remittance and settlement, and trade restrictions for banks establishing branches within the zone. Given the rising use of the RMB in international transactions, it holds the promise of making Shanghai an international financial center rivaling Hong Kong and Singapore.[144]

Transportation Equipment

The story of transportation equipment in China is largely a story of automobiles. In nowhere is the transformation of China more apparent than on its roads. Swarms of bicycles propelled by people exhaling only carbon dioxide have been replaced by automobiles, bumper to bumper in traffic jams and helping to create the smog that hangs over nearly every major Chinese city. Crowded roads, however, are part of the Chinese dream of a house and a car, two wants that go along with a good education, a computer, and a baby boy.

FIGURE 8.2. A STREET SCENE IN SHANGHAI

Photograph by D. Nanto

In just three decades, China has become the largest and fastest growing automobile market in the world. In 2010, automobile sales in China reached 17.1 million, while those in Western Europe were 14.4 million and 11.8 million in the United States. In 2014, vehicles sales in the PRC reached 19.4 million. China, moreover, is fueling the boom in demand for automobiles throughout the world. In 2002, the global auto industry sold 58 million vehicles with 3 percent of them in the PRC. By 2012, global sales had reached 82 million vehicles with 24 percent in the PRC. By 2020, worldwide sales are forecast to reach 109 million vehicles—32 million in China alone. If achieved, sales in China could be more than those in North America and Europe combined.[45]

Unlike much investment in China, investment in the automobile and truck industry is primarily to serve the local market, although China is slowly developing into an exporter of vehicles. In 2012, Chinese automakers exported $9.5 billion in automobiles and trucks. Chinese producers of automobile parts, however, have become highly aggressive in seeking export markets. In 2012, they exported $22.6 billion in motor vehicle parts to the world.

When Beijing decided to open China's auto market to international companies, it was aware that domestic manufacturers would not be able to compete with their foreign rivals. China's automakers traditionally have been sponsored by provincial or local governments, and most are too small to be competitive. A large number of the 80 or so larger automobile makers in China are slated to disappear. China's economic planners would like to see the current number of automakers reduced to only a few dozen tier-one and tier-two producers by 2022 or so.

In order to develop the industry, the government strategy was to invite the leading global automakers to form joint ventures with the strongest domestic companies. The import duty would be kept high and the domestic side would absorb the technology and learn how to build motor vehicles that would clearly be Chinese. Foreign automakers could own no more than 50 percent of any joint venture.[46] Government control would be maintained through two mechanisms. The first would be through the state-owned partners in the joint ventures. The second would be through the approval process. Beijing had to grant approval for major joint ventures and also for any models that were to be produced.[47]

The Chinese government hoped, initially, that such arrangements would allow Chinese car producers to tap the technological and managerial expertise of their foreign partners. In exchange, foreign automakers would gain access to the vast Chinese market. However, a quarter century later, based on market shares, foreign automakers are considered by domestic automakers to have benefited more than their local partners from these link-ups.[48]

In 2009, I was part of a delegation visiting Chengdu, a second-tier city in Sichuan province. The purpose of the visit was to travel to the countryside to see the rebuilding after the great Sichuan earthquake in 2008. Our Chinese hosts warned us that Chengdu was not Shanghai. It was in the interior where modernization was just taking hold. This was to be a taste of traditional China. The city was near the mountainous area famous for its Panda Bear Reserve. As we rode from the airport into the city center on a modern arterial expressway, we encountered a virtual auto dealers row. There were lines of cars being displayed in dealerships for Volvo, Mazda, Jeep, Buick, Volkswagen, Toyota, and Nissan plus a smattering of domestic brands. One afternoon, I decided to go for a run from the modern Shangri-la Hotel where our group was staying. As I reached the intersection below the hotel, imagine my surprise when I came face to face with a dealership for Bentley luxury motorcars. Later, I discovered that Greater China had become the largest market for Bentley Motors. In 2012, the company delivered 2,253 cars to Chinese customers (including those in Hong Kong and Taiwan) out of a total of 8,510 luxury vehicles sold worldwide.[149]

FIGURE 8.3. A BENTLEY DEALER IN CHENGDU

Photograph by D. Nanto

Foreign investment in China's automotive sector entered in three waves. Between the mid-1980s and late 1990s, a few well-controlled foreign joint ventures by American Motors, Volkswagen and PSA Peugeot Citroen dominated China's market. From the late 1990s to 2001, GM and Honda entered the market, and then, after China's accession to the World Trade Organization in December 2001, other foreign automakers followed course.

American Motors was an early entrant into the China market. In 1984, it formed the Beijing-Jeep joint venture with an initial investment of only $8 million that bought it 37 percent of the resulting company. Within five years, even with low production rates, it was able to turn profits of $90 million per year by both selling knocked-down kits (essential parts and components shipped from the Jeep plant in the United States) to the venture and then receiving its share of the profits from Jeep sales. The venture, however, was run like a state-owned enterprise. It received a production quota from the state planners, and the planners set the price for the Jeeps. This meant that there was no marketing necessary and no incentive to improve the quality of the vehicles. Each year, the main challenge for management was to negotiate the price of the knocked-down kits. This was a zero-sum game, since the higher the kit price, the more Jeep (by 1987 owned by Chrysler) earned and the less there was in profits for the joint venture. Instead of cooperating to build a better vehicle, the venture regressed into acrimonious squabbles over profits (determined by the price of the kits).1[50]

Jeeps, however, are highly popular in the PRC market. Some potential buyers lament that it is so much easier to find shirts, shoes, belts, and backpacks with the Jeep logo than to find a Jeep itself. Jeep gear is so popular in China that there are more than 1,500 licensed Jeep clothing outlets in the country, but only 120 auto dealers sell the real vehicles. Three decades of troubles at Chrysler/Jeep headquarters in the United States have left it without local production and missing out on surging demand for SUVs. Production of Jeeps in China ceased in 2006 as its new owner Chrysler faced bankruptcy at home. Now Jeeps have to navigate a restrictive import market and tariffs that raised the starting price of a Jeep Grand Cherokee in 2012 to 575,900 RMB, or $91,000, compared with $27,000 in the United States. The top-of-the-line Grand Cherokee went for $189,750. Despite the high price, in 2011 there were 19,013 Jeeps sold in China, but this was but a fraction of the number of vehicles sold there by General Motors.1[51]

Volkswagen has joint ventures with Shanghai Automotive Industry Corp. and First Automotive Works Corp. (FAW). The SAIC-VW venture was formed in 1985 and made the well-known Santana that dominated Chinese passenger car sales for many years. The Santana, however, never kept up with the times, and Shanghai Automotive did not accomplish a primary goal—to learn how to build its own cars. Even after ten years of operation, Volkswagen controlled the design, engineering and manufacture of the Santana while SAIC managers took charge of distribution, handled the regulatory side of the business and worked together on finances.[152] In the mid-1990s, domestic Chinese companies still could not build a world-class car, even a basic, entry level model. SAIC and other Chinese automakers clearly needed help.

Initially, in the FAW-VW joint venture, Volkswagen set a record for foreign automakers by investing $150 million in the operation, although most of its contribution came in the form of a used VW Jetta production line that was dismantled in Westmoreland, Pennsylvania and shipped to China.[153] Since production of the Jetta began in 1991, the venture has produced six more models, including the Audi and Passat, on production lines that were not secondhand. In 2013, Volkswagen said it would build an additional seven car plants in China. That would bring the total to 19, and by 2018 increase production capacity from 2.5 million to 4 million vehicles a year.

The listing of luxury vehicle brands in the PRC illustrates the importance of China to foreign players. Volkswagen's luxury car brand Audi's global success is greatly attributed to its prosperous sales in China. Audi has almost exclusively controlled China's high-end official car market since 1999 when it locally produced its flagship model, the A6. Its image as an official car boosted its sales and helped Audi for years beat its rivals, BMW and Mercedes-Benz, to top China's luxury car market.[154]

There is an old saying in China, "Drive BMW, seat Benz." The meaning is that BMW gives the best in driving experience while Mercedes-Benz is the most comfortable for sitting or being chauffeured around. BMW came to China in 1994 and formed a strategic management alliance with Hua Chen Car Holding Ltd., and the two companies created Hua Chen BMW. BMW also has a joint venture with Brilliance Auto, a listed arm of Hua

Chen, which manufactures its vehicles in China. BMW made a splash by becoming a sponsor of the Chinese Olympic Committee. More than a third of China's gold medal Olympic champions have chosen to drive a BMW. BMW has advertised with the slogan, "Gold medal people with a gold medal car."[55] In 2012, BMW sold 326,000 vehicles in the PRC.[56]

General Motors has the largest U.S. presence in the PRC. In 2014, the company had 11 joint ventures and two wholly owned foreign enterprises as well as more than 58,000 employees there. In 2014, GM China sold 3,539,970 vehicles under the brand names of Buick, Cadillac, Chevrolet, Baojun, Wuling and Jiefang nameplates. [57]

GM first entered China in the 1920s with a Chevrolet dealer in Shanghai. In the 1930s, one out of every six cars in China was a Buick. It was the preferred car of the last Emperor of China, Puyi. This partiality toward Buicks continued with the ensuing revolutionaries despite their political differences. Sun Yat-Sen, the founder of the Republic of China and its first president, was chauffeured around in a Buick. Even the leaders after the Communist victory in 1949 preferred this American car. Mao Zedong and Zhou Enlai both had Buicks.[58]

General Motors scored a veritable coup in 1997 when it won regulatory permission to open a Buick assembly plant in Shanghai. At the time, foreign entry into the Chinese auto market was severely restricted, but GM parlayed its connection to Sun Yat-Sen and portrayed Buick as returning to a market where it had a large presence in the 1920s and 1930s. General Motors established a joint venture with Shanghai Automotive Industry Corporation (SAIC). SAIC General Motors offers over 20 product lines under the Buick, Chevrolet and Cadillac brands. Its products include luxury vehicles, economy and premium sedans, MPVs and SUVs, as well as hybrid and electric vehicles. In 2010, the joint venture became China's first passenger car maker to sell 1 million vehicles in a single year.[59] In 2014, it had record domestic sales of 1,710,025 units. GM has been selling more Buicks in the PRC than it has in the United States.

SAIC-GM-Wuling Automobile Company is a joint venture that was founded on November 18, 2002 with GM China holding 44.0 percent, SAIC 50.1 percent and Wuling Motors 5.9 percent. The joint venture manufactures commercial vehicles under the Wuling nameplate and cars under the Baojun brand. These vehicles are designed specifically for the Chinese market. Its manufacturing bases are located in the Guangxi Zhang Autonomous Region (southwestern China), in Shandong and in Chongqing. In 2014, this joint venture had domestic sales of 1,787,931 units.

In 2009, General Motors joined with China FAW Group (formerly First Auto Works) in a 50-50 joint venture to produce light-duty trucks and vans. The venture also has engaged in R&D, exports and aftersales support. In 2014, FAW-GM sold 41,702 vehicles in China, down from 88,000 vehicles in 2010.

Ford has found itself far behind the curve in China, although it is catching up quickly. This is ironic since on June 12, 1924, Sun Yat-Sen wrote to Henry Ford stating that if Mr. Ford visited China, it would give him great pleasure to welcome him in South China where much of China's intelligence, energy, and wealth can be found. Sun Yat-Sen went on to say, "I know and I have read of your remarkable work in America. And I think you can do similar work in China on a much vaster and more significant scale." At the time Ford Motor was the market leader in the United States. In the reply to Sun Yat-Sen, an assistant in Henry Ford's office sent a terse note acknowledging receipt of the invitation but stating, "We desire to advise, however, that Mr. Ford has made no plans for visiting China in the very near future."[160]

Ford has been expanding both its manufacturing capacity and sales in China. Still, far behind General Motors, in 2014, its wholesale deliveries topped one million for the first time. Ford has increased its sales by adding eight models to the five it previously had and producing more locally. The company has about 400 dealers for cars and another 200 for trucks.

Ford's main production operation in China is a 50-50 joint venture between Ford and Chongqing Changan Automobile Company called the Changan Ford Automobile Corporation (CAF). CAF currently operates three assembly plants with total annual production capacity of about 1 million vehicles, an engine plant and a transmission plant. Another assembly plant in Hangzhou with capacity for an additional 300,000 vehicles was slated for completion in 2015.[161] Ford has long held shares in Japan's Mazda Motors. In China, the two companies have joined to form another venture with Chongqing Changan Automobile Company to produce engines for Ford and Mazda vehicles manufactured in China. Ford also has a 32 percent share of JMC, a joint venture between Changan and Jiangling Motors Company. This company assembles the Ford Transit van, Ford diesel engines and non-Ford vehicles for distribution in China and in other export markets.

Ford along with other American and European automakers have benefitted from the diplomatic and military tensions between Japan and the PRC. Toyota, Honda, Nissan, and Suzuki often face collateral damage when there are incidents involving islands claimed by both Japan and China or when historical issues arise that relate to Japan's invasion of China in World War II. It is difficult for Chinese consumers to shop for a Japanese brand automobile when Chinese newspapers and television stations are criticizing Japan for clashes and there are protests on the streets. Recent incidents over the Senkaku/Daioyu islands include a Japanese naval ship ramming a Chinese fishing boat and Japan threatening to shoot down a PRC drone flying between the islands.[62]

In 2012, the Japanese government arranged to buy back three of the five Senkaku/Daioyu islands from a Japanese deed holder, and Japanese nationalists landed on one of the islands and unfurled a Japanese flag. Protests erupted in China. Japanese cars, dealerships, and restaurants were attacked, and sales of Japanese cars in the PRC dropped by as much as 40 percent.[63] The anti-Japanese protests led Toyota to change its name in Chinese to China Toyota (meaning China's Toyota) rather than Toyota China (meaning Toyota's Chinese Branch). The anti-Japanese sentiment in China has caused Toyota to face an uphill battle for market share.

Toyota began exporting to China in 1964 but lagged behind rivals in the country, choosing instead to concentrate on the markets in the United States and Europe. It wasn't until 2002 that it rolled out its first locally produced, Toyota-brand car. Toyota has two joint ventures in the PRC: FAW Toyota and Guangqi Toyota. These two joint ventures have production capacities of 460,000 and 360,000 vehicles, respectively. In 2012, Toyota and its local partners sold 883,400 vehicles in China.

Although anti-Japanese protests have been a problem for Toyota, its strategy of not introducing a low-cost model tailored for the China market also had been questioned. In 2013, Toyota unveiled such a car projected to cost around $10,000 to compete with GM's Chevy Sail and Nissan's Tiida. Toyota had opted to produce such a car for the market in India and import the Yaris model to sell in China. Import duties, however, pushed the price for the Yaris above competing, locally-produced models. The Yaris also was said by insiders to lack what the Chinese call "daqi" or "road presence." Compared to the Tiida, they said, it felt cramped and was short on pizzaz.[64]

Toyota discovered the hard way that over the past decade, the Chinese automobile market has grown from a backwater for outdated models to the largest auto market anywhere with much of the world's leading technology being delivered there first. Nowhere is competition more severe. Buyers are looking for cars with cutting edge technology and looks. The luxury market is booming, but volume sales are found in lower- and mid-priced cars aimed at China's rising middle class.

Nissan first tested the waters in the PRC in 1973 by introducing its Cedric model. In 1993, the company established Zhengshou Nissan Automobile Co. and began manufacturing light commercial vehicles. Nissan's strategy for China has been to partner with the Dongfeng Motor Corp. both in production and sales of passenger cars. In 2003, Nissan and Dongfeng Motor Corporation founded Dongfeng Nissan Passenger Vehicle Company. This venture gives Nissan partial cover from the outbursts of anti-Japanese sentiment in the PRC. During protests in 2012, however, even its cars and some of its dealerships were attacked. Nissan has assured its buyers that it would reimburse owners for damage to vehicles during protests, including future demonstrations.[65]

In 2012, Nissan sold 1.18 million vehicles (773,000 cars) in China, including imported models such as the Infiniti. The Chinese market has accounted for one quarter of Nissan's sales worldwide. The company plans to boost production capacity in the PRC to 2.3 million units.[66]

Honda has taken a bifurcated route in its China business. Like other automobile makers, it has teamed with domestic Chinese companies to manufacture there. Honda, however, also exports some of its China-produced cars. Wuyang-Honda Motors (Guangzhou) began operations in 1992 making five models of which one of them, the Lead, went to Japan. The Guangqi Honda Automobile Co. began production in 1999 and makes seven models, including the Accord, Odyssey, and Fit. The Dongfeng Honda Automobile Co. began production in 2004 and makes six models, including the CR-V and Civic. Honda Automobile (China) began production in 2005 and makes the Jazz for export to Europe.1[67]

For South Korean automakers Hyundai and Kia, the protests against Japan coincided with a push to gain market share in the PRC. Hyundai joined with Beijing Motors in 2002 to form Beijing Hyundai Motor Co. This was the first automobile joint venture approved by the Chinese government after the country entered the World Trade Organization. In 2012, Hyundai sold 854,000 vehicles in the PRC.

Hyundai also owns a 33 percent interest in Kia, South Korea's second largest automaker. In 2002, Kia joined with the Dongfeng Auto Group to create Dongfeng Yueda Kia Motors. In 2012, Kia sold 480,000 vehicles in China.

Other global automakers, such as Mercedes-Benz, Porsche and Leland, also have a large presence in the PRC. No global automobile manufacturer can overlook the PRC, not only because of its size but as a leader in automobile technology and design. In addition to the fierce rivalry among the joint ventures, China's domestic competitors are pushing the envelope to try to win market share and are compelling global automakers to introduce some of their latest models and technology in China. At first, the accepted wisdom was that the joint ventures with foreign companies would make upscale cars while China's domestic competitors would serve the low-cost segments. Competition, however, has forced the joint ventures to try to capture even the low-cost market. This has pushed the major Chinese domestic car companies more into the upscale market.

Computers and Electronic Products

For the person on the street, China is best known for its computers and electronic products. A large share of consumer electronics sold throughout the world is assembled in China, as are many of the components that go into them. As indicated in the chapter on Taiwan's investments in the PRC, most large American computer companies source many of their Chinese-made products from Taiwanese assembly plants rather than from their own subsidiaries in the PRC. Apple, Dell, Hewlett Packard, Oracle, Intel,

Cisco, and other companies source most of the computers, cellular phones, and tablets they sell primarily from Taiwanese equipment makers who have their factories in both the PRC and on Taiwan.[168] Some, however, also have built their own assembly plants.

Foreign companies also are active in investing in supplying parts for electronic products, particularly those embodying the latest in high technology. For example, nearly every high-tech electronic device has a computer chip and memory device embedded somewhere in its core. For supplying such semiconductors, Intel Corporation opened its first manufacturing facility in China in 2010. It was a $2.5 billion semiconductor plant in Dalian. Named Fab 68, the facility covers an area the size of 23 football fields, potentially is to have 1,500 workers, and drew in two dozen other companies that located there to supply the fabrication plant. When opened, Intel's CEO stated, "This manufacturing facility helps deliver on our vision to contribute to sustainable growth in China while giving us better proximity to serve our customers in Asia."[169]

IBM has operated in China since the 1970s. In addition to direct sales, it set up some joint venture factories as part of Beijing's attempt to develop an indigenous information technology industry. Eventually, the government abandoned the effort to build mainframe computers and focused on microcomputers and peripherals. In 1995, IBM set up its China Research Laboratory. At the time, many state-owned enterprises, universities, and government research facilities wanted to partner with them, but IBM decided that they would dance with everyone but marry no one. The lab has more than 100 Ph.D. scientists employed and has grown to be an integral part of IBM's eight-lab network.[170]

In 2007, Micron Technology opened its first semiconductor fabrication and test facility at a cost of $250 million in Xi'an in Shaanxi province in western China. In 2010, Micron announced its second semiconductor Test and Module Assembly building to complement its existing facility in Xi'an at an additional cost of $300 million. Micron also has an integrated circuit design center in Shanghai.[171]

The Dell Computer company operates two computer manufacturing plants and an enterprise command center in Xiamen. In 2013 Dell opened a second operations center in Chengdu in western China. The center has the capacity to produce up to seven million units a year and will manufacture computers and other electronics not only for the Chinese market but also for markets in Europe and the United States. At the opening ceremony, Michael Dell, the company's chairman and CEO, stated that the company's commitment to China has never been stronger, and its ongoing investment demonstrates the importance of China to Dell's strategy and future.[72]

The mobile phone market in the PRC has exploded in size, and global communications companies are vying to capture shares of the growing market. While domestic companies tend to be favored by the government, foreign firms have been able to carve out pieces of the market. One of the foreign players is Sony Ericsson China, a joint venture between Japan's Sony and Sweden's Ericsson. In 2004, the company took a majority interest in an existing Ericsson manufacturing plant and renamed it Beijing SE Putian Mobile Communications Co. Ltd. The new joint-venture manufactures mobile phones designed partly in Sony Ericsson's R&D operation center in Beijing.[73]

Siemens (Germany) began doing business in China in 1872, a quarter century after the company was founded. The company supplied China's first telegraphs, buses and x-ray machines. It opened its first permanent office there in 1904. Siemens even survived the tumultuous years of the Mao regime from 1949 to 1970. During both the 2008-09 global financial crisis and the European Sovereign Debt Crisis of 2011-12, Siemens' expanding China footprint helped it to maintain stability during unstable times. The product line of Siemens in China has expanded to include items such as power generators, combination MRI (magnetic resonance imaging) and PET (positron emission tomography) scanners, high-speed rail equipment and fire protection systems.

Of Siemens' global workforce, 31,000, or 8 percent, are in China. Siemens has invested heavily in research operations there. The company has more than 2,000 persons spread over some 16 R&D centers in the PRC. Of the 57,000 Siemens patents worldwide, there are approximately 3,400 active in China.[74] The company has 65 subsidiaries or joint ventures in the PRC, including Seimens Industrial Automation, Ltd., Siemens Medical Equipment, Ltd., Shanghai Electric Power Generation Equipment Co. and Shanghai Electric Wind Energy Co.[75]

Chemicals

Another sector that has attracted foreign investment has been chemicals. Since 2005, China's chemical production has trailed only that in the United States and Japan. Following the PRC's entry into the World Trade Organization, FDI in China's chemical industry has been high. Some chemicals, such as silicone, polyurethane and engineering plastics were considered to be new materials by domestic Chinese companies but were mature technologies for foreign players.

Dow Corning and also Germany's Wacker have set up factories in China to produce siloxane and fumed silica, two new materials to Chinese producers. Another new material is titanium dioxide made with chlorination technology. This is cleaner and cheaper than the old sulfate method used traditionally in the PRC. Paint, paper, toothpaste, plastics, cosmetics, and just about any other item colored white uses titanium dioxide. DuPont owns the patent on the chlorination technology. DuPont China was established in Shenzhen in 1984 and operates through nearly 40 subsidiaries and joint ventures in the country. It has refused to license the technology to China but built a titanium dioxide facility using its chlorination process in Shandong province.

According to U.S. court documents, in the 1990s, Walter Lian-Heen Liew (aka Liu Yuanxuan), a naturalized American citizen, met with the government of the PRC and was informed that the PRC had prioritized the development of chloride-route titanium dioxide (TiO2) technology. DuPont's TiO2 chloride-route process also produces titanium tetrachloride, a material with military and aerospace uses. Liew was aware that DuPont had developed industry leading TiO2 technology over many years of research and development, and he assembled a team of former DuPont employees, including Robert Maegerle, to assist him in his efforts to convey DuPont's TiO2 technology to entities in the PRC. Liew executed contracts with the Pangang Group companies in China for more than $20 million for chloride-route TiO2 projects that relied on the transfer of illegally obtained DuPont technology. He later was found guilty of economic espionage and theft of trade secrets.[176]

MDI-based polyurethane[177] and polycarbonate production also have received foreign investment. Polyurethane is used in an extensive range

133

of everyday products, and polycarbonate appears predominantly in the automotive, electrical and construction industries. Huntsman Chemical and Germany's BASF as well as Bayer have established facilities in the Shanghai Chemical Park to produce MDI-based polyurethane. Bayer also has built a polycarbonate plant in Shanghai. GE Plastic has been cooperating with China National Petroleum Company to build additional polycarbonate plants.[78]

China's modern chemical industry could scarcely have developed without foreign investment and foreign technology.

Retail

Western companies have entered the highly competitive retail market in the PRC. Market leaders in retail include Walmart, Sun Art Retail Group (a joint venture of the Taiwan conglomerate Ruentex Group and the privately held French retailer Groupe Auchan) and China Resources Enterprise, a company that teamed up with the British retailer Tesco in 2013. France's Carrefour and Japan's major department stores also are there.

Walmart operates more than 400 stores in China and in 2012 bought control of Yihaodian, a leading Chinese e-commerce website that claims 24 million registered users and provides same-day delivery. In the early 1990s, I visited a Walmart Sam's Club located in Shenzhen in Guangdong province. The parking lot looked just like any Sam's Club, Costco, or BJ's in the United States. It was full of SUVs and vans. Our host explained that the difference between the vehicles there and those in the United States was that the vehicles at the Chinese Sam's Club were owned mainly by small businesses rather than by households. Heading out the exit door and to a van in the parking lot was a man pushing a flatbed cart piled so high with toilet paper that when he hit a bump, the load started to fall off the cart. The inside of the store looked much like any wholesale club, but it had more Chinese items. I asked the manager what the most popular products he carried were. He said that by far, the most sought after was Peking duck during the New Year celebration. The line at the counter selling the duck snakes through the store and out the front door. The most popular non-seasonal item was a five-gallon bucket of laundry detergent made in Utah.

Our host said that Chinese businesses that had to launder clothes or hotel sheets and towels love American detergent. It gets things clean.

Walmart relies on more than 20,000 Chinese manufacturers for its global operations. In the United States, Walmart has cut costs by bypassing the middlemen and going directly to the manufacturer. In 2004, Walmart alone imported $18 billion worth of merchandise from China, nearly as much as did Germany. This volume has allowed Walmart to receive large discounts and to offer low prices. It also has put pressure on its suppliers to cut costs, at times in ways that are allegedly in violation of labor laws.[179]

Not all of the existing Walmart stores in the PRC, however, are profitable. The company already has closed many of its outlets.[180] As Chinese consumers have become wealthier, they have become more discerning. Walmart stores are known for selling inexpensive merchandise, but many of the modern consumers in the PRC want something better. Chinese tastes are going upscale, and Walmart has been taking measures to account for this change in taste, particularly in food. Chinese customers are increasingly discerning about food, so the company is opening new distribution facilities to ensure fresher food and produce.[181]

This mistrust in food safety was heightened by a baby milk powder scandal in 2008 that resulted in six babies dying and 300,000 infants sickened. Suppliers in China were adding the industrial chemical melamine to milk powder in order to cause it to appear to have higher protein content and command a higher price. In a conversation I had with a supplier of American-made baby formula, the supplier said that his company had to ration stocks of baby formula in retail outlets in Hong Kong. Professional carriers from the PRC were going into Hong Kong stores and buying all the baby formula they could find and taking it back home to sell. As soon as his company re-stocked stores in Hong Kong (or the PRC), the formula would fly off the shelves.

The more discerning Chinese customers also are accustomed to seeing knockoff products and imitations of brand name merchandise. They know they have to check spelling and labels carefully and not assume anything. Savvy Chinese customers are not fooled by "Arm and Hatchet" baking soda, "Blackbelry" cellular phones, "oMC McDnoald" hamburgers, or "Hike" (not Nike) shoes.[182] They expect foreign stores to carry real merchandise and often check to make certain.

Department stores and other retail outlets from Japan also have entered the China market. Sogo and Isetan Mitsukoshi, both companies with leading department stores in Japan, have opened similar stores in China. The stores, however, face dual challenges. The first is competition from online retailers, a factor that is bedeviling all bricks and mortar retailers. Sales at department stores is being hit hard enough that Isetan Mitsukoshi has closed three of its department stores in China and is opening a chain of smaller stores aimed at catering to fashion-conscious women.

The second challenge is the same anti-Japanese sentiment that has affected Japan's automakers. Even Japanese-owned stores with names that appear to be Chinese have not escaped damage. During the 2012 protests over the Senkaku/Daioyu Islands, Heiwado Department store suffered about $6 million in damages and more than that amount in lost business at three of its stores in Hunan province. After the protests, Heiwado's company president met with Communist Party executives of the province who promised that Japanese citizens and companies would be protected. The protests were somewhat ironic because in the 1990s, local governments in the province had eagerly recruited Heiwado to open stores there.[183]

Other retail outlets from Japan faced similar protests but are proceeding with expansion plans. Aeon Group, another operator of supermarkets and other outlets in Japan, also had its Jusco outlet in Qingdao in Shandong province damaged, but it opened a new supermarket a month later. Likewise, Fast Retailing Co., operator of the Uniqlo casual wear shops, is going forward with its plan to open numerous outlets in China. One of Japan's flagship department stores, Takashimaya, opened its Shanghai store, its first in the PRC, in December 2012 following the street protests.

The competition in the retail market in China is fierce. From street hawkers to exclusive Louis Vuitton boutiques, everyone wants to cash in on the *nouveaux riches* and their wannabes in China. One example of the extent to which Chinese competitors will go to attract customers is a women's restroom in La Perle Shopping Centre, a high-end shopping complex in Guangzhou in the southern province of Guangdong. The Centre was designed to attract only the richest Chinese consumers and includes the most famous luxury brand names from around the world. The women's restroom truly is a place to rest. Each cubicle consists of a sound-proof toilet room with the latest in high-tech commodes (two in each space) plus a small powder room complete with vanity mirrors and floor-to-ceiling wall mirrors plus a padded seat to use at the sink counter while freshening up. The entry area features a huge mosaic made from tiny ceramic tiles pieced together to form the face of a stylish Chinese woman.[184] Perhaps this is a metaphor for the modern China: a nation pieced together from thousands of shops and businesses catering to millions of people who suddenly find themselves in a position of relative luxury that was only a dream less than a half century ago.

FDI Company Performance

Has the rush to invest in the PRC paid off for foreign investors? Are profits being made, or are the investments long-term with meager current returns but looking for profits at some point in the future?

The American Chamber of Commerce in Shanghai conducts a business climate survey each year among its member companies. The survey in 2014 found that most companies responding to the survey reported growing profits and general optimism regarding their business prospects in China. Among respondents, 67 percent reported revenue growth over the previous year, and 74 percent of companies said their China operations were profitable. Seventy-five percent also reported a positive cash flow in their China operations, up 3 percentage points from the previous year.

Other findings from the survey were that 86 percent of the companies reported an optimistic or slightly optimistic outlook for their five-year business prospects in the PRC. Among the common trends reported by U.S. companies were:

- 59 percent of the companies said they primarily are in China to compete in the growing domestic market;
- Growth is slowing, but profitability is spreading;
- Increasingly strong competition exists from both Chinese and international players and

- More U.S. companies, including a growing number of small and medium-sized enterprises, are tapping into a fast developing services economy in the PRC.[85]

Lessons

The general themes running through the experience of Western and other companies in China are many. They include:

- The China market is for real. Every company must have a China strategy, one component of which could be to invest in production or research and development in the PRC.
- Competition is fierce, not only from domestic Chinese companies but from other foreign companies as well. No longer can global corporations start factory operations in China by shipping outmoded equipment to make past-generation products already being replaced in their home countries.
- The Chinese consumer is moving upscale and is tech savvy.
- International political or territorial disputes can severely disrupt the operations of foreign investors.
- Socialism with Chinese characteristics means that the government in the PRC at all levels plays a major role in the operation of businesses and industries. Ignorance of government policy is never bliss. In China, ignore it at your own risk.

CHAPTER 9. CHINA'S INDUSTRIAL STRATEGY AND POLICY

In 2011, U.S. photovoltaic solar panel maker Solyndra declared bankruptcy and laid off 1,100 Silicon Valley workers. The company had raised more than $1 billion from investors and secured a $535 million loan guarantee from the U.S. government to equip its factory with state-of-the-art robotics. Even robots, however, could not compete with the drastic price cuts on solar panels imported from China.[186] The failure of this half-billion-dollar loan guarantee became a point of contention between U.S. candidates for President in the 2012 U.S. general election.

The Solyndra case turned out to be collateral damage from China's industrial policy. In 2010, China's government-controlled China Development Bank extended an estimated $30 billion in credit to the country's largest solar manufacturers. This amount was about 20 times larger than the comparable U.S. figure for that year.[187] Some 100 companies in China had rushed into this high priority market being targeted for growth by the PRC government. Production quadrupled, and soon China became the world's largest exporter of photovoltaic cells. By 2009, Suntech Power Holdings Ltd., a Chinese startup company founded in 2001, rose to become the world's largest solar panel maker. The surge in production capacity led to cut-throat competition, and between 2008 and late 2011, the wholesale price of solar panels fell by 50 percent.[188] This drove competitors all over the world into bankruptcy, including several from China. By 2012, even Suntech Power Holdings was bankrupt.[189]

China's industrial policy gave its solar panel industry a huge lift. China leads the world in installations of clean solar energy, but solar energy is just one of many sectors that Beijing targets for favorable treatment, subsidies and growth. Industrial policy and the role of government in the economy form an important element of socialism with Chinese characteristics.

This chapter provides an overview of China's industrial strategy or policy as it affects foreign direct investors there. Foreign companies often say that they want the playing field in the PRC to be level. They claim that government policy often is tipped toward assisting domestic enterprises and hampering foreign companies. A crucial part of operating a business in the PRC is to understand and cope with government intervention into the economy. While a large part of socialism with Chinese characteristics consists of government ownership of certain enterprises, an equally large part is government influence over non-state-owned corporations through its industrial policy and also through its licensing and regulatory process. To ignore government policy in China is to risk being blindsided by actions that could threaten your operations or, alternatively, to miss government programs that subsidize or favor certain types of economic activity that also may be open to foreign companies.

Industrial Strategy

China's industrial strategy or policy consists of government intervention into the economy to promote specific companies or sectors often by changing the conditions under which they compete. It fits well into the PRC's three core national interests: (1) the Communist Party of China and its rule, (2) territorial sovereignty and (3) economic development. Robust industrial development is necessary to protect all three core interests. Industrial policy also helps China realize its centenary goals of wealth and power. The government aims to double gross domestic product and per capita income by the 2021 centenary of the Communist Party of China and to achieve a great rejuvenation of the Chinese nation by 2050 the centenary of the founding of the People's Republic of China in 1949.

Industrial policy often is designed to give domestic companies an unearned competitive advantage. Industrial policy also may promote technological or structural change. The instruments of China's industrial policy stretch across the gamut of government action both at national and local levels. While many such activities are considered normal functions of government, such as providing infrastructure and funding for research and development, other activities are considered to be mercantilist or beggarthy-neighbor policies that are intended to benefit China at the expense of its trading partners. Industrial policy is directly intertwined with international trade policy.

The PRC's industrial policies are not without a plan. China's 12th Five-year Plan ran from 2011 to 2015. In it Beijing targeted seven strategic emerging industries that are intended to become the backbone of China's economy in the future and industries needed to be able to compete well on a global scale. They were: (1) biotechnology; (2) new energy; (3) high-end equipment manufacturing; (4) energy conservation and environmental protection; (5) clean-energy vehicles; (6) new materials and (7) nextgeneration information technology. As part of its industrial policy, the government intended to spend from 10 trillion to 14 trillion yuan ($1.5 trillion to $2.1 trillion) on these industries over the five years of the plan. The intent was to increase their contribution to GDP from 5 percent in 2011 to 8 percent by 2015 and 15 percent by 2020.[90] This plan will be discussed further in Chapter 10.

China's industrial policies also include consolidating firms and closing unprofitable state-run enterprises that are unable to compete. The degree of intervention into an industry depends on the strategic value of the industry to the state. The major determinants of strategic value are the relationship of the industry to the military, the contribution of the industry to political control by the central government, whether the industry represents highlevel technology, whether the industry tends to be monopolized and whether the industry is emerging and could become a core industry in the future.

The most strategic industries in the PRC tend to be dominated by state-owned enterprises and are highly regulated. These include aircraft and aerospace, military equipment, telecommunications, the media, energy, insurance, financial services and chemicals. The least strategic industries tend to be less regulated, have many firms competing and are more open to foreign investors. These include electronic equipment, machinery, logistics, retail, tourism and consumer goods. In the middle are industries such as automobiles and pharmaceuticals that are heavily regulated and have stateownership but also have been fairly open to foreign investment.[91]

The Challenge of Industrial Policy

For the United States, the economic challenge from Chinese industrial policy is multifaceted. The focus of the U.S. public debate tends to be on the huge and continuing U.S. trade deficit with China, the arguable undervaluation of the Chinese currency, whether trade with China is fair, and how and to what extent support should be given U.S. businesses to assist them in competing with products from China. The economic policy issues include ensuring access to the huge Chinese market, making certain that U.S. companies are not placed at a competitive disadvantage with respect to those from China, protecting the intellectual property of U.S. companies, protecting U.S. companies from Chinese government cyber espionage to benefit Chinese companies, making certain that Beijing abides by the commitments it made when it joined the World Trade Organization and dealing with an economic system in which the state not only is the owner of major Chinese corporations but also actively uses government power to bolster the success of its companies. The United States would like the PRC to adopt principles that would lead to competitive neutrality, or an equal competitive footing, for all companies operating there.

Manufacturing Industrial Policy

Chinese industrial policy is aimed at both manufacturing and service industries, but manufacturing usually garners the most attention. The conventional view of China's manufacturing economy is that of an export powerhouse that is highly competitive in world markets partly because of an undervalued exchange rate and an unending supply of low-cost labor. In 2009, China's average hourly compensation costs were an estimated $2.85 for manufacturing employees in urban areas and $1.74 nationwide. This cost for compensation was far below comparable costs in neighboring countries, such as Japan ($30.03), South Korea ($15.06) and Singapore ($17.54), but it was roughly on par with those of the Philippines ($1.70).[192]

The fact of Chinese manufacturing, however, is that it not only benefits from low labor costs but that it is part of a global supply chain that includes direct investments from many countries of the world. In this supply chain, the Chinese economy is critical to the profitability and viability of multinational corporations whose products are generated by the supply chain. The final link in the manufacturing process often is an assembly plant in China, but content of the resulting export may hardly be Chinese at all, even though it carries a Made in China label. The final assembly usually constitutes but a small share of the total costs of manufacture. For example, in the case of the iPhone 3G S handset with 16 gigabytes of memory that was assembled in China in 2009, the manufacturing cost for assembly accounted for only $6.50 of the total $178.96 cost at the factory. The $172.46 bill for materials was for parts and components supplied by companies such as Toshiba, Samsung and Infineon. Apple sold this iPhone for $600. The situation was similar for the iPhone 4, the ensuing generation of iPhones. Its final assembly cost in Shenzhen in 2010 was estimated to be about 7 percent of the ex-factory cost of production.[193]

For Beijing, a goal of industrial policy is to capture more of the value in a product that is assembled in China. The key is to nurture Chinese companies that can manufacture more of the parts and components that go into the assembly process and to move them upstream and downstream into the design and marketing segments of the supply chain that leads to the final customer purchase.

China's strategy has been to start by promoting manufacturing. Manufacturing has been critical to the development of the country and to the maintenance of the existing political system. It has been essential for economic growth which, in turn, has generated rising incomes and has pulled millions out of poverty. The resultant Chinese economic miracle has provided legitimacy to the ruling regime and has augmented the resource base needed to achieve the country's political and security goals.

The ruling Communist Party understands well that unless it can deliver a rising standard of living, the resulting discontent could spell trouble for its position as the sole ruling party. For Beijing, the rapid economic growth experienced over the past quarter century and the transformation of the Chinese economy was driven mainly by the growth of industries which, in turn, depended largely on Chinese industrial policy and foreign firms that took advantage of it. The policy of reform and opening under Deng Xioaping not only has been a critical part of Beijing's industrial policy, but it also has been a major driver of that policy.

Ethnocentric Economic Nationalism

PRC industrial policy is conducted against the backdrop of a type of ethnocentric economic nationalism. As China has risen, an innate Chinese ethos appears to be re-emerging. For many Chinese, the natural state of the world is for China to be the Middle Kingdom and for vassal states to pay tribute to it, rather than for the country that is the center of the world to pay tribute to foreigners. For centuries, Chinese have viewed their Middle Kingdom as the center of a universal civilization surrounded by concentric circles of barbarians. The further from China, the more barbaric the people.

For millennia, the nexus that bound China together has not been a sense of nation but an irradicable sense of belonging to a superior civilization—the Chinese civilization. This thinking is being renewed for much of modern China. After more than a century of being subjugated by Western powers and being on the receiving end of unequal treaties, China is feeling its new-found power based on the goods that pour from its modern factories, its accumulation of foreign exchange reserves, the rockets that it now can launch into space and its new blue-water navy.

What Chinese ethnocentric nationalism implies for foreign investors is that they will always face headwinds in China. Even though local jurisdictions will encourage foreign investment and foreign manufacturers, the central government and other businesses with the help of government policy could well be trying to edge the foreign company out of the market. Non-Chinese will always be outsiders—foreigners in a foreign land.

Industrial Policy Measures

Industrial policy is aimed at promoting certain industries or companies. In contrast to macroeconomic policy that is directed toward the economy as whole, industrial policies are intended to stimulate growth in specific sectors or by particular firms. They also may promote technological or structural change.I[94] At a minimum, industrial policies are designed to foster collaborative, rather than antagonistic, relations between government and private industry.

China's industrial policies can be divided roughly into four overlapping categories: (I) policies intended to promote the competitiveness of specific companies or industries, (2) policies to facilitate domestic technological development, (3) policies to promote efficiency in production and transportation, and (4) policies to promote exports or provide protection from foreign competition. The policies include measures such as:

- promoting the development of domestic industries and national champion companies by providing subsidies, monopoly positions, or preferential government procurement policies;
- restricting foreign direct investment or requiring that foreign firms partner with domestic companies in order to limit competition from foreign companies;
- forcing the transfer of technology from foreign companies to domestic entities often by requiring joint ventures or the establishment of research centers in China in return for access to China's market or other market right;
- using the government approval process to impose requirements on foreign direct investors and delaying or refusing approval for those not cooperating;
- creating Chinese-centric standards, especially for high technology products, that are intended to benefit domestic firms over foreign firms that use internationally accepted standards;
- using national security considerations to protect and foster the growth of domestic producers;
- using the tax code to favor domestic producersI[95] or to provide tax incentives for enterprises with foreign investment that meet certain criteria;
- failing to provide adequate protection of foreign intellectual property or technology (or even using government entities, particularly the military, to cyber-spy on foreign companies to gain commercially useful information) in order to enable domestic firms to become more technologically advanced, more innovative, and more globally competitive; and
- imposing barriers to imports in order to foster the growth of infant industries or provide protection from international competition.

Coordinated Government Policy

In the PRC, there also is an additional consideration that relates to industrial policy. Since the Chinese Communist Party has a monopoly on all segments of government, it can marshal any or all government resources to achieve a particular goal. Government policy often is coordinated across the various parts of the central government. Beijing can use the whole gamut of government policy in order to accomplish a particular industrial policy goal, even if the policy tool is not directly related to the goal in question. Japan has often been the victim of such action.

The PRC, for example, curtailed shipments of rare earth metals to Japan as the two countries clashed over claims to disputed islands. China asserted that it was merely preserving a scarce natural resource. Japan claimed, however, that the shipments halted by Chinese customs authorities were done as retaliation. China also admitted that it wanted to spur development of electronic car batteries and was providing an incentive for Japanese battery makers that use the rare earth metals to locate their manufacturing facilities in China.

Another example of the use of disparate government actions to support industrial goals has occurred in antitrust reviews. Beijing appears to be using its new anti-monopoly law to implement its industrial policy. In antitrust reviews of merger cases involving multinational corporations, the Chinese antitrust authorities seem to be taking an unconventional route. In certain cases, China has used the protection of its domestic firms rather than protection of consumers as a major criterion in considering merger applications. As antitrust experts note, "there is a real sense that Chinese companies are not held to the same merger standards as China turns the screws on foreign companies, trying to create space for its domestic firms to grow." In addition to problems of long delays, as Daniel Sokol, professor of law at the University of Florida, explained, "Sometimes the remedies have nothing to do with antitrust concerns, but you are so desperate to close a deal that you give up the store to the Chinese. Firms will make all kinds of concessions. If this were the United States, people would say: I'll see you in court [but] no one is going to do that in China."[96]

Beijing's antimonopoly law apparently has been used in the digital cold war between the United States and the PRC. Accusations have been thrown back and forth over hacking into U.S. computer systems by the Chinese military and U.S. surveillance of electronic communications in China. In 2014, a hundred Chinese investigators raided Microsoft Corporation's offices in four Chinese cities claiming that Microsoft may have broken its antimonopoly laws by not disclosing relevant information about some security features and how it ties its software products together. The question remains over whether these actions were actually aimed at preserving competition under the antimonopoly law or whether they were designed to gather information related to cybersecurity and to weaken Microsoft.

Other foreign companies that have been investigated include Mercedes-Benz, a dozen Japanese makers of auto components, Chrysler, Audi and Qualcomm. In August 2014, the National Development and Reform Commission fined the Japanese auto parts makers a record 1.235 billion yuan ($201 million) for manipulating prices. In April 2014, the U.S. Chamber of Commerce wrote a letter to U.S. government officials stating, "The Chinese government has seized on using the [antimonopoly law] to promote Chinese producer welfare and to advance industrial policies that nurture domestic enterprises."[97]

Another way that the PRC looks after the interests of its industries is to retaliate against companies from a particular country if that country has taken adverse action against a Chinese company. For example, China may impose additional duties on American exports if there has been antidumping duties imposed on Chinese exports to the United States. In 2009, China was found to be dumping (selling below cost) tires in the U.S. market, and the United States imposed antidumping duties of 35 percent to curb imports of such tires. China retaliated by raising the duty on imports of U.S. chicken, nylon, and automobiles.[98]

In another case, in 2013, the U.S. government effectively banned China's networking equipment companies, Huawei and ZTE, from supplying telecommunications equipment for use in American telephone and digital communication networks for fear that it could be used as a portal for cybersyping. Later, after Edward Snowden leaked documents on U.S. spying programs that included electronic eavesdropping on China, Cisco Systems, an American networking equipment maker, reported that its sales in China dropped steeply. Beijing apparently retaliated against the banning of Huawei and ZTE based on the rationale that Cisco equipment posed similar cybersecurity risks. The Snowden documents bolstered that claim.I[99]

The Snowden documents and the PRC's anti-terrorism campaign have opened new avenues to force disclosure of industrial secrets. In 2015, the PRC enacted a new national security law that has sent ripples through the global technology industry. The law calls for a national security review of the technology industry, including networking and other products and services, and foreign investment. The law also requires technology that supports crucial sectors to be secure and controllable, a catchphrase that multinationals and industry groups say could be used to force companies to build so-called back doors which allow third-party access to systems and provide encryption keys or even hand over source code.[200] Foreign technology firms fear that, if disclosed, such codes would find their way into the hands of state-owned corporations or other domestic Chinese competitors.

Partly as a result of this policy development, IBM has reversed its China policy. In 2015, IBM announced that it would now share its technology with Chinese firms and allow them to design software and hardware based on its products. IBM apparently decided to accept the proposed disclosure requirements as a necessary part of doing business there, but many other foreign companies have opposed them. They are reluctant to provide the latest and most sophisticated software codes to potential competitors and fear that their operations in other countries could be threatened by giving China back-door access to their products.[20]I

Foreign companies in China are caught between protecting their technology and doing business in the expanding Chinese market. The PRC has twice the number of Internet users as does the United States and has accounted for about half of global information technology spending. Chinese regulators know full well that foreign companies cannot risk losing customers in such a large market and companies often will accede to Chinese demands to disclose technology. If the Chinese regulators can just get one company to give in, others will follow rather than be left behind. For example, as the use of cloud storage took hold, foreign information technology companies had a tacit agreement not to give in to demands that they store data in China. However, in 2012, Microsoft capitulated, cooperating with a local company to store data there and to help its customers meet Chinese legal requirements. Soon after, IBM, Amazon and Apple followed suit.[202]

New Directions in Industrial Policy

In looking forward, China's policymakers see problems and limits to the country's economic growth. They recognize that foreign-invested enterprises have accounted for more than half of the country's exports and that the manufacturing sector has been too concentrated in low-technology, labor-intensive, and often high-polluting assembly plants. Even though the products assembled in China might be highly sophisticated, the amount of value originating in China is only a small percentage of the total export value of the product. They see wages rising (particularly along the eastern coast); the labor force peaking; income disparities widening both across and within regions; and society aging quickly because of the one-child policy. Chinese policymakers fear that the country could become old before it becomes rich. Many of China's current economic problems stem largely from its unbalanced economic growth model, a model that has made exporting and fixed investment, rather than consumer demand, the main sources of economic growth.

The Chinese government is attempting to address these problem areas. In October 2006, the government formally outlined its goal of building a harmonious socialist society by taking steps (by 2020) to lessen income inequality, improve the rule of law, enhance environmental protection, reduce corruption, and improve the country's social safety net by such means as expanding health care and pension coverage to rural areas. The Chinese State Council in 2006 issued guidelines on a national medium- and long-term program for science and technology development for 2006-10. The guidelines stated that a central goal of the government was to change China from a major manufacturing center to a major global source of innovation and to reduce the country's reliance on foreign technology within 15 years.

Beijing, therefore, sees a need for major changes in China's industrial structure. According to the government, their industries must move up the value chain to higher valued-added products, innovate on their own and rely less on foreign-invested enterprises. China needs to shift more resources into service industries that pollute less and to shift growth to industries that are based on domestically-generated intellectual capital rather than on manual labor working overtime hours. Former Chinese Premier Wen Jiabao summarized the problem when he characterized the Chinese economy as suffering from the paradox of the Four Un's—an economy whose strength on the surface masked a structure that was increasingly unstable, unbalanced, uncoordinated and ultimately unsustainable.[203]

The 2007-09 global financial crisis reinforced the view by Beijing's policymakers that the Chinese economy is *sui generis*, quite unlike any other in the world. The crisis provided a huge boost of confidence to China's leaders in their economic system because while North America, Japan and Europe fought recession, China continued to grow at more than 9 percent per year and to run large surpluses in its international trade. Not only did this add to the nearly $2 trillion in China's foreign exchange reserves at that time, but it apparently convinced policymakers in Beijing that their brand of socialism was superior to the market capitalism of the United States, Europe and other industrialized countries. This generated a surge of economic nationalism and a tightening of control over the development of the Chinese economy. It also brought about a new focus on Chinese industrial and innovation policies that was manifested in more reliance on central government direction and intervention, larger subsidies for targeted industries, more emphasis on indigenous innovation, more growth in state-owned enterprises and overt picking of winners and losers among companies and industries.

In 2012, a new set of leaders entered China's stage. These leaders included Xi Jinping as President and General Secretary of the Communist Party and Li Keqiang as Premier. They have been building on existing industrial policies, particularly those contained in the Five-Year Plans. However, the focus of their new industrial policy is directed toward energy-saving and eco-friendly industries and on the greening of traditional industries. They also have stressed the information technology industry as applied to traditional industries and the expansion of information consumption. They recognized the need to rely less on exports and more on domestic consumption as an engine of growth. They placed high priority on the service sector to spur consumption and to reduce reliance on foreign export markets. The leaders also have seen urbanization as a driver of the country's modernization as well as more creative destruction in industries with overcapacity. The key principles governing China's industrial policy for the ensuing decade seemed to center on industrial modernization, informatization, globalization, urbanization, environmental protection and the extension of the service sector.[204]

The short-hand for Beijing's economic plan is 3-8-3. The first number three covers reforms in three areas: the market, government, and companies, with the goal to reduce the role of government in the economy. The number eight refers to a focus on eight core sectors: finance, taxation, state assets, social welfare, land, foreign investment, innovation and good governance. The final three refers to three reforms: relaxing control over market access, launching social security and allowing sales of collectively-owned rural land. The household registration system (*hukou*), which continues to discourage migration, is to be phased out in third-tier cities.[205] The Shanghai Free-Trade Zone is one manifestation of this policy direction. It remains to be seen, however, whether China will succeed in significantly reducing the role of government in the economy.

Avoiding Instability

Given China's turmoil during the Great Leap Forward and Cultural Revolution, a corollary to Beijing's industrial policy is the prevention of political instability. Over the past three decades, the PRC has been able to avoid major political instability. However, much could happen over the next quarter century to throw the PRC off course. According to Minxin Pei, "rising inequality and endemic corruption in China could fuel social unrest and cause its economic growth to sputter. And if a democratic breakthrough somehow forces the Communist Party from power, China is most likely to enter a lengthy period of unstable transition, with a weak central government and possibly mediocre economic performance."[206]

The Party knows well that the more affluent and well-traveled the population, the greater the probability that challenges to its authority could spread and throw the nation into chaos. The first priority for Beijing is to maintain the supremacy of the Communist Party. It does this partly by undertaking sufficient reform to placate critics and to keep the economy moving forward. It also cracks down on any signs of dissent or criticism while attempting to alleviate some of the sources of discontent.

Cracking down on dissent has become a science in the PRC. Beijing suppresses dissent by first crushing it before it spreads and by attempting to silence critics whether they are domestic or international. If demonstrations do occur, the police are quick to quell them.

For Beijing's policymakers, dealing with the approximately 105 million ethnic minority groups in the country poses a particularly difficult challenge. Beijing's underlying strategy for ethnic groups seems to be assimilation and cooptation by creating ethnic minority stakeholders in the larger political system and allowing Han Chinese to move into traditionally minority areas.

I was in China shortly after the rioting and clashes in July 2009 between members of the Xinjiang Region's native Muslim Uighurs and China's majority Han population that left more than 200 dead. The new factor in the equation had been electronic communications. In my conversations with government officials in Beijing, they said that they were surprised that an incident at a toy factory in the Southeastern province of Guangdong could trigger unrest in the far western region of Xinjiang. Social media and the Internet had played a key role in communicating the feelings of unrest.

The PRC's repression of the Uighurs in the Xinjiang Region is gradually escalating into violent attacks that have shocked China's policymakers. Between April 2013 and February 2014, more than 100 people had been killed in clashes between Uighur militants and Chinese authorities. While most of the violence was in Xinjiang and Kunming, Beijing residents were particularly unnerved when militants crashed a car into a group of tourists on Tiananmen Square killing two tourists and three persons in the car.[207]

There is concern in Beijing that certain militant separatists from the PRC possibly are being trained by jihadists factions affiliated with al-Qaeda and the Taliban in Afghanistan and Pakistan. If so, terrorist attacks in China could become more sophisticated and deadly.[208] The 2014 incident in the Kunming railway station that left at least 29 dead and scores wounded was done by knife wielding attackers. Suicide car bombers in Xinjiang used propane gas cylinders as bombs. These crude weapons of attack could be replaced by sophisticated terrorist devices that could spell trouble for the PRC. Beijing's nightmare is that the ethnic Muslim population will become radicalized and turn to weapons and methods honed in the Middle East and Afghanistan.

To the credit of Beijing and local governments, they have discovered that ethnic culture can be a huge tourist draw. They are rebuilding temples, constructing cultural parks showcasing ethnic life and producing shows based on ethnic culture mainly as tourist attractions. The rebuilt temples, however, also provide places of worship for believers and, along with the cultural theme parks, provide some opportunities for ethnic groups to preserve their heritage.

In Shangri-La, for example, the Song Zan Lin Buddhist temple is almost completely reconstructed after being destroyed in the Cultural Revolution. It reportedly has 800 monks and is the largest Tibetan temple outside of Tibet. During a 2009 visit to this temple, I asked how much the government interfered with the religious operation of the temple. A temple official said that one major problem was that government approval was necessary for assignments of monks to various Tibetan temples and that monks were not able to stay as long or come as often to study at this temple as would traditionally be the case. I also asked our local guide if he was ethnic Tibetan? He said, "No, I am Han Chinese."

FIGURE 9.1. THE REBUILT SONG ZAN LIN TEMPLE IN SHANGRI-LA

Photograph by D. Nanto

In 2011, during the Arab Spring uprisings in the Middle East, a loosely organized protest movement dubbed the Jasmine Revolution began to bubble up in the PRC. In February, U.S. Ambassador John Huntsman was photographed at one anti-government rally near a McDonald's restaurant in Beijing, although he quickly left the scene once he was recognized.[209] The police responded with an overwhelming presence at rallying sites and by blocking Internet sites and searches for words such as Huntsman, Jasmine and Egypt. Means of communication, such as Facebook and Twitter, already had been blocked, and Sina Weibo (the Chinese equivalent of Twitter) does strict self-censoring of content.

I was in Shanghai at the time of this Jasmine non-Revolution. The word got out that there was to be a walking-around demonstration (non-violent demonstration with no signs, only people walking around) on Sunday near the Starbucks Coffee Shop across from People's Square in the center of the city. I decided to see what was happening. When I emerged from the subway in front of the Starbucks, there was a drizzling rain. Lined up under the building overhang were rows of young people just standing around while crowds passed by on the sidewalk. A number of policemen were watching carefully. I took a few pictures and acted like a tourist. Soon a policeman stopped me and asked me something in Chinese. When I answered in English, he asked to see my passport. When he saw my official passport, he then asked if I was an American diplomat. I said that I was an American official but not a diplomat. His colleague wrote down my name and passport number. I assured them that I was just enjoying the sights, markets, and museum, but I wondered if I was to be taken into custody. The policeman then asked if I knew the number to call if I needed help from the police. He gave me the number and let me go with a wry smile. (See **Figure 9.2**)

FIGURE 9.2. A WALKING-AROUND DEMONSTRATION IN SHANGHAI, MARCH 2011

Photograph by D. Nanto

The Chinese government frequently arrests people critical of the government and blocks access to Internet sites that provide foreign news, books and video. In 2016, Beijing imposed new rules that banned foreign ownership and joint ventures in online publishing and stipulated that all content had to be stored on servers located in the country. Government officials say that Internet rules are needed to ensure security in the face of rising threats, such as terrorism and foreign ideology, that could destabilize China.[210]

Beijing now has learned well how to quash organized threats to Communist Party rule. Whether by jailing dissidents, not renewing visas for foreign journalists who have reported on government corruption, censoring communications, banning organizations that might provide a platform for dissent (such as Christian churches governed from abroad or the Falun Gong religious sect), or by stifling the first signs of anti-government activity, the Chinese government is able to suppress dissent. The question, however, is how much longer Beijing can keep a lid on a pot that has long been simmering and may start to boil?

Does Industrial Policy Work?

Many Western economists and industry analysts are skeptical of industrial policies and doubt that governments can do a better job than the market in picking winning and losing firms or technologies, particularly if political considerations hover in the background. They assert that such policies can create economic inefficiencies and may help one firm at the expense of another, thereby failing to produce net benefits for the economy as a whole. Michael Porter, the business professor who has written extensively on the competitive advantage of nations, has stated, "Government should not overplay its role in national competitive advantage. If it does, it will create an economy of dependent, backward-looking, and ultimately unsuccessful firms."[211] In a study for the World Bank, Dani Rodrik concluded that there is no shortage of economists who believe that Taiwan as well as South Korea, China, and other East and Southeast Asian countries would have come out further ahead if their governments meddled less in industry.[212]

Some economists argue that heavy support of the state sector is creating significant distortions in the Chinese economy, and that, at some point, these will begin to weigh it down.[213] Kim Eng Tan with Standard and Poor's argues that the main risk to China's future economic growth is failure to address obstacles to productivity, such as price controls and excess incentives for state-owned enterprises, and he warns: "If the central government makes little or no progress, due to strong resistance from interest groups, China's economic growth over the next five to ten years could slip from levels to which it has become accustomed."[214]

The current interest in Chinese industrial policy is reminiscent of the 1980s and the debate over Japan's industrial policies. Some in the United States claimed that Japan was displacing the United States to become number one in the world or that the United States and Japan were "trading places."[215] Japan's growth rates from 1960 to 1990 eventually slowed from rates similar to those currently being reported in China to what has become known as the lost decades from 1990 to 2010.

The difference with China, however, is that China's population at 1.3 billion is four times that of the 312 million in the United States and ten times that of Japan's 128 million. Even though Japan's per capita income has risen to the level of that in the United States, the income in Japan is held by a smaller population base, so Japan's GDP has been second, and since 2010, third, in size to that of the United States. China's annual per capita income of $6,091 in 2012 was roughly one-ninth that of the $51,749 in the United States. However, it is spread over a larger population, so China's GDP at $8.2 trillion is roughly half the $16.2 trillion of the United States. Once per capita GDP in China reaches a quarter of the level of that in the United States, approximately where Brazil or Poland is now, The GDP of the PRC will surpass that of the United States. China, then, will be the largest country in the world (although India may surpass it in population).

Figure 9.3. Growth Rates in Japan, S. Korea, and China under Rapid Economic Growthshows economic growth rates for Japan, South Korea, and China beginning when each started growing at about 7% per year—the rate at which an economy doubles over ten years. A three-year moving average of growth rates is used to smooth the series.[216] Japan's data begins in 1957, South Korea's in 1964, and the PRC's in 1978. The growth rate in each country generally rose at first, reached rates exceeding 10%, had temporary dips, and, for Japan and South Korea, gradually declined after about 30 years of rapid growth. China now is around that 30-year point. It is not surprising; therefore, that the country has adopted an industrial strategy to attempt to maintain growth as its economy approaches a probable slowing of economic growth and, perhaps, even a recession.

FIGURE 9.3. GROWTH RATES IN JAPAN, S. KOREA, AND CHINA UNDER RAPID ECONOMIC GROWTH

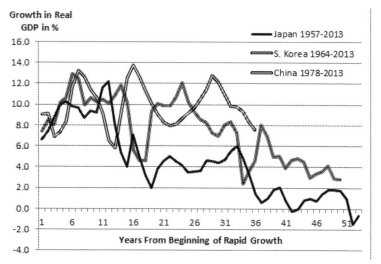

Source: Underlying data from Japan Statistics Bureau, World Bank, Global Insight.

Note: Data for each country begins the year when growth reached around 7% or more. Data are three-year moving average growth rates.

In China's case, industrial policy seems to have resulted in some successes. Justin Lin, the Chief Economist of the World Bank, said that export incentives aided Chinese companies in gaining a foothold in competitive global markets, and he credits active industrial policy with much of China's recent success.[217]

A World Bank-commissioned study that examined industrial policy, particularly in China, concluded the following: A main implication from our analysis is that the debate on industrial policy should no longer be for or against having such a policy. As it turns out, sectoral policies are being implemented in one form or another by a large number of countries worldwide, starting with China. Rather, the issue should be on how to design and govern sectoral policies in order to make them more competition-friendly and therefore more growth-enhancing.[218]

Dani Rodik, in another World Bank-commissioned study, found that industrial policy may look good in theory, but in practice has two major constraints. The first is that in the absence of omniscience—that is, almost always—an activist government will miss its targets, support economic activities with no positive spillovers and waste the economy's resources. The second objection is that industrial policy is an invitation to corruption and rent-seeking. Once the government is in the business of providing support to firms, it becomes easy for the private sector to demand and extract benefits that distort competition and transfer rents to politically connected entities. Entrepreneurs and business executives spend their time in the capital asking for favors rather than looking for ways to expand markets and reduce costs.

In reflecting on the experience of countries with respect to industrial policies, Rodik comments, however, that governments may not be the greatest stock-pickers (able to select future winners), but "it beats being taken to the cleaners."[219]

Chapter 10. The Governmental Forces Behind China's Industrial Policies

In China, much of the economy is the state, and without a thriving economy the state would be hard pressed to rule. In the absence of democratic elections, the viability of continued Communist Party rule depends on sufficient support from the people to ensure that no populist movement arises to depose them. A rapidly growing economy helps to provide that support. In addition, the industrial sector plays a key role in generating revenues for the state and provides managerial positions and training for elite players and rising stars in the Party. China's industrial strategy, therefore, transcends the country's core national interests. It also is a primary interest to the ruling Communist Party.

The influence of the government in China's economy is too pervasive to catalog here. The Chinese say their economy is socialism with Chinese characteristics, but in reality their economy is market capitalism with some key aspects of socialism mixed in. The major Chinese characteristics are not uniquely Chinese but are common to other mixed economies. The two major socialist characteristics in China's economy are, first, that the government controls key industries and intervenes directly in the economy and, second, that officials look out for the Party's economic interests at all levels of society. The market and competition still play a major role in economic decision making by businesses and households, but the government has learned well how to use the market to benefit the country and Party.

Government Control of the Economy

In 1949, when the Chinese Communists ousted the Nationalists, Beijing set out to create a Soviet-type command economy. Post-revolutionary China, therefore, always has had industrial policies. Under the Maoist brand of communism, the government controlled nearly all aspects of life, including the whole supply chain and prices for most major products. Since 1978, the process of reform and opening of the Chinese economy has established a more modern, market-based system, but the long arm of government still prevails.

Beijing's current economic strategy has been to create an economy in which the government guides, intervenes and directly controls key sectors but leaves many of the basic economic functions to markets, firms, and individuals. This strategy has required the creation of a commercial code, a banking system, a judicial system, and other institutions to support market transactions as well as membership in international organizations such as the World Trade Organization. Laws and regulations being adopted by Beijing often mirror those in Western industrialized countries, but implementation tends to be uneven. In any dispute, the question is whether the rule of law or the rule of the Party will prevail.

The shadow that the government casts over the economy poses distinct challenges for foreign direct investors. Not only are numerous enterprises financed and operated by both the central and local governments, but competition from foreign firms can be limited through the approval process for foreign investment, by limiting foreign ownership or by restrictions on the scope of their operations. Government, at both the central and local level, also can channel bank credit to targeted industries, intervene in private joint ventures with foreign companies, provide subsidies to favored companies and enforce buy-Chinese policies in government procurement. Foreign companies have to seek a balance between maintaining good relations with the government and competing head-to-head with state-owned and state-financed enterprises in markets that can suddenly become tilted against them.

In addition to state ownership of many enterprises, socialism with Chinese characteristics essentially refers to the authority of the governing Communist Party. This is also true of one-party governments in other countries. The government claims the right to intervene directly whenever it deems such action necessary and downplays Western notions of democracy, human rights and the rule of law, even though these ideals are spreading in Chinese society and some are being adopted as they serve the interests of the Party and contribute to social stability. Since the Party also controls the judicial system and often censors the press, there often is no recourse against government actions that are arbitrary, corrupt or protectionist, although the advent of the Internet and social media is rapidly creating ways to mobilize public opinion among China's wired generation. Not only foreign companies, but Chinese citizens also, are often victims of arbitrary and self-serving actions by governments, particularly local governments.

Industrial Structure

Much of the Chinese economy resembles the market-based economies of industrialized countries of Asia, Europe, and the Americas. There are both state-owned and private companies, entrepreneurs, a huge retail sector, intense competition among companies and a plethora of both global brand-name goods and primarily domestic brands. On the surface, industries in China and those in other parts of the world may look alike, but they differ in many of their important respects.

China's current industrial structure illustrates the nature of the mixed socialist and market system. About a half million medium and large manufacturing enterprises comprise the core of the industrial economy. Of these, more than half are privately owned, about a quarter have all or some state ownership, and about a fifth are foreign firms (including firms from Hong Kong, Macao, and Taiwan.)

In 2012, there were 343,769 enterprises engaged in manufacturing that had revenues over 20 million yuan ($3.17 million). (See **Figure 10.1**) As discussed in the section below on the ownership and supervision of state-owned enterprises, with the exception of enterprises solely owned by the state (central government), it is difficult to determine which companies are government-owned (including local and provincial government), partly state-owned, or state-influenced. Categories overlap, and companies are continually evolving.[220]

FIGURE 10.1. INDUSTRIAL ENTERPRISES IN THE PRC

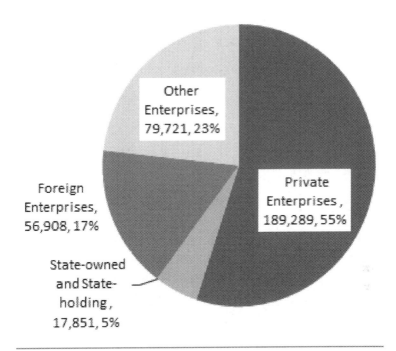

Source: 2012 China Statistical Yearbook, Tables 14-1, 14-5, 14-6, 14-10.
Note: Industrial enterprises with revenues exceeding 20 million yuan
($3.17 million) in 2012.

As shown in **Figure 10.1**, state-owned enterprises numbered 17,851
(5.0% of all enterprises). These included enterprises that were collective-
owned (owned mostly by local or provincial governments), cooperative and
joint-ownership as well as limited liability corporations in which the state
was the sole investor. There were an additional 79,721 enterprises, mainly
limited liability corporations, in which the state or local and provincial
governments may have invested funds.

More than half of the industrial enterprises or 189,289 (55%) were
privately-owned firms (not foreign-invested) that have taken a variety
of organizational forms. The combination of all these state, collective,
cooperative, limited liability and privately-owned enterprises comprise the
category of domestically-funded enterprises and totaled 286,861 or 83.4

percent of all manufacturing enterprises with revenues over 20 million yuan ($3.17 million).

In addition to these domestically-funded enterprises, China reported 56,908 (16.5% of total) foreign-invested enterprises. Of these, 25,935 (7.5%) came from Hong Kong, Macao and Taiwan, while 30,973 manufacturing enterprises (9.0%) came from a variety of countries of the worldFigure 10.2. Distribution of Total Industrial Assets by Type of Enterprise in China **10.2** shows the types of industrial enterprises by asset values. The types of enterprises with relatively larger asset values included state-owned enterprises with 5 percent of the number of enterprises along with 41 percent of the assets and foreign funded firms with 17 percent of the total number of enterprises and 22 percent of the assets. Private enterprises tended to have smaller asset values. They accounted for 55 percent of the number of enterprises but only 20 percent of the asset values. Foreign industrial enterprises were worth more in asset values than private firms and had more than half as much in assets as state-owned enterprises.

In other sectors of the economy, there also is a mix of state-owned, private and foreign enterprises. In construction, of the 75,280 enterprises, 9,242 were state-owned or collectives while 680 were foreign (including those from Hong Kong, Macao and Taiwan). In hotels, of the total 17,109 corporations, 3,789 were state-owned or collective, and 980 were foreign.

In 2012, 767.0 million persons were employed in China, with 9.2 million unemployed in the urban areas for an urban unemployment rate of 4.1%. Those employed were divided almost equally among the three economic sectors. Primary industry (agriculture, forestry and fisheries) had 257.7 million or 33.6 percent of the total employed. Secondary industry (manufacturing) had 232.4 million or 30.3 percent, and tertiary industry(services) had 276.9 million or 36.1 percent of the total employed. The labor force is expected to peak in 2016 at about 831 million workers.[222]

FIGURE 10.2. DISTRIBUTION OF TOTAL INDUSTRIAL ASSETS BY TYPE OF ENTERPRISE IN CHINA

Billion U.S. Dollars and Percentage of Total Assets

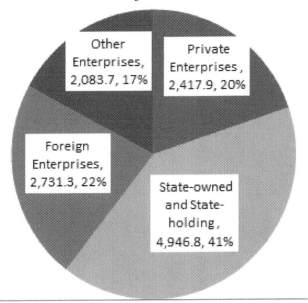

Source: Underlying data from *China Statistical Yearbook 2013*, Tables 14-1, 14-5, 14-6, 14-10.

Notes: Total Assets for industrial enterprises with revenues over 20 million yuan ($3.17 million) in 2012.

State-Administered Capitalism

Under Marxism, government is supposed to be a dictatorship of the proletariat as society transitions from capitalism to communism. Following a revolution, the proletariat (working class) should rule. In the PRC, however, the system is a dictatorship of the Party. Rule is top down. Foreign investors might wish that top-down in the PRC referred not to the structure that administers the economic system but to their ability to cruise by government constraints like a car with its top down on an autobahn. Unfortunately, that is not the case. The Chinese government often digs potholes or throws detours in their way, even though, at times, they might be provided with high octane gasoline in the form of investment and other incentives.

In most top-down political structures, at the apex stands a dictator, czar, or perhaps a ruling family that has descended from monarchy. For those at the top, their interest in maintaining the existing order usually outweighs their interest in promoting the general welfare. Policies directed downward from the top tend to be biased toward benefitting those above rather than the minions below.

China has tempered its top-down rule in the economic sphere by several ameliorating policies. It has imposed term limits on top leaders to preclude a strong-man ruler from becoming entrenched. Although the party is not a perfect meritocracy, merit and ability are important factors in advancement. Party leaders often have experience either in state-owned enterprises or dealing with businesses. Still, the torrent of policies emanating from Beijing is evidence that when it comes to the economy, the Party thinks it knows best. The vestiges of a command economy remain, and the commands emanate from Beijing.

The State Council

At the top of the system of state-administered capitalism sits the State Council, the highest executive and administrative body in the Chinese government. Membership in the State Council includes the premier, vice-premiers, state councilors, and the heads of ministries, commissions, and other top government arms. The 65 organizations under the State Council include all 22 ministries, 9 commissions, 15 administrations, 9 offices, 4 bureaus, and 6 other organizations such as the People's Bank of China, Xinhua News Agency, and Chinese Academy of Sciences. The State Council has broad responsibility over the nation. It deals with internal politics, diplomacy, national defense, finance, economy, culture and education. The Council's powers include submitting legislation, managing the economy and society, and conducting international affairs.

The Council members most influential on matters of industrial policy include the Ministers of Industry, Commerce, Finance, Environment, Transportation, and Science and Technology as well as the head of the National Development and Reform Commission (NDRC). The various ministries, such as finance and transportation, oversee industries within their sectors and perform functions similar to those in other governments.

Directly under the State Council are numerous organizations that deal with specific economic and political activity. For industrial policy, quite important is the State-Owned Assets Supervision and Administration Commission that supervises state-owned enterprises and investments in sectors other than banking and finance. The State Council also controls various administrations with responsibility for customs, taxation, environmental protection, civil aviation, media, sports, statistics, industry and commerce, and intellectual property.

The National Development and Reform Commission

The NDRC is part of the State Council, but in formulating industrial policy outranks the ministries and coordinates industrial policy among them. It works in conjunction with the ministries in devising and administering industrial policy.

The NDRC essentially is the top economic planner and regulator of industries for China. The official role of the NDRC is to formulate, coordinate, and implement strategies for national economic and social development, compile national economic plans, regulate the overall price level, carry out economic research and analysis, put forward targets and policies for the national economy and recommend the use of various economic instruments and policies. In particular, the NDRC drafts laws and regulations concerning national economic and social development, economic system restructuring, and opening up to the outside world.

The NDRC has broad authority with respect to foreign investments. It plans major construction projects and formulates regulatory targets, policies and measures concerning the total size and structure of fixed asset investment in the country. The NDRC also approves, authorizes, and reviews key construction projects, key foreign-funded projects, key investment projects for overseas resources development and investment projects using large amounts of foreign exchange. It also guides private investment and puts forward strategies and plans for foreign capital utilization and overseas investment. [223] A new role for the NDRC is to police compliance with the PRC's antimonopoly law with respect to pricing. The other government agencies that enforce the antimonopoly law are the Ministry of Commerce which deals with mergers and the State Administration for Industry and Commerce which deals with potential abuse of market power. Among the three government entities, however, the NDRC seems to have the most resources and has been the most aggressive in targeting foreign companies. The NDRC is responsible for some of the most high-profile investigations, such as those of baby-formula producers, eyeglass makers, foreign automakers and the Microsoft Corporation.[224]

The NDRC actively promotes China's industrial policy. For example, in March 2011, the NDRC reported that it was in the process of building 50 national engineering centers, 32 national engineering laboratories, and 56 key national laboratories. These were located within enterprises in industries such as digital television, next-generation Internet, advanced-generation liquid-crystal display panels, large-scale integrated circuits and regional aircraft. It had moved forward with 7 projects to apply high technology to production, built 18 national high-tech industrial bases and set up 13 venture capital funds. The NDRC also had allocated a fund of 20 billion yuan ($3.1 billion) for invigorating industries and upgrading their technologies and supported 5,051 technological upgrading projects.

The NDRC has been behind the government's policy of forced mergers and dissolution of certain companies as part of its plans for industry restructuring. Among the rationales for its actions are to reduce excess capacity, to eliminate sources of pollution and to rid the government of companies operating at a loss. It shut down what it called backward production facilities, thereby eliminating 12.1 million kilowatts of capacity at thermal power plants, 9.31 million tons of capacity at steel mills, 40 million tons at iron foundries, 116 million tons at cement plants, 552,500 tons at plate glass plants and 4.7 million tons at paper mills.[225] In a sense, the NDRC is both the creator and destroyer in Joseph Schumpeter's process of creative destruction that describes progress in capitalism as the emergence of new technology or industries and the destruction of the old.[226]

On April 26, 2011, the NDRC announced a revised (from 2005) *Catalogue of Industrial Structure Adjustment* (effective June 1, 2011) that provided a list of sectors the government should promote, curb, or ban in coming years to promote industrial restructuring and upgrading and the development of a modern industrial system. The catalog provided a guide for Chinese regulators as they steer investment, levy taxes, and determine financial, land and trade policies that affect these industries. Industries newly targeted for expansion include new energy, city rail infrastructure, public safety and emergency response equipment. In the service sector, the number of favored industries increased from 33 to 112 to include upcoming sectors such as logistical, financial, and information technology services.[227]

Ministries

The State Council also includes ministries directly responsible for sectors of the economy. These include the Ministries of Finance, Commerce, Construction, National Defense, Education, Science and Technology, Labor and Social Security, Transportation, Railways and Agriculture. In 2008, the government created a new Ministry of Information Industry responsible for industries that manufacture electronic and information products, the telecommunications industry, and the software industry. These ministries draft laws and prepare regulations related to their industries and coordinates policies with the National Development and Reform Commission.

Ownership and Supervision of State-Owned Enterprises

China's State-Owned Assets Supervision and Administration Commission (SASAC) is a special institution directly controlled by the State Council. SASAC serves as controller of state investments in sectors other than banking and finance. By law, it performs the responsibilities of an investor in state-owned enterprises (SOEs). It supervises and manages the assets of SOEs; guides and pushes forward the reform and restructuring of SOEs and evaluates, rewards, and punishes top executives of the enterprises under the direct supervision of Beijing. By law it is to maintain and improve the controlling power and competitive power of the State economy in areas which have a vital bearing on the lifeline of the national economy and State security, and to improve the overall quality of the State economy.[228] The SASAC also is attempting to bring some local state-owned assets under its supervision.

In 2003, when the SASAC was established, there were 196 state-owned enterprises under its supervision. SASAC immediately set out to close or force mergers of unprofitable enterprises. By the end of 2007, 152 were left, and by the end of 2012 the number had diminished to 117 firms. By 2015, SASAC reportedly intended to reduce the number of SOEs to 30 to 50 national champion enterprises. These would have their own intellectual property, have globally-recognized brand names, and would be internationally competitive.[229]

Although the leading state-owned enterprises can be identified easily because they report directly to Beijing, thousands more fall into a gray area of mixed public and private control. These include the subsidiaries of the large state-owned enterprises, companies owned by provincial and municipal governments, and companies that have been partially privatized yet retain the state as a majority or influential shareholder.

Fortune Magazine's 2013 listing of the top 500 global companies[230] included 89 Chinese companies, up from 73 in 2012, 63 in 2011 and 34 in 2008. Three Chinese companies made it into the top ten—more than either the United States or Japan. The top 20 of these firms are listed in Table 10. These companies were largely concentrated in oil and gas, power, construction, autos, insurance, and telecommunications. Several Chinese firms were major employers, including China National Petroleum (at 1.66 million workers) and Sinopec Group (1.02 million). Dongfeng Motor employed about the same number of workers (163,990) as Ford Motor Company, a company that had 166,000 employees worldwide.

TABLE 10.1. MAJOR CHINESE COMPANIES LISTED IN FORTUNE GLOBAL 500 FOR 2013

Name	Global Rank	Assets ($ billions)	Employees	Comments
Sinopec Group	4	314.1	1,015,039	Oil producer
China National Petroleum	5	547.2	1,656,465	Oil and gas
State Grid	7	374.5	849,594	Power company
Industrial & Commercial Bank of China	29	2,815.6	427,356	Banking
China Construction Bank	50	2,242.7	348,955	Banking
Agricultural Bank of China	64	2,125.8	481,431	Banking
Bank of China	70	2,035.3	302,016	Banking
China Mobil Telecommunications	71	204.8	222,431	Mobile services
Nobel Group	76	19.7	15,000	Supply chain manager
China State Construction Engineering	80	105.5	203,761	Construction & real estate
China National Offshore Oil Corporation	93	131.3	102,562	Offshore crude oil/gas
China Railroad Construction	105	78.2	290,907	Engineering contractor
China Railway Group	102	88.4	289,343	Railways
SAIC Motor	103	50.9	105,953	Automaker
China Life Insurance	111	370.2	141,932	Insurance
Sinochem Group	119	46.0	47,718	Chemicals, fertilizer, oil
China Southern Power Grid	134	89.0	300,863	Power networks
China FAW Group	141	39.1	85,552	Automaker
Dongfeng Motor	145	36.7	176,480	Automaker
China North Industries Group	161	45.7	260,021	Defense, petroleum

Sources: *Fortune* Global 500, 2013 Annual Rankings of the World's Largest Companies, and various company websites. Rankings are based on 2012 revenues. Excludes Hong Kong firms.

Note: All are 50% or more government owned except for the Nobel Group and the China North Industries Group. Chinese banks report the gross amount of derivative assets while U.S. banks report net amounts.

Of the Chinese firms on the *Fortune* Global 500 list, the vast majority were described as having government ownership of 50 percent or more. Those private Chinese firms listed with government ownership of less than 50 percent include the Nobel Group, China North Industries Group, Ping An Insurance, Huawei Technologies, Jiangsu Shagang Group (China's largest private steel enterprise) and Lenovo Group (a major global computer company). It is not clear, however, the extent to which these firms actually are privately owned and operated and the role of the central government in their development.[231] For example, many analysts contend that Huawei has received extensive financial aid from the central government, and some have alleged that it has links to the Chinese military.[232] (Huawei denies having such ties.) The Chinese Academy of Sciences, China's highest academic research organization and a member of the State Council, is thought to be the largest shareholder of Lenovo Group.[233]

One observer estimates that about three-quarters of 1,500 Chinese firms listed on China's stock exchanges are state-owned. He explains the problem of differentiating between the state-owned sector and the private sector as follows:

> Examining what companies are truly private is important because privatization is often confused with the spreading out of shareholding and the sale of minority stakes. In China, 100 percent state ownership is often diluted by the division of ownership into shares, some of which are made available to nonstate actors, such as foreign companies or other private investors. Nearly two-thirds of the state-owned enterprises and subsidiaries in China have undertaken such changes, leading some foreign observers to relabel these firms as nonstate or even private. But this reclassification is incorrect. The sale of stock does nothing by itself to alter state control: dozens of enterprises are no less state controlled simply because they are listed on foreign stock exchanges.[234]

The sale of stock in state-owned enterprises is partly a result of the government's attempt to separate government functions from business operations. The policy has been applied gradually since the 1980s, first to manufacturers of consumer goods, then to high-technology firms and heavy manufacturing, and, more recently, to banking. As a result, some government favoritism toward state-owned companies is fading, but it still exists. The stock market and shareholders also may be able to exert some market discipline on company management, particularly in generating profits and keeping executive compensation from becoming excessive.

Beijing, however, still looks after the interests of its enterprises. The large SOEs enjoy oligopolistic status (characterized by a few rather than one monopoly firm in an industry) in certain protected or favored sectors. The government maintains relatively strong state control over certain pillar and backbone industries. These include the automotive, chemical, construction, electronic information, equipment manufacturing, iron and steel, nonferrous metal, science and technology, and survey and design industries. State capital also plays a leading role in seven strategic sectors: aviation, coal, defense, electric power and grid, oil and petrochemicals, shipping and telecommunications. The railroads, grain distribution, and insurance industries are also dominated by the state.[235] Moreover, the People's Bank of China, along with the state-owned banks and the Finance Ministry, greatly influence the lending activities of China's private banks.

Since salaries in state-owned enterprises are relatively high, positions there are major plums for Communist Party Members. The managers of many of the large state-owned holding companies—the central SASAC enterprises—are senior party cadres, some of whom sit on the Party's central committee as ordinary or alternate members.

Profits of SOEs under SASAC are divided three ways. Some are taxed; some go to SASAC, and the rest are retained. Since 2008, the corporate tax rate in the PRC has been 25 percent, down from the previous 33 percent. However, because of various tax breaks and incentives, on average domestic firms paid rates of about 24 percent and foreign firms roughly 14 percent. SASAC enterprises remit between zero and 10 percent of their profits to SASAC through the Ministry of Finance. This gives SASAC the resources needed to purchase companies, pay the costs necessary to restructure particular firms or sectors and buy out workers and social services in bankrupt enterprises.[236]

In 2001, when China joined the World Trade Organization, several countries had expressed concern over China's state-owned enterprises.

With respect to this issue, China's representative to the Working Party on Accession stated:

> State-owned enterprises had been reformed by a clear definition of property rights and responsibilities, a separation of government from enterprise, and scientific management. The state-owned enterprises basically operated in accordance with rules of market economy and were responsible for their own profits and losses. The government would no longer directly administer the human, finance and material resources, and operational activities such as production, supply and marketing. The prices of commodities produced by state-owned enterprises were decided by the market and resources in operational areas were fundamentally allocated by the market. The state-owned banks had been commercialized and lending to state-owned enterprises took place exclusively under market conditions. China was furthering its reform of state-owned enterprises and establishing a modern enterprise system.[237]

While some aspects of this statement seems to accord with the current situation related to state-owned enterprises, China appears to be far from fully implementing what the country claimed in 2001.

Many countries have raised concerns about SOEs in China and elsewhere. The Organization for Economic Co-operation and Development (OECD) has called for guarantees of competitive neutrality with respect to SOEs. This means that government-supported business activities would not enjoy net competitive advantages over their private-sector competitors in three key legally and geographically distinct markets: a party's home market, the other parties' home markets, and third-country markets.[238]

One objective of foreign governments with respect to the PRC is to ensure that their firms are accorded national treatment. National treatment, however, does not only mean treating foreign-affiliated companies the same as domestic firms. It also means putting private firms, whether foreign-affiliated or not, on an equal footing with state-owned enterprises. For example, in August 2010, an alliance of 16 state-run firms was established to accelerate the development of electric vehicles in China. These included China FAW Group Corp., Dongfeng Motor Group Co., and the State Grid Corp. of China. The government reportedly planned to inject 1.3 billion yuan (about $200 million) into the organization. Meanwhile, private companies, including foreign companies and even the Chinese electric vehicle maker BYD Co., had not been permitted to join the alliance.[239]

In April 2011, the World Trade Organization's Appellate Body issued a report on a case brought by the PRC in which it argued that the U.S. Department of Commerce incorrectly found in its final anti-subsidy determinations that Chinese state-owned enterprises provided subsidized inputs to Chinese exporters. The United States argued that SOEs constituted public bodies because the enterprises were majority-owned by the government of China and, therefore, bestowed subsidies on behalf of the government when providing inputs (such as steel, rubber, and petrochemicals) at less than market prices. However, in a March 11, 2010, report, the WTO Appellate Body reasoned that majority ownership alone is insufficient to determine if a state-owned enterprise is a public body. Rather, it stated that an SOE is a public body only if it possesses, exercises, or is vested with governmental authority.[240] In short, it must perform a government function and not merely be majority-owned by the government.

The Trans-Pacific Partnership Agreement (TPA) is an Asia-Pacific regional trade agreement among the United States and eight trading partners that was waiting final approval in 2016. It contains a chapter on state-owned enterprises principally engaged in commercial activity. These provisions were some of the most hotly debated parts of the agreement. If approved, the assistance that TPA governments could provide to enterprises with more than 50 percent state ownership would be reduced. Although China was not a participant in the TPA negotiations, the final language on state-owned enterprises will likely provide an important template for any future negotiations with China on this topic.[241]

Dick K. Nanto

Local and Regional Government Industrial Policy

Provinces, counties, cities, towns, and even villages share a common goal of fostering economic growth and development. This goal requires that they pursue an active industrial policy. Economic growth is so important to local and regional government officials that they often can quote from memory a variety of statistics on local GDP, investments and trade. Banquets for visiting dignitaries usually begin with a litany of statistics on the local economy. While foreigners find this somewhat befuddling, it reflects the incentives for promotion within the Chinese Communist Party. A major criterion for moving up in the party hierarchy is to foster economic growth while serving as a Party Secretary in a location, the mayor of a town or governor of a prefecture.

A key difference between local officials in the PRC and those in more democratic countries is that those in China are appointed by the Communist Party and not elected by the local citizens (except at the village level). These local administrators usually are party officials (particularly party secretaries), military leaders or powerful businessmen. They usually serve for five-year terms and often are not from the local area. They secured their appointment by showing their ability to generate revenues, manage government operations and demonstrate their loyalty to the Party.

At times there are conflicts between Beijing and local governments as to who will be appointed as leaders. During a visit to Guangdong province in 1992, I was introduced to the Acting Governor Zhu Senlin. After the meeting, I asked our host why there was only an Acting Governor and not a permanent governor. He said that there was a dispute with Beijing over who should be the next governor. Beijing wanted to appoint someone not from the area even though, traditionally, each governor of the province usually had local roots. Zhu had been mayor of Guangzhou. He served as Acting Governor from 1991 to 1993 before his appointment became official.

Given considerable autonomy, local officials often engage in corrupt deals to enrich themselves and other insiders. Since local governments have control over land, they can engage in land deals that frequently require confiscating real estate from existing farmers or residents and leasing it to businesses for development. Also, since local governments levy taxes and enforce one-child policies and religious prohibitions (under the direction

176

of Beijing), they have several ways to intimidate people. They also manage the police and have great influence over local judges, so there often is little recourse against corrupt and unfair practices except to mobilize demonstrations or appeal directly to Beijing.

Another problem that local governments face is that the number of government officials continues to proliferate in the rural areas. This requires that farmers and other local residents pay more and more for their support rather than investing in productive enterprises. In the Han Dynasty (206 B.C. to A.D. 8) there were 8,000 people working the land for every official. In 1987 the ratio was 87 to 1. In 1998 it was 40 to 1 with the number of officials continuing to increase. The number of people running the town of Yi Xian in Hebei province, one of the poorest in the country, increased from 5 in 1980 to 400 in 1997. To pay their salaries, the local population faced higher taxes and costs for electricity that were 10 times higher than those in Beijing.[242] On the other hand, the concentration of power in the hands of local officials means that they can not only create obstacles for foreign investors, but they also can shake up the bureaucracy and remove obstacles if needed.

Five-Year Plans

China's industrial policies appear to be both situational and designed to achieve the goals set forth in the country's Five-Year Plans. These plans are comprehensive, complex, and have far-reaching effects. The five-year plan is the major vehicle for the government to establish broad economic goals for the time period under consideration, to coordinate investments between the central and local governments, and to oversee implementation of policy. Not only does the plan influence investments by government entities, it also provides direction for bank lending and government approvals and regulation of private and semi-private industries. The CEO of General Electric once stated that his company studies each five-year plan closely in order to align its company initiatives with the government's plan.[243]

Of course, not everything goes according to plan, but since the plan is an agglomeration of local plans, it is as much a bottom-up as a top-down process. The central government determines the major parameters, goals, and financial resources, but there also is a process for local and regional governments to submit their plans and for consideration of special issues, such as the environment. Local, regional, and special plans are required to be consistent with the national plan. When the plan is announced, most of its content will have already been vetted, and it usually has support from local government officials who often will attempt to exceed the goals of the plan in order to gain recognition within the Chinese Communist Party.

Much of China's economy, however, operates in spheres only loosely influenced by the plan. As many as half of the businesses in China, particularly smaller enterprises and farms, are privately run and are only indirectly affected by the targets and parameters in the plan. For foreign-invested companies, the plan tends to be most influential in securing initial approvals, in structuring joint enterprises, in mandatory technology transfers, in government procurement, and in securing local financing.

The 12th Five-Year Plan (2011-2015) contained three broad themes or areas of focus: (1) economic restructuring, (2) promoting social equality, and (3) protecting the environment. Chinese industrial policy comes into play primarily in economic restructuring but also is apparent in the other areas of focus. Particularly noteworthy is the targeting of seven strategic emerging industries that are intended to become the backbone of China's economy in the future and to enable Chinese industries to compete well on a global scale. These seven industries are: (1) biotechnology, (2) new energy, (3) high-end equipment manufacturing, (4) energy conservation and environmental protection, (5) clean-energy vehicles, (6) new materials, and (7) next-generation information technology. The government reportedly intended to spend from 10 trillion to 14 trillion renminbi, or $1.5 trillion to $2.1 trillion, on these industries during the 12th Five-Year Plan with the aim of increasing their contribution to GDP from 5% in 2011 to 8% by 2015 and 15% by 2020.[244]

Some of the highlights of the plan that pertain to industries included:

- consolidating inefficient sectors and promoting the services industry;
- promoting energy-saving and new-energy industries;
- welcoming foreign investment in modern agriculture, high-technology, and environmental protection industries;

- turning coastal regions from "world's factory" to hubs of research and development, high-end manufacturing, and services;
- lengthening high-speed railway to reach 28,000 miles, expanding the highway network to reach 51,000 miles, and building a new airport in Beijing;[245]
- creating more than 45 million jobs in urban areas;
- keeping urban registered unemployment no higher than 5%;
- expanding service sector output to account for 47% of GDP, up 4 percentage points;
- increasing expenditure on research and development to account for 2.2 percent GDP, with an average of 3.3 patents registered per 10,000 population;
- expanding non-fossil fuel to account for 11.4% of primary energy consumption;
- cutting water consumption per unit of value-added industrial output by 30%;
- cutting energy consumption per unit of GDP by 16%;
- cutting carbon dioxide emission per unit of GDP by 17%;
- increasing the minimum wage by no less than 13% on average each year;
- encouraging qualified enterprises to get listed in stock markets; and
- reforming monopoly industries for easier market entry and more competition.[246]

Macroeconomic Policies

China maintains a number of macroeconomic policies that appear to broadly support many of its industrial policies. Two examples include China's managed currency peg and policies that encourage high domestic savings.

In order to halt or slow the appreciation of the renminbi relative to the dollar, the Chinese central bank has intervened heavily in financial markets by accumulating foreign currency assets. This undervaluation of the currency makes Chinese exports less expensive in world markets and their imports more expensive to the Chinese consumer than that which would occur if the renminbi were a freely traded currency. To some critics of the PRC, China's currency policy acts as a *de facto* subsidy to its export industries and as an additional "tariff" that is imposed on imports into the country. Some contend that the PRC's currency policy has made its economy too reliant on exports. A 2009 International Monetary Fund study estimated that fixed investment related to tradable goods plus net exports together accounted for over 60 percent of China's GDP growth from 2001 to 2008. This was significantly higher than that in the Group of Seven (G-7) countries (16%), the euro area (30%), and the rest of Asia (35%).[247]

China maintains the highest savings rate of any of the world's major economies. In 2012, its gross savings as a percent of GDP was 51.6 percent (versus 15.7% for the United States). The largest source of Chinese domestic savings is from households, followed by corporations and government. Chinese households are believed to be high savers largely because of the lack of an adequate government social safety net (such as pensions, health insurance and social security). The decline of the iron rice bowl (in which food and employment were assured by the state) also has forced households to save a large amount of their income to pay for retirement and medical costs and as a cushion in case they become unemployed.

With so much in savings, Chinese householders have to find somewhere to invest their accumulated funds. Investing overseas is one obvious solution. The Chinese government, however, places tight restrictions on capital outflows partly to enable it to maintain its fixed exchange rate system. These capital restrictions imply that Chinese households are limited largely to domestic choices with respect to where they can invest their savings, and most deposit them in a Chinese bank. However, deposit rates are set at relatively low levels by the government. Michael Pettis with the Carnegie Endowment for International Peace contends that Chinese government's financial repression policies have kept real returns to deposits low and sometimes negative (inflation rates are higher than interest rates on deposits) in China in order to keep real lending rates artificially low for Chinese firms, especially state-owned firms. He contends that this constitutes a forced transfer of income from Chinese households to Chinese producers and that this has led to overinvestment and overcapacity by Chinese firms (because the interest rate they pay is substantially below what a market rate would be), and much of that excess capacity is being exported.[248] In short, China's growth policies are benefitting firms at the expense of consumers.

Pollution

Along with industrial development in China has come pollution. In many parts of the PRC, there simply is no clean air to breathe. Chinese are inhaling the results of being the largest coal consuming country on earth and also the world's largest automobile market. Air pollution levels in many parts of the country, particularly along the industrialized Eastern coast, not only are above hazardous levels, but they are life-threatening.

Around the turn of the twenty-first century, people in China were almost proud of smog because it meant that they were industrializing. They were becoming a real country and had the problems of modernity rather than the problems of the middle ages. Smog then was regarded as progress, but not anymore.[249]

During the 2008 Beijing Olympics, Chinese were highly critical of athletes who showed up wearing face masks and of the foreign news articles raising the threat that smog would impair the performance of the Olympians. Beijing spent $17 million dollars on pollution abatement and took drastic countermeasures—even shutting down factories and reducing automobile traffic for two months during the Olympic and Paralympic games. This was perhaps the first time the government actually had to battle the high levels of air pollutants rather than just criticize the U.S. Embassy in Beijing and foreign journalists for dwelling on it. A later study found that the interlude with lower pollution levels had led to a temporary boost in heart health only to worsen after the games were over and pollution levels rose again.[250] Now pollution levels have reached a point where they are forcing school children to stay indoors and are causing a rise in the incidence of lung disease. As shown in **Figure 10.3**, visibility often is worse than in a London fog. Given that the Communist Party has monopolized government in the PRC, the people know whom to blame.

FIGURE 10.3. SMOG SHROUDS THE TOWERS OF SHANGHAI

Photograph by D. Nanto

A basic conflict exists between GDP growth and environmental quality. China's problem is that its environmental regulators have little authority over those who are undertaking projects that will lead to more economic growth. For example, in 2012, nine railway projects failed to pass their environmental impact statement. However, because of the pressure to continue to grow, none of the projects was completely stopped. The reality is that the Ministry of Environmental Protection cannot do much if projects are not in compliance with its environmental regulations.[251]

Corruption

The heavy hand of the Communist Party and government in business matters opens great opportunities for officials to enrich themselves. Many Party members have become affluent by holding high-level management positions in state-owned enterprises and by using their political positions to gain wealth and through corruption. The sudden wealth flowing through the Chinese economy has become irresistible to many. Corruption has become rampant. The case of Bo Xilai was instructive. He was a popular Party chief of Chongqing in south-western China and a member of the politburo. Although other factors, such as his wife being accused of murder and the embarrassment it caused the Party, also came into play, the official indictment on July 25, 2013 charged him with bribery, corruption and abuse of power. He had allegedly taken advantage of his office to accept an extremely large amount of money and properties.[252]

The PRC is not a signatory to the OECD Anti-Bribery Convention. This convention establishes legally binding standards to criminalize bribery of foreign public officials in international business transactions. It is the first and only international anti-corruption instrument focused on the supply side of the bribery transaction. The 34 OECD member countries and six non-member countries—Argentina, Brazil, Bulgaria, Colombia, Russia, and South Africa—have adopted this Convention.[253] Another five non-OECD countries adhere to the OECD guidelines on combating corruption.

PRC President Xi Jinping has made an anti-corruption campaign one of the hallmarks of his tenure and a means to consolidate power. He has targeted the tigers and the flies. The tigers are high-level corrupt officials, and the flies are those in lower positions who also are corrupt. In addition, he has moved to curb conspicuous consumption with government funds. Gone is the red carpet, and officials cannot spend massive amounts of money on banquets. When they dine out on official business, they are allowed only four dishes and one soup. They also are not allowed to use official cars for their personal gain or to be paid a bonus. Officials often paid themselves generous bonuses. Also, they no longer can work overtime in their spare time for extra pay.[254]

While the campaign has snared many flies, it also has ensnared some tigers, including a senior Chinese Communist Party official, Jiang Jiemin, the former head of the China National Petroleum Corporation. In August 2013, four senior managers of C.N.P.C. and PetroChina were dismissed as part of a party investigation into reported disciplinary violations, a term that usually means corruption. Days later, Jiang was publicly accused of the same violations and dismissed from his job running the government agency that administers state-owned companies.[255]

In 2013, 30,420 people were punished by Chinese disciplinary authorities for violating what is called the eight-point rules of the Communist Party's Central Committee. The rules are aimed at cleaning up undesirable work styles and include extravagance, formalism, bureaucracy and hedonism.[256]

As has been the case in North Korea and other authoritarian states, anti-corruption campaigns also can be a tool to consolidate power. Since almost all officials can be accused of some sort of corruption, it can be used to remove political competitors completely or merely to put the fear of being targeted into the hearts of all government officials. Currently, however, in addition to imposing discipline, Beijing seems to have been compelled by public opinion to clean up its act or risk losing the legitimacy it relies upon to continue Communist Party rule.

For foreign investors, China's anticorruption campaign, if effective, is probably welcome. This could help to level the playing field in the PRC. However, practices common in China could hurt American companies. For example, Americans are subject to the Foreign Corrupt Practices Act (FCPA). The FCPA prohibits paying a foreign official anything of value to obtain or retain business or gain an improper advantage. A problem in the PRC is that the definition of a government official becomes blurred because of state-owned enterprises. It is not clear, *a priori*, whether a particular employee in a state-owned enterprise is a government official under FCPA definitions. The enterprise, itself, may be considered to be a government entity or a particular employee may actually be a government official working in the company. Any member of the Chinese Communist Party potentially could be considered to be a government official, since the party's structure parallels that of the government and virtually all government officials are members of the party. This ambiguity raises the risk for U.S. corporations in trying to win approvals, gain influence, provide marketing incentives or secure contracts in China.

The long arm of the FCPA also extends to what many would consider to be prudent business practices in the PRC. For example, in 2013, U.S. prosecutors and regulators were examining whether JPMorgan, the largest U.S. bank, had violated the FCPA by hiring children and other relatives of well-connected Chinese politicians in hopes of steering business to the firm. In a country where princelings with *guanxi* are prized for their access and relationships, it may come as a surprise that hiring such people would be a violation of U.S. law.

Beijing's anti-corruption push also has targeted foreign companies. In 2013, Chinese police investigated several foreign pharmaceutical companies, and accused the U.K.'s GlaxoSmithKline of using fraudulent invoices to funnel up to 3 billion yuan ($490 million) to travel agencies to facilitate bribes to doctors and officials. In 2012, Eli Lilly encountered similar issues as its sales force in China was submitting expense reimbursements used to get cash to pay for bath houses and meals for government doctors in return for the doctors purchasing Eli Lilly products.[257]

For foreign investors, corruption can grease the skids but eventually may cause one to skid on grease. Foreign investors in China that recognize the risks of and potential penalties for engaging in corruption and invest in robust compliance programs may be able to avoid the expenses associated with investigations, adverse publicity and potential fines or even imprisonment. U.S. companies that are successful in the China market tend to have significant investment in complying with the FCPA and the PRC's anti-corruption laws. Compliance is an essential part of their overall strategy.

The Visible Versus the Invisible Hand

The jury is still out as to whether Adam Smith's concept of the invisible hand guiding decision-making in market economies or the PRC's quite visible hand of government will prove superior in generating economic growth and prosperity over the long term. In many respects, Beijing has backed off from directly controlling large swaths of its economy. Beijing no longer determines prices and quantities to be produced for a wide variety of consumer goods and services. Still, for the central government's strategic sectors and state-owned enterprises or for local government champion companies, the government still works as an owner, a protector, a financier, an advocate and final arbiter of disputes.

One study in 2007 summarized the situation as follows:

> In transitional China there has been a move to a mixture of legal, administrative, and market mechanisms where the traditional "iron hand" of central state control has not been entirely relinquished, but it has been replaced by a less controlling "visible hand" at most levels of government and an "invisible hand" of mainly market control at the furthest edges of local governments. This decentralization has not been uniform, thus creating a heterogeneous institutional environment.[258]

In Michael Porter's study of the sources of national competitive advantage, he posited that the role of government is to act as a catalyst and challenger. It is to encourage, or even push, companies to raise their aspirations and to move to higher levels of competitive performance. Governments also play a role in creating specialized factors of production, such as skilled labor, capital, and infrastructure. In these areas, the PRC is playing catch-up with the rest of the world, but it is doing so with bravado and urgency and with ample loans and subsidies. Governments also influence several underlying factors that contribute to creating internationally competitive companies: dynamic competition that impels firms to increase productivity and innovate and the existence of upstream and downstream industries that cluster around core producers that facilitates the exchange of information, technology, and efficiency in production.[259]

When the PRC government selects winning industries, however, it distorts resource allocation. It generates a headlong drive to invest in the selected and favored industries of the moment. The American baseball player Yogi Berra was often quoted as saying, "It ain't over 'til it's over." This seems to be the maxim for China's economic planners. They are willing to push industrial growth until "it's over." The result is that industries then suffer from overbuilding, overcapacity, and overborrowing.

When I visited Germany in 1986, a haze of industrial pollution hung over many of the industrialized parts of the country. On a wall in one city was graffiti that was a play on the World War II slogan of "Deutschland über alles" (Germany over all). It read, "Smog über alles." That graffiti certainly applies to the PRC today. The haze hanging over eastern China is gradually turning industrial policy away from growth at any cost to growth within environmental bounds. Going back to the original German slogan, the Chinese leaders of today have not been heard to say, "Volksrepublik China über alles" (the PRC over all), but that dream seems to be a driving force in the minds of many of Beijing's policymakers. They would like nothing better than to reclaim the glory status that China had centuries ago as a leading economic power in the world. In order to accomplish that status, the PRC needs to first become a leader in technology and innovation. This has become a large component of China's new industrial policy.

Chapter II. Scaling the High-Technology Ladder

A key to China's continued industrial development and independence from foreign firms is to create innovations and inventions on its own. Without becoming a center for technological change, the PRC will remain primarily a manufacturing platform for products conceived, designed and engineered elsewhere in the world.

Global supply chains have fundamentally altered the access by countries to technology and innovation. Traditionally, economies had to climb the technology ladder through their own efforts. In the range of countries in the global marketplace, economies once could be categorized as being advanced industrial, newly industrialized, developing, and least developed.

Each country began with low-technology products such as traditional crafts, apparel, shoes, and simple toys. As industries developed, the countries moved into smelting steel, tool making and assembling consumer electronics. The ultimate goal of industrial visionaries in countries was to be able to produce automobiles carrying their own brand names, aircraft, cutting-edge pharmaceuticals, computers or telecommunication equipment. The climb up the technology ladder was slow and arduous with many failures along the way. Technology had to be created, bought, reverse engineered, or stolen.

Companies from one country competed directly with companies from another. Competition was a zero sum game. One country's gain was another country's loss. Progress was piecemeal, and countries that had superior technology often ruled over those without. The industrial revolution and

European technology, such as steam ships and cannon, were central to creating a British empire so vast that indeed the sun never set on it.

Now, however, the nature of production and organization of companies has changed. In 1776, Adam Smith wrote about the making of pins in his book, *The Wealth of Nations.* Today, Adam Smith would scarcely recognize the modern manufacture, not only of pins, but products such as laptop computers and motorcycles. He wrote of the division of labor and the productivity gains that it brought in the early years of England's industrial revolution. What he did not mention was that the factories that used the division of labor often had separate entrances and compartmentalized manufacturing areas so that no worker could see the entire process and take the technology for his own. A worker came from the outside through a door into a room where he would work on one step of the process walled off from the rest of the factory. The mechanics of mass production were still a secret. There was no visible production line or conveyer belt connecting one person's work to another's.

Today, the production process is both more integrated yet even more compartmentalized. The final assembly line is a marvel to behold. The product moves along conveyers with parts and components arriving just in time and added to the body of the product either with or without human hands. The manufacture of parts and components is a process unto itself. A tire or wire assembly, for example, will have its own production line, usually in a separate company. Compartmentalization today is more by supplier and location rather than by rooms in a factory.

Modern supply chains span the world. For a laptop computer, the software and microprocessor may come from the United States, the memory chips from Taiwan, and the hard drive from Japan, while the final assembly may be done in China for shipment to markets all over the world. In global supply chains, the company doing the final assembly may not own or even have knowledge of the technology that goes into the item being manufactured. Its workers may merely snap or glue components into place, polish and package the final product and let shipping companies do the rest.

As was indicated in chapter 6 on investment clusters, China has benefitted greatly by attracting assembly plants that then drew in suppliers to form industrial clusters. However, even when supplier companies move their manufacturing facilities into a country to be near the point of final assembly, the suppliers still own and control their technology and manufacturing processes. This largely is the case with the PRC, and this is what China wants to change. It not only wants to do final assembly of products but to provide the components with technology owned or originated in China. Beijing also wants the final product to have a label bearing a Chinese brand name recognizable around the world and being sold by a large, Chinese national champion company.

China's economic planners understand well the so-called smile curve that describes the returns to the stages involved in a product's value chain. A shown in **Figure II.I**, a product begins with research and development (R&D) and subsequently progresses to product conceptualization, design, manufacturing, branding, marketing and distribution, and finally to consumer service. As proposed originally by Stan Shih, the founder of Acer in Taiwan, manufacturing is the least profitable stage of the value chain. The more profitable activities are found in the upstream and downstream segments that encompass more intellectual property. The curve of profitability begins high with R&D, drops to a low in manufacturing, and then rises again in branding and marketing.[260] These higher profitability activities are the ones that China is aiming to capture. Instead of being primarily the manufacturing platform of the world, China wants to move aggressively into R&D and product conceptualization on the upstream side of manufacturing and also into branding and marketing on the downstream side. It wants innovation to be indigenous and for its domestic companies to control the process all the way to the consumer.

FIGURE 11.1. THE SMILE CURVE OF PROFITABILITY

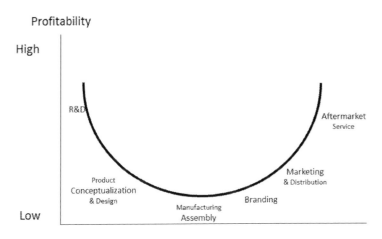

China does not have to look far for examples of Asian companies that have scaled the technology ladder and succeeded in the global marketplace. Many Japanese, South Korean, and Taiwanese corporations have developed world-class brand names, conduct extensive R&D, control distribution and have become national champions. Japan's Toyota began by making looms but moved into automobiles. The first Toyota car imported into California in 1958 boiled over when taken for a test drive up a mountain. The American Big Three treated the early Toyopet car as a clumsy knockoff whose engine and gearbox had been copied from those in a Chevrolet. Now Toyota vies with Volkswagen to be the largest auto manufacturer in the world.

In the 1980s, as offices became computerized, there was much discussion about the paperless office. An executive in the United States commented that there was about as much chance of a paperless office becoming a reality as a paperless toilet. This executive apparently had not been to Japan where the bathroom fixture company Toto was selling commodes equipped with a system of water jet bidets and blow dryers that did the job better than paper. The so-called Washlet system also included heated toilet seats that were the delight of women. By the turn of the twenty-first century, such toilets were commonplace throughout Japan and South Korea and rapidly making inroads into other countries of the world. Toto had transformed itself into a high-technology company.

Likewise, South Korea's Samsung began as a small trading house exporting dried Korean fish, vegetables and fruit to China. It made its first black-and-white television sets in 1970 and later branched out into heavy industries, semiconductors, and electronics. Samsung was the first to offer large, curved-screen television sets and has become the largest cellular phone manufacturer in the world. Its Galaxy tablet computer caught up quickly with Apple's popular iPad in unit sales and even surpassed it in some high-tech features.

Taiwan's Giant Manufacturing Company began in 1972 manufacturing bicycles to be sold under brand names such as Schwinn and Nishiki. Now Giant is the largest bicycle maker in the world and is known for its high-end racing bikes.[26]I

Toyota, Toto, Samsung and Giant: these are the types of companies China would like to build.

Indigenous Innovation as an Industrial Policy

No country can move up the technology ladder without acquiring the technology existing on the next higher rung. That technology, however, is always changing. The technology ladder itself is not set. It is more like an infinite extension ladder in which the top keeps getting pushed upwards as companies innovate and new technologies are discovered.

To a large extent, the model used to introduce high-technology into the PRC has been successful. The technology was brought into the country by foreign investors, purchased, imitated, or stolen. For China's economic planners, however, the time now has come for the PRC to develop technology on its own. Innovation has to begin occurring more in China, by Chinese, and in Chinese companies or research institutions. It is time for innovation to be indigenous.

The goal of the PRC's indigenous innovation program is simple—to make China the center of innovation as it was in the 13th century when Marco Polo brought back tales of the kingdom's riches. At that time, China considered itself the center kingdom of the world and had such wealth and advanced technology that Marco Polo reported being overwhelmed by the city of Hanzhou. He referred to it as beyond dispute the finest and noblest city in the world and was amazed at the enormous wealth of the merchants and the amount of goods that passed through their hands.[262]

China's push for indigenous innovation began in 2006 but the implications of that policy took a few years to become manifest. Indigenous innovation policy may sound heavenly in concept, but it can be devilish in its details. After all, who could be opposed to encouraging Chinese companies to innovate or to generate higher levels of technology? The question, however, has been how precisely that is to be accomplished.

Although the program for indigenous innovation began in Beijing, the ideas for implementing it went beyond mere polemics and promises. They already had been debated in Chinese policy circles, and major objections had been heard and overruled. Many Chinese users of foreign technology shuddered at the thought of suddenly being required to rely on domestic innovations that were not likely to appear for some time. How, for example, would decreasing dependence on imported technology be achieved? If it were left to market forces, there would be no problem, but if it were achieved by artificially limiting foreign technology, then that would be a barrier to economic progress. For Beijing's planners, however, the dream of generating a Chinese technological renaissance took precedence over all such protestations.

The essence of the indigenous innovation policy was embodied in the Medium- to Long-term Plan for the Development of Science and Technology. The goal was to turn the Chinese economy into a technology powerhouse by 2020 and a global leader by 2050. The plan envisaged expenditures for research and development that could exceed those in other leading nations. It called for an investment of 2.5 percent of China's GDP in research and development by the year 2020 (up from 1.3% in 2005), an increase in the contributions to economic growth from technological advance to more than 60 percent and a limit to PRC dependence on imported technology of no more than 30 percent. The scientific aims of the plan were to move China into the top five nations in the world in the number of invention patents granted to Chinese citizens and for Chinese-authored scientific papers to become among the world's most cited.[263]

The tools of indigenous innovation include:

- providing financial incentives in the form of grants, low-interest loans, and tax breaks for companies and research organizations to engage in research and development and develop high-technology products;
- increasing the filing of patents, copyrights, and trademarks in China by Chinese owners in order to capture more returns from advances in technology and to incorporate Chinese technology into technology standards adopted in China and in international standards organizations;
- compelling foreign companies to reveal commercial secrets through compulsory licensing of technology, mandatory joint ventures, requiring transfers of technology that are in the national interest, and requiring submissions of source codes and other trade secrets in order to obtain the Chinese Compulsory Certification; and
- developing catalogs listing indigenous innovation products that would be eligible for special benefits.[264]

Beijing launched the indigenous innovation program with obvious measures, such as increasing government expenditures for targeted activities and incentives, such as rewards for patents. Soon, however, the devilish aspects of the details began to reveal themselves in areas such as government procurement.

Government Procurement and Indigenous Innovation Products

The Chinese government procures from $100 billion to $200 billion in goods and services per year. China is not a signatory to the World Trade Organization's Government Procurement Agreement (GPA), although it is an observer to the WTO Committee on Government Procurement. In 2007, the PRC initiated GPA accession by submitting its application and an initial offer of coverage, but the United States and other countries indicated that significant improvements would be needed. Its offers in 2011 and 2012 also were deemed insufficient, and in 2014, China submitted its fourth bid to accede to the GPA. This version was to improve on its offer of market access and take into account the requests made by the parties to the GPA.[265]

China has promulgated a Government Procurement Law (GPL) that generally reflects GPA provisions, but this law also directs central and sub-central government entities to give priority to local goods and services, with limited exceptions. The law also does not cover tendering and bidding for public works projects. These projects represent at least half of China's government procurement market.

Indigenous innovation came into play when the regulations were being issued to implement the GPL. Because Beijing had agreed to have some degree of transparency in the Chinese regulatory process, U.S. and other foreign business interests were able to see some of the draft regulations before they were finalized. The draft rules on government procurement, in particular, raised alarms. The essence of indigenous innovation in government procurement was nothing more than a strong buy China policy and bordered on blatant protectionism. It would have limited government procurement to products based on Chinese inventions and manufactured domestically except in limited circumstances. In short, the rules as drafted were intended to channel economic activity toward domestic Chinese firms and away from foreign companies.

The rules also were not clear on what constituted local or domestic products. How were they to be defined? Most countries consider products domestic if they contain a certain percentage of their value from domestic sources or they have been substantially transformed in-country. The PRC government, however, eschewed the international definition and adopted a highly restrictive approach to what was to be considered indigenous.

China's National Development and Reform Commission, in cooperation with the Ministry of Science and Technology and the Ministry of Finance, has been responsible for issuing rules on the accreditation of indigenous innovation products for government procurement. Initially, accredited products had to meet certain criteria, such as conforming to national industrial and technology policies, and their manufacturers had to own the intellectual property rights in China pursuant to their own innovation or license the use of the intellectual property right in China.[266] The government created a catalog of such products and proposed that government purchases be restricted to indigenous versions of the listed items unless the product could not be produced in country, purchased on reasonable commercial terms in China or was for use outside of the country.

In the original 2009 draft of the government procurement law, a product's intellectual property would have had to be initially registered (patented) in China in order for the product to qualify as indigenous innovation. It could not be patented in the United States, for example, and subsequently patented in China. It had to be patented in China first. The United States expressed serious concerns to China about this measure, as it would provide preferential treatment in government procurement to products developed by Chinese enterprises. In December 2009, more than 30 businesses, representing the world's major technology firms, wrote to the Chinese government claiming that the policies were discriminatory because of three key rules linking government procurement to indigenous innovation by domestic firms. Foreign companies viewed the policies as preventing them from accessing the Chinese market.

The issue also was addressed in bilateral talks. In January 2011, President Hu Jintao of the PRC paid a state visit to the United States. In the U.S.-China joint statement following the Hu-Obama Summit meeting, China said that it will not "link its innovation policies to the provision of government procurement preferences." This reflected an earlier agreement in December 2010 that neither the PRC nor the United States would adopt or maintain measures that make the location of the development or ownership of intellectual property a direct or indirect condition for eligibility for government procurement preferences for products and services.[267] The three rules that the 30 technology firms had protested were officially dropped as of July 1, 2011.[268] The question, of course, is whether the essence of the rules will remain the *de facto* policy even though they are not *de jure*.

A related problem with the policy is that provinces and municipal governments have issued their own indigenous innovation catalogs related to local government procurement. Some municipal governments have listed certain products in the catalogs primarily to protect their local manufacturers from all competition, not only from foreign companies but from other producers in China.

Intellectual Property Right (IPR) Protection

The protection of intellectual property and the process of indigenous innovation dovetail onto each other. In the early stages of a country's economic development, IPR protection tends to be lax and innovation scarce. When per capita income is less than $1,000 per year, few can afford to pay world prices for software or have the training and skill to invent and patent things on their own. China has been no exception. The lack of effective and consistent protection of intellectual property has been cited by U.S. firms as one of the most significant problems they face in doing business in China. China has been on the U.S. Trade Representative's Priority Watch List and, therefore, is subject to special monitoring. A wide range of American intellectual property rights holders have reported serious obstacles to protection and enforcement of all forms of IPR in China, including patents, trademarks, copyrights, trade secrets and protection of pharmaceutical test data.[269]

In 2013, China was the number one source of counterfeit products that were seized at the U.S. border. According to one copyright industry association, the piracy rate in China at more than 90 percent remains one of the highest in the world. U.S. companies lose over one billion dollars in legitimate business each year to piracy. On average, 20 percent of all consumer products in the Chinese market are counterfeit.[270]

The U.S. International Trade Commission estimated that U.S. intellectual property-intensive firms that conducted business in China lost $48.2 billion in sales, royalties and license fees in 2009 because of IPR violations there.[271] The Business Software Alliance estimated that in 2011 China's illegal software market was worth nearly $9 billion as compared to the legal market of less than $3 billion. This amounted to a piracy rate of 77 percent. When considering the situation on the basis of personal computers (excluding monitors) purchased, businesses and consumers in China spent an average of $542 per unit but just $8.89 on legal software to run them. This was less than a quarter of the amount spent per unit in Russia, India, or Brazil and just 7 percent of the amount spent on software per personal computer in the United States.[272]

While IPR piracy is often cited in music, movies and software, it is just as large a problem in product design and production processes and is often seen in the outright counterfeiting of popular items. While imitation might be the sincerest form of flattery, businesses are less concerned about flattery and more about ensuring that they receive their due returns from investment in research, development, design and marketing.

In 1985, at the Tsukuba Expo in Japan, the robot maker Fanuc showed a 25-ton ambidextrous robot that could assemble a tiny model of itself. In 2005, a British mechanical engineer designed a self-replicating rapid prototyper, or RepRap, based on rapid prototyping technology commonly used to manufacturer plastic components in industry from computer-generated blueprints.[273] What stirred the imagination of people then has now become simpler and involves considerably less weight. In the 21st century, with 3-D printers and coordinate measuring machines capable of copying tangible products, a machine can replicate itself or just about anything else. When 3-D printers are combined with cyber-thefts of computer models of industrial products, they make the counterfeiting of almost any item possible. The copy can be precisely machined to nearly the same tolerances as the genuine product, even though it may be constructed of inferior materials.

A Belgian restaurateur who has been in Beijing since early in the period of reform and opening said that his restaurant has had numerous and frequent inspections by local government officials. He noticed that the inspectors visited only Western restaurants and did the inspections mainly to learn Western restaurant management and methods of operation. They then passed the information on to domestic competitors.

The extent to which Chinese imitator companies can produce knock-off products both rapidly and with advanced features is illustrated by the Apple smart watch. In January 2015, months before the genuine product was revealed, Chinese competitors were showing near-identical copies of the $350 watch at the Consumer Electronics Show in Las Vegas for as little as $60 apiece. "The brazen forgery at the world's largest technology fair shows the speed, boldness and uncanny accuracy with which China's counterfeiters can mimic even pioneering products."[274]

The Semiconductor Industry Association's Anti-Counterfeiting Task Force has reported numerous instances in which counterfeit semiconductors have potentially caused health, safety, and security issues. These instances included counterfeit semiconductor components in an Automated External Defibrillator; in a vacuum cleaner for residential use that caused a fire; in a power supply used for airport landing lights that failed; in microcontrollers intended for use in braking systems in high-speed trains in Europe and in automobiles; in automated medication applications (including intravenous drip machines); and for components intended for use in nuclear submarines.[275] The Task Force did not specifically identify China as the source of the counterfeit semiconductors, but such semiconductors have been found in shipments from the PRC.

Primarily as a result of the foreign complaints, Beijing has improved its IPR protection regime significantly over the past few years. It has beefed up its IPR laws and has conducted periodic IPR-focused campaigns, such as raids against major IPR infringers and public displays of the destruction of pirated video disks. The authorized movie and video industry has struck directly at pirated copies of films and television programs by lowering the prices of authentic products enough that they compete directly with illegal copies. Still, U.S. industries complain that piracy rates in China remain unacceptably high.

Intellectual Property Laws

On the international side, the PRC is a member of the World Intellectual Property Organization and is a signatory to the Bern Convention for the Protection of Literary and Artistic Works, the Universal Copyright Convention, the Geneva Phonograms Convention, the Patent Co-operation Treaty, and the International Classification of Goods and Services.

Domestically, the PRC has enacted numerous laws directed at protecting intellectual property. Among them are the Trademark Law of the PRC (1982, revised 1993 and 2001), the Patent Law of the PRC (1985), the Copyright Law of the PRC (June 1991, amended 2001), Regulations for the Administration of Import and Export of Technology (2002), Regulations on Protection of Computer Software (2002), and Implementing Rules of Madrid International Registration of Trademarks (2003). There also have been several laws or regulations issued on implementing the basic laws.

Trademarks are protected for ten years from the approval date for registration and are renewable. The first party to register gains an exclusive right to a trademark. Since 1984 when China joined the Paris Convention, nationals of other member nations may claim priority use[276] of trademarks within six months of the date of the first filing.

For foreign companies, anticipating selling products in China, the timing for registering the trademark can be critical. Before applying for a license to sell the product in the Chinese market or even before contacting potential distributors, it may be prudent to register the trademark. However, if a company does not anticipate using the trademark in China for more than three years, it may be a waste of money to register it because if a registered trademark has not been used for three consecutive years, it may be cancelled for non-use.[277]

Copyrights are protected for the life of the author plus 50 years, or for 50 years from the first publication. Copyright holders can license their rights for ten years (renewable upon expiration), after which the rights revert to the original owner. If the author develops the item in a work-for-hire situation or as a result of his employment, the copyright belongs to the author, except for computer programs, engineering designs, drawings of product designs and product specifications (which belong to the employer).

Copyright protection can be granted for written, spoken, recorded, broadcast, and artistic works; construction and product drawings; maps and charts and computer software. Newspaper and media reports are not covered, and the law is not clear on whether databases (such as directories and lists) can be copyrighted.[278]

Copyright violations abound in the PRC. For example, in 2007, Beijing's Shijingshan Amusement Park turned out to be an imitation Disneyland complete with Disney-like characters and a castle that resembled Disney's Sleeping Beauty castle. A sign over the entrance said, "Disney is too far." The Chinese owners claimed that the Minnie Mouse character was really a cat with large ears and pointed out that the Cinderella character had a Chinese-like face. Not everything was copied correctly, however, as the seven dwarfs were seen following Sleeping Beauty instead of Snow White. After negotiations with Disney, many of the characters were removed.[279]

Patents

Originally adopted in 1984, China's modern patent law has undergone three major changes to bring it closer to those in advanced industrialized nations. In 1992, China enacted a round of amendments to the patent law primarily in response to foreign pressure to improve patent protection. The second round in 2000 was required by China's WTO commitments. The third round was a series of amendments to PRC Patent Law that took effect Oct 1, 2009, and that contain important changes that attempt to align Chinese patent practice with much of the rest of the world.

The current patent system provides 20 years of protection for inventions and 10 years for utility models and designs. Neither is renewable. As for novelty, no identical invention or utility model may have been previously disclosed in publications, publicly used in the country or filed previously with the PRC's State Intellectual Property Office. Scientific discoveries, rules and methods of intellectual activity, methods of diagnosing and treating diseases, animal and plant varieties, and substances obtained through nuclear transformation are all not patentable. However, patents may be granted for processes used in producing animal and plant varieties.

Article 20 of the Patent Law no longer requires a first filing in China, but it requires that all applicants (Chinese or foreign) report to the State Intellectual Property Office for a confidentiality examination before filing for a foreign patent if the invention was completed in the PRC. The stated goal of the confidentiality exam is purported to be to protect China's national defense interests or other vital national interests. The amended Patent Law also raises the standard for patenting a design and includes a provision on damages that aims to strengthen patent protection.

Compulsory licenses for an unused patent may be granted if another entity requests and is denied permission by the patent holder. Terms must be reasonable. A compulsory license also may be obtained if the use of a patent is necessary to exploit a new, more technically-advanced patent, or during a state of national emergency.

In the 2009 amendments to the Patent Law, China retained utility model patents but provided rules and regulations for exploiting these utility patents both alone and in conjunction with a more traditional invention patent. A utility patent may be for a new and useful method, process, machine, device, manufactured item, or chemical compound, or any new and useful improvement to the same. The utility patent can, for example, provide protection for a product's shape or structure or combination thereof. Utility patents are available in many countries worldwide but not in the United States. The U.S. Patent Office does grant what it calls utility patents, but these are patents for an invention. The American utility patent is equivalent to the PRC's invention patent.

Until 2001, utility model applications in the PRC required no substantive application examination, and rights were normally granted within one year from the filing date. Since 2001, China's amended patent law provides that if the utility-model patent holder has cause to defend his patent against an infringement, the courts or the patent administrative authorities may require the patent holder to show the report issued after a substantive examination. A substantive examination deals with the novelty, inventiveness, and usefulness of an item for which a patent has been applied, while the nonsubstantive examination deals with procedural, format, and timing issues.[280]

Utility patents, however, are real patents and can be used in lawsuits. In a landmark court case, CHINT Group Co. Ltd sued Schneider Electric (Tianjin), a French company, for infringement of a small circuit breaker utility model patent. This appeared to be retaliation for some 20 patent lawsuits initiated by Schneider Electric in Europe in hopes of pressuring CHINT to agree to a takeover by Schneider. In September 2007, the Intermediate Court of Wenzhou City awarded $48 million to CHINT— the highest amount ever awarded to date in a Chinese IP lawsuit. Schneider then appealed to the High Court of Zhejiang province. The High Court did not issue its decision for a year while the two parties worked at mediating a settlement. Eventually the two sides settled for about $23 million (157.5 million yuan).[281] Even though it is generally known that the courts in Zhejiang province tend to favor local companies over both state-owned and foreign enterprises, this case served as a warning to foreign investors to take utility patents seriously.

An integral part of indigenous innovation is the push for more patentable innovations and inventions. The PRC's 2011-2015 Five-Year Plan established a goal of an average of 3.3 patents registered per 10,000 citizens. This goal has generated a new numbers game among Chinese corporations and innovators. As with most numerical targets, quantity tends to take precedence over quality. The push for more patents combined with government subsidies and company remuneration for patent applications has provided incentives for a plethora of "frivolous" filings. Some applicants apparently have filed for patents more to obtain subsidies or cash rewards than for the intrinsic value of the patent.

The number of patents granted in the PRC to Chinese applicants surged from 6,923 in 1990 to 501,786 in 2009, to 740,626 in 2010 and to 1,163,226 in 2012. Most of the Chinese patents granted, however, were utility or design patents. For non-utility and non-design patents in 2012, domestic Chinese applicants were granted 217,105 patents, while foreigners were granted 73,258 of them.[282] For patent applications in the United States in 2012, China ranked seventh according to nationality of the applicant. Out of a total of 302,948 U.S. patents granted in 2013, the United States accounted for half, at 147,652, while China had 6,597. The most for any foreign nation was Japan, at 54,170, followed by Germany with 16,605 and South Korea with 15,745.[283] In Europe, out of a total of 65,687 patents granted in 2012 by the European Patent Office, 32,684 went to European Patent Office member states, and 33,053 to other countries, including 793 to China, 14,699 to the United States, and 12,852 to Japan.[284]

Enforcement

The enforcement of intellectual property rights in China has long been suspect because courts are under the jurisdiction of the Communist Party and not independent. *Fortune Magazine* once sued a Chinese knockoff magazine for copyright and trademark violation. The magazine used the identical *"Fortune"* masthead with the addition of *"New"* in the magazine title. As the case was being heard, a Chinese acquaintance of a *Fortune* editor told him in private that his company should drop the case because it would lose in court—even though the evidence was overwhelmingly on *Fortune's* side. *Fortune* went ahead with the case but lost. This was an example of how Party connections and Party pressures on judges can affect legal cases.[285]

On the other hand, in 2009, Chinese courts imposed criminal liabilities upon the creators of a modified Windows XP software operating system called Tomato Garden. It was being sold by Chengdu Share-Software Net Science and Technology Co. Ltd. without Microsoft's authorization and allowed users unrestricted access to certain Microsoft software programs, technical support, and access through free downloads online. The court fined the offending company nearly 9 million yuan ($1.3 million) and ordered it to forfeit all 2.9 million yuan ($0.4 million) of illegal earnings. The president of the company and manager of the program's website were both sentenced to three and a half years in prison and fined 1 million yuan ($0.15 million). Two of their software developers also received fines and two-year prison sentences. This was the first time criminal penalties were imposed for copyright infringement in China.[286]

Given China's highly fragmented and large bureaucracy, enforcement of trademark rights by foreign companies has been an expensive and time-consuming task. Even when raids and seizures of counterfeit goods succeeded, the fines and sanctions imposed at the government's discretion were hardly a deterrent (in one year, the fines averaged only about $700 per case, with the trademark owner receiving about $40 in compensatory damages). The counterfeit goods were stripped of their infringing marks, but were then resold at public auction, often to be rebranded and sold by the same or another counterfeiter.[287]

In the fall of 2010, former PRC Premier Wen Jiabao introduced a campaign to combat intellectual property rights infringement in China. Running from October 2010 to June 2011, it was called the Special Campaign to Combat IPR Infringement and the Manufacture and Sales of Counterfeit and Shoddy Commodities. The special campaign focused on copyright, patent, and trademark protection by targeting products in the agricultural, high-tech, and entertainment industries (such as audiovisual materials, auto parts, books, mobile phones, pharmaceuticals, software and seeds).

Through the campaign, China's government sought to strengthen the confidence of foreign investors in the government's ability to provide IPR protection and to improve the domestic intellectual property environment. The State Council Information Office reported that during the special campaign, administrative agencies investigated 156,000 cases of IPR infringement and the manufacture and sale of pirated goods worth 3.4 billion yuan ($532.2 million), closed more than 9,130 illegal plants making pirated and counterfeit goods and shut down 12,854 underground factories. Chinese police reportedly arrested 9,031 suspects. These relatively large numbers seem to attest more to the wide breadth of IPR violations rather than the extent of the crackdown.

Counterfeit pharmaceuticals came under particularly close scrutiny, since their potential effects can be fatal and they have been appearing in export channels. As a result of the special campaign, China reported that it has made an effort to reduce illegal sales of counterfeit pharmaceuticals, including medicines sold illegally through online web sites, by conducting raids of criminal manufacturing sites and making arrests. PRC law, however, still requires proof that violations in any counterfeit activity exceed threshold values before any action is taken by authorities beyond arrest. These criminal thresholds thwart attempts at prosecution.

Pirated music is a perennial problem in all countries, but it is so in China in particular. In 2010, total music revenue (for both legitimate physical and digital sales) in China amounted to $64.3 million. This was unusually small compared with $178.4 million in South Korea and $68.9 million in Thailand. If Chinese sales were equivalent to Thailand's on a per capita basis, music sales would have been almost $1.4 billion. It is difficult to imagine that young Chinese are so less hip and not into music compared with their counterparts in Thailand.

In 2011, China reportedly sanctioned 14 websites for providing illegal music downloads and required those web sites to remove links to offending files which had been identified by the government. Nevertheless, illegal downloads still accounted for an estimated 99 percent of all music downloads in China.[288]

In November 2011, as part of the IPR infringement campaign, officials shut down the music portals Qishi.com and 5474.com and subjected the site operators to fines and criminal sentences. One of the Qishi.com operators was sentenced to five years imprisonment and fined 1.5 million yuan ($234,750). In January 2011, one of the largest perpetrators, VeryCD, reportedly disabled all of its links to infringing music and movie content.

The Chinese Internet giant Baidu also reached a landmark agreement with Universal Music, Warner Music and Sony Music to distribute legal content on its online music platform. Following that agreement, the U.S. Trade Representative removed Baidu from its Notorious Markets list.

As for illegal software, PRC authorities reported that, during the campaign, legal software had been implemented in each of its 135 central governmental agencies and that the agencies had spent a total of 140.9 million yuan ($22.1 million) to purchase 176,763 legitimate software packages.[289] More than government offices, a larger IPR violator is the state-owned enterprise sector. These leading companies in China not only set an example for other companies but the low cost of pirated software can give them an unfair commercial advantage when competing with companies that pay to acquire their software legally.

This enforcement campaign was directly linked to China's indigenous innovation policies. If foreign and domestic companies are to invest in developing technology in China, they need some assurance that their rights will be protected. Time will tell whether Beijing is serious about permanently protecting intellectual property or whether this campaign was just another knee-jerk reaction to a pervasive and potentially crippling problem. One positive indicator was that in November 2011, Premier Wen Jiabao announced that the special campaign would be made permanent through the creation of the National Intellectual Property Enforcement Office. The office was to be led by the Vice Premier and staffed by the Ministry of Commerce and its Market Order and Supervision Division. This arrangement provided a permanent mechanism under senior leadership for IPR enforcement and investigation.

Foiling Counterfeiters

In March 2012, at a conference panel sponsored by the Richard Paul Richman Center for Business, Law, and Public Policy at Columbia Business School, the panelists noted that multinational companies have grown more sophisticated in efforts to foil Chinese counterfeiters. Their strategies included the following:

- **Modular manufacturing.** Instead of contracting with one manufacturer to make all the components, spread different aspects of a product among different factories—competitors if possible.
- **Withholding key components.** Even if making an important part is more expensive outside the PRC, some multinational companies are withholding key components to foil copycats.
- **Practice secrecy.** Beyond having in-country meetings in parks or restaurants rather than in the offices of joint venture partners, some executives go so far as to leave their personal computers, tablets and smart phones at home. They bring only pristine laptops without e-mail trails that can be hacked.
- **Innovation.** The panelists pointed out that most Chinese copiers have learned how make exact copies of a product but lack the scientific know-how to understand how it works. Even in the West, many electronic manufacturers, in particular, have more or less given up on patents, a system which promises market exclusivity in return for product disclosure. By continually tweaking a product, they frustrate counterfeiters and competitors alike with innovation.
- **Branding.** Despite the large number of counterfeit products sold in the PRC, Chinese consumers do not like knockoffs and often do not recognize that they are not buying the real thing when they purchase a copied product. Western and Japanese auto manufacturers and makers of luxury goods have had success by stressing their quality and product performance, encouraging consumers to shop for the real thing.[290]

Hogan Lovells, a large international law firm with offices in Shanghai, provides the following advice for fighting counterfeiting:

- Register rights for which protection is sought. Do not complain if there is infringement of unregistered rights.
- Focus on intellectual property enforcement strategy. Do not delegate intellectual property enforcement to junior level paralegals with no support. Invest appropriate resources into

anti-counterfeiting. Go after main counterfeiters. Invest in investigation. Do not judge success or failure of program on the number of goods seized.

- Use the civil litigation system.
- Educate your workforce on the enforcement of intellectual property rights. Do not tolerate the purchase of counterfeit products, even for personal use. (Clients often come to China quite agitated about infringement of their intellectual property. Those same people will then ask for directions to the Silk Market in Beijing or Yatai market in Shanghai—places notorious for sales of counterfeit merchandise.)[291]

Cybersecurity

The twenty-first century Trojan horse is the cable connecting the company to the Internet. Computer hackers, many located in China, reportedly have stolen proprietary information from companies such as DuPont, Johnson & Johnson, General Electric, and NASDAQ, and they are suspected in hundreds of other cyber-attacks.[292] It is not clear, however, whether the attacks are by students (as part of their school projects), criminals, government agencies, the Chinese military or some combination of them.

The former Director of National Intelligence in the United States and two co-authors have stated that "it is much more efficient for the Chinese to steal innovations and intellectual property—the source code of advanced economies—than to incur the cost and time of creating their own. They turn those stolen ideas directly into production, creating products faster and cheaper than the U.S. and others." They also state that cyber-espionage is an ideal tool for stealing intellectual capital. Hackers can penetrate systems that transfer large amounts of data, while corporations and governments have a very hard time identifying specific perpetrators.[293]

Richard Clarke, a former cybersecurity and cyberterrorism advisor to the White House stated that his greatest fear is that rather than having a cyber-Pearl Harbor event, U.S. industries will lose their ability to compete internationally by having the results from their research and development siphoned away by the Chinese completely under the radar. There is no single event that shocks the country into doing something about it; the theft remains just below our pain threshold. Company after company in the United States spends millions, hundreds of millions, in some cases billions of dollars on R&D, but that information goes free to China. After a while you cannot compete anymore.[294]

In 2013, The Commission on the Theft of American Intellectual Property reported that the impact of international theft of intellectual property on the American economy ran into hundreds of billions of dollars per year. These estimated losses are comparable to the current annual level of U.S. exports to Asia—over $300 billion. The members of the Commission agreed with the assessment by the Commander of the United States Cyber Command and Director of the National Security Agency, General Keith Alexander, who stated that the ongoing theft of intellectual property is "the greatest transfer of wealth in history."[295]

In February 2013, Mandiant, an information security firm, released a report that detailed extensive cyber-crime activities that it attributed to Unit 61398 of China's People's Liberation Army. This organization was found to have systematically infiltrated 141 companies in over 20 major industries, including 115 U.S. companies. The investigation covered several years beginning in 2006 and found the theft of "technology blueprints, proprietary manufacturing processes, test results, business plans, pricing documents, partnership agreements and emails and contact lists from victim organizations' leadership." In one instance, the cyber attacker was able to steal 6.5 terabytes of compressed data from a single organization over a ten-month period. The industries most frequently targeted included information technology, aerospace, public administration, satellites and communication, scientific research and consulting, energy, and transportation. Four of the seven industries targeted had been listed by the PRC as "strategic" emerging industries that needed to be fostered and encouraged as part of its 12th Five-Year Plan.[296]

Despite the tension in relations with the PRC over cyber-enabled theft, the Chinese turned deaf ears to U.S. complaints about state-sponsored cybersecurity intrusions into American businesses to help Chinese businesses gain competitive advantage. Ultimately, it was the prospect of a significant sanctions package that changed the value proposition of hacking. In the weeks prior to the 2015 state visit by President Xi Jinping to Washington, Beijing dispatched a top party official to negotiate, and ultimately the PRC promised to end state support for cyber theft for commercial purposes.[297]

Technology Transfer

When China joined the World Trade Organization, its representative to the working group on accession gave assurances that the PRC "would only impose, apply or enforce laws, regulations or measures relating to the transfer of technology, production processes, or other proprietary knowledge to an individual or enterprise in its territory that were not inconsistent with the WTO Agreement on Trade-Related Aspects of Intellectual Property Rights (TRIPS Agreement) and the Agreement on Trade-Related Investment Measures (TRIMs Agreement)." The Chinese representative also confirmed that "the terms and conditions of technology transfer, production processes or other proprietary knowledge, particularly in the context of an investment, would only require agreement between the parties to the investment."[298] In other words, the government would not impose additional conditions on any private deal. However, it does not appear that China has been fulfilling this commitment. In 2011, U.S. Treasury Secretary Timothy Geithner stated, "We're seeing China continue to be very, very aggressive in a strategy they started several decades ago, which goes like this: you want to sell to our country, we want you to come produce here ... if you want to come produce here, you need to transfer your technology to us."[299]

According to a specialist in intellectual property at Tufts University, "Chinese companies, once they acquire the needed technology, will often abandon their Western partners on the pretext that the technology or product failed to meet Chinese governmental regulations. This is yet another example of a Chinese industrial policy aimed at procuring, by virtually any means, technology in order to provide Chinese domestic industries with a competitive advantage."[300]

Often, foreign firms with desirable technology are required by the Chinese government to enter into a joint venture (JV) arrangement with a government-selected, state-owned company (which usually then takes a 50% or more controlling stake in the venture). The JV arrangement generally requires the foreign company to transfer some level of technology to the Chinese firm and sometimes to establish research and development centers in China.

To illustrate, in 2003, General Electric (GE) negotiated with the Chinese government for a $900 million contract to supply gas turbines for power plants in China. GE won the bid, but only after it first agreed to enter into JVs with two Chinese state-owned enterprises that involved a commitment by GE to transfer technology to its new partners. A press release by GE at the time called the agreement a win-win for both GE and China. However, the *Wall Street Journal* quoted a GE official as saying: "It was a difficult negotiation. They're interested in having total access to technology, and we're interested in protecting the technology that we made significant financial investment in."[301]

Another case in point is Goldwind Science & Technology Co It began as a research institution but has transformed itself into a formidable wind-turbine manufacturer. It initially received its technology from a Danish company in 1989, then from German-based Jacobs Energie GmbH in 1996 and then from Repower Systems AG, another German company in 2001. In 2000, Goldwind formed VENSYS Technology in Germany, a subsidiary company that relied on German scientists and engineers to develop permanent-magnet generator direct-drive turbines for efficient electricity generation. Goldwind is now China's largest wind-turbine manufacturer and the fourth largest in the world with a 9.2 percent global market share in 2014. Although much of Goldwind's recent success possibly can be attributed to technology developed by VENSYS, the company relied heavily on technology transfers from Denmark and Germany to begin its operations.[302]

The underlying concern of foreign governments is that Chinese demands for technology and joint production will lead to significant job losses in advanced technology industries in their home countries. On the other hand, some observers counter that greater cooperation between foreign and Chinese firms, such as through joint ventures, could have some positive benefits for the foreign firms. This includes greater access to capital from Chinese banks, the ability to draw on intellectual property developed by Chinese partners and greater overall cooperation from the Chinese government for the protection of IPR in China.

According to a professor at the National University of Ireland Galway, China has decided that it is no longer willing to be the minor partner in terms of added value and profitability in any industry while the lion's share goes to the owners of intellectual property in the form of royalties and license fees. The demands by Beijing for indigenous innovation represent, he says, a kind of gamble for multinational corporations. In order to gain access to the huge Chinese market, foreign firms put their innovations on the line.[303]

Research and Development (R&D)

Spending for research and development constitutes an integral part of China's industrial strategy to foster invention and innovation at home. According to an observer in 2009, "China's R&D investment over the past decade has been history making. This nation can no longer be considered an 'emerging nation' when it exceeds and challenges both the U.S. and Europe in terms of the intellectual property it generates and the financial and infrastructure commitments it continues to make in science and technology endeavors."[304]

As indicated in **Table II.I**, in 2000, China spent $27 billion (on a purchasing power parity basis) in total R&D expenditures or about a tenth as much as did the United States. This amount, however, was at about the same level as that of the United Kingdom and more than that in South Korea. By 2011, however, China with $208 billion in R&D spending had passed Japan and ranked second to the $429 billion spent by the United States. In 2011, China spent the equivalent (on a purchasing power basis) of the amount spent by France, Germany and South Korea combined. China's R&D spending as a percent of GDP was 1.4 percent in 2009 and has been rising steadily at a time when GDP also has been increasing at high rates. On a nominal (non-purchasing power parity) basis, China's National Statistical Agency reported that China's total expenditures on R&D in 2011 had surged by 21.9 percent to $140 billion. This amount was equivalent to 1.83 percent of GDP.[305] The central government has set the goal of raising this rate to 2.5 percent of GDP by 2020.

TABLE 11.1. SPENDING ON RESEARCH AND DEVELOPMENT IN SELECTED COUNTRIES

$Billions

	1990	2000	2005	2006	2007	2008	2009	2010	2011
U.S.	152.4	269.5	328.1	353.3	380.3	407.2	406.0	409.6	429.1
China	NA	27.2	71.1	86.6	102.3	120.7	154.0	178.2	208.2
France	23.2	33.0	39.2	41.9	44.0	46.5	49.5	49.9	51.9
Germany	35.3	52.3	64.3	70.1	74.0	82.0	82.4	86.3	93.1
U.K.	19.6	27.9	34.1	37.0	38.7	39.4	39.2	39.5	39.6
Japan	69.0	98.7	128.7	138.3	147.7	148.7	136.0	139.6	146.5
S. Korea	NA	18.6	30.6	35.3	40.7	43.9	46.7	52.8	59.9

Source: U.S. National Science Board, *Science and Engineering Indicators 2014*, Appendix Table 4-13.

Note: On a PPP (purchasing power parity) basis. Purchasing power parity attempts to reflect the relative purchasing power of a currency domestically when expressed in U.S. dollars. NA=Not Available

The role of businesses in funding China's R&D has come to resemble that in other industrialized nations. In 2011, business provided 74 percent of the gross expenditures on R&D with 22 percent originating from the government and only 1 percent from private/nonprofit groups. In that same year in the United States, 59 percent came from business, 31 percent from the government, 6 percent from higher education, and 4 percent from private/nonprofit groups. Businesses accounted for 76 percent of R&D funding in Japan, 66 percent in Germany and 74 percent in South Korea.[306]

The question for the PRC is whether the government subsidies for R&D, innovation, and cutting-edge technology are seed money being thrown on rocky ground or whether they are actually bringing results. One indicator is in academic articles published in journals. The European Union, the United States and Japan have been major producers of academic articles for several decades. China emerged as a major producer in the mid-2000s. **Figure 11.2** shows the number of science and engineering articles in all fields for the United States, Germany and China. The United States has the clear lead with about 200,000 articles per year. In the year 1997, China had 12,172 articles or less than a third of Germany's 41,415 articles (or Japan's 51,462). By 2006, the number for China surpassed that for Germany (and the United Kingdom). By 2011, China's 89,894 articles were nearly twice the level as Germany's 46,259 (or Japan's 47,106 articles and the United Kingdom's 46,035 articles. China's science and engineering article count is rising fast. Even though the raw numbers tell little about quality and substance, in sheer quantity, China clearly is becoming a major contributor to the body of science and engineering knowledge.

FIGURE 11.2. SCIENCE AND ENGINEERING ARTICLES FOR THE U.S., GERMANY AND CHINA

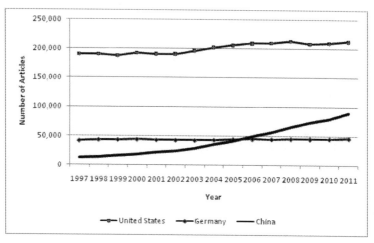

Note: Articles in all fields. Counts from a set of journals covered by Science Citation Index and Social Sciences Citation Index. Articles classified by year of publication and assigned to country on basis of institutional addresses listed on article. Articles on fractional-count basis.

Source: National Science Foundation, National Center for Science and Engineering, Science and Engineering Indicators 2014, Appendix Table 5-6.

These numbers on articles in science and engineering help to confirm a comment by a manager at Huawei Technologies. I asked him if the data that showed the high number of engineering graduates in China were for real. In the United States there was considerable skepticism about the quality of engineering education in China. The number of graduates might be rising, but what about their education? Were these real engineers trained in the hard sciences or were they like the so-called engineers who operate trains or merely do research for real engineers? The Chinese manager said that while the quality of graduates does vary, the huge number of new graduates means that among them are a large number people with truly first-rate minds. His company had no problem finding bright, young and well-trained engineers to hire.[307]

The role of foreign investment in the output of science and engineering articles from China, however, should not be overlooked. Microsoft established its research center for Asia in Beijing in 1998 following a visit by Bill Gates to Chinese universities. He said that he was deeply impressed by the talent, enthusiasm, and creativity of the Chinese students he met. Over its first ten years of existence, Microsoft Research Asia stated that it had filed patents for more than 1,000 technologies and had published over 3,000 papers for top international journals and conferences. Microsoft's researchers in China also come from other countries, but most of the principals are Chinese.[308]

Foreign Investment in R&D

Foreign-invested firms have become a growing source of R&D in China and are estimated to account for a quarter of China's current business enterprise R&D.[309] According to the PRC government, in 2009 China had more than 1,200 R&D centers set up by multinational companies. Of these, 465 of them were established as independent legal entities with the approval of the Ministry of Commerce. These centers had a total investment amounting to $12.8 billion and registered capital of $7.4 billion. They were concentrated mainly in Shanghai, Beijing, Guangdong, Jiangsu and Zhejiang.[310] The list of companies with R&D facilities in China reads like a tally of the top high-technology multinational corporations in the world. The list includes IBM, Motorola, Nokia, Siemens, Microsoft, Intel, Samsung, Nortel, GE, AT&T, P&G, DuPont, Ericsson, Matsushita, Mitsubishi, Lucent-Bell and GM.[311]

The early foreign investments in R&D facilities were partly for creating goodwill but mostly for training local staff and localizing products. Training tended to be related to management and sales rather than technology. Even those centers actually performing R&D work did so on a fairly rudimentary level. Most of the early products coming from foreign-funded R&D facilities in China tended to be software upgrades or systems integration solutions.[312]

The U.S. National Science Foundation found that, in 2007, there were 105 U.S. multinational corporations that had 173 majority-owned R&D facilities in the PRC. These facilities performed $1,146 million in R&D and had 189,000 employees in China. These amounts were up considerably from the $646 million in R&D and 135,000 employees in 2005. The amount U.S. multinationals spend on R&D in China is rapidly approaching the level being spent in other major industrial countries of the world. In 2005, the amount being spent in the PRC was roughly equal to that being spent in Italy, Brazil and Singapore. By 2007, the amount being spent in the PRC was roughly double the amounts used in these three countries.[313]

After the great recession of 2008-09, overseas R&D spending by U.S. multinationals stagnated somewhat. By 2010, spending by U.S. multinationals in China had reached $1,453 million, still less than that in Germany ($6,713 million), Canada ($2,749 million), France ($1,984 million), Israel ($1,948 million), Japan ($1,885 million) and India ($1,644 million).[314] There were 189,000 R&D employees of U.S. multinational corporations in China. This was fewer than those in Germany, the U.K., or Canada where U.S. companies have had a presence for a long time. The number of such employees in China, however, is larger than those in France, Italy, India, Brazil, or Mexico and is increasing quickly.

IBM

One example of foreign R&D in China is that by IBM. The company has a long history of activity in modern China. Beginning with sales of mainframe computers from 1979 and joint ventures with the Chinese government to jump-start its information technology industry, IBM has had a keen interest in this rapidly growing economy. In 1995, IBM established the IBM China Research Laboratory (CRL), the first multinational corporation to establish such a research center in the PRC. Located near

National Tsinghua University in Beijing, the lab initially planned to hire 15 to 17 researchers. The hope was that being there first meant that it would have first crack at the local talent available. The lab had a modest beginning with a budget of $3 million and only two personal computers with an Internet connection. People had to wait in line to check their e-mail.[315] It now has about a hundred researchers and support staff and currently is focusing on the technology and innovations associated with Analytics, Cloud Computing, and the Internet of Things.

Initially, IBM's CRL focused on China-specific areas of research. By 1997, for instance, researchers had overcome substantial obstacles to make ViaVoice for simplified Chinese the first continuous speech-recognition product in China. The research agenda has grown over time. In addition to Chinese speech and language technologies, it also works on next-generation computing systems, distributed computing, and information intelligence and knowledge management. The lab has pioneered HotVideo innovations that allow hyperlinks to hot spots in digital videos. It also explores e-business solutions that help businesses extend their reach beyond national boundaries.[316] It has become an integral part of IBM's global research organization.

As with foreign manufacturers in China, foreign research centers and laboratories exert influence beyond their company-specific activity. They work with universities, the government, and with local research institutes in collaborative projects and in training scientists, developing courses and curricula, and broadening the horizons of students. CRL, for example, has established joint research labs/institutes with Chinese universities and research institutes to conduct long-term collaboration in cutting-edge research areas. After jointly identifying research areas, CRL sponsors the research with the grants and researchers. It also provides scholarships, opportunities for visiting scholars, research grants, and equipment for research projects. CRL also delivers series of technical talks and opens courses in universities in various research topics. It collaborates with government agencies and universities in curriculum development and degree offering. Some of this outreach activity circles back to benefit IBM. But it also establishes training benchmarks and educational benefits to non-IBM personnel.

Pfizer

Pfizer is the number one multinational R&D based biopharmaceutical company in China. The company established its China Research and Development Center in Shanghai in October 2005, sixteen years after building its first manufacturing plant in Dalian. The facility provides global drug development support capabilities, including support for Phase I-IV clinical trials, and research collaborations and strategic alliance opportunities for China and the Asia region. In October 2010, Pfizer opened another R&D presence in Wuhan Biolake.

Since its establishment, Pfizer's China R&D Center has also worked to develop the skills and talents of local scientists, biostatisticians, medical professionals, pharmacists, and others with expertise in life sciences. The Center collaborates with leading academic researchers and top institutions in China, including Peking University, Tsinghua University, Fudan University, the Chinese Academy of Science Institute of Biophysics, and the Chinese Academy of Sciences' Shanghai Institute of Biochemistry and Cell Biology. This is another example of a foreign R&D center working with Chinese educational institutions to raise their level of education and training. Pfizer works to create an environment in China that will nurture research and innovative drug development.[317]

ABB

The experience of the Swedish-Swiss power and automation technology giant ABB Group is perhaps indicative of the future of R&D in China. ABB operates in more than 100 countries around the world. It is a market and technology leader in robotics with more than 160,000 robots in operation—the largest installed base of any robotics manufacturer. The company also makes grids for electrical transmission and is a leader in designing smart grid transmission systems that conserve on electricity losses through transmission. It also makes efficient engines that conserve on inputs of electrical power.

ABB first supplied a steam boiler to China in 1907 and invested in a joint venture in Xiamen, Fujian province in 1992. Since then, ABB has established a full range of business activities in China, including research and development, supply chain management, engineering, manufacturing, sales, and services. It has 18,300 employees in China, 35 local companies, and an extensive sales and service network across 80 cities.

The story goes that ABB Chairman of the Board, Hubertus von Grunberg, once picked up a tablet computer and read the inscription on the back that said, "Designed in USA, assembled in China." He remarked that this was not the strategy that ABB would pursue, nor is it a strategy that would work in the future. The approach for ABB was to be "designed in China and made in China" and the slogan was to be "In China, for China and for the world." ABB's strategy was to find markets in China and also to export to other countries of the world.[18]

ABB has become the first robotics company to localize both its manufacturing and robotics R&D in China. It established the group's third robotics R&D facility in China following facilities in Sweden and Norway. Since its inception in 2005, the local robotics R&D team has increased in size tenfold. Seeing the huge potential and great importance of the China market, the company moved its robotics global headquarters from Detroit to Shanghai in 2006.

An Innovative China?

When the modern Hollywood movie "Kung Fu Panda" hit China, Beijing's political leaders were appalled that their film industry could not have conceived and produced such a blockbuster movie using quintessential Chinese culture and characters. Chinese business leaders and officials routinely lament the country's lack of innovation. "Our ability to copy is far greater than our originality," Zhang Xin, chief executive of real estate group Soho, once said. "The society we live in needs original things badly."[19]

Can China innovate and climb the high-technology ladder? This is not the question. Rather, the question for multinational corporations throughout the world is how fast China's ascent will be and whether the ladder can be extended to keep the top out of reach of Chinese industries in hot pursuit of the world's best.

In a 2015 study of innovation in China, the McKinsey Global Institute concluded that China has the potential to evolve from an innovation sponge—absorbing and adapting global technologies and knowledge—to an

219

innovation leader. The study found that Chinese companies are performing well in some types of innovation, by filling consumer needs with better products and services and wielding the power of China's manufacturing systems to make innovations in production processes. However, China has yet to take the lead in more challenging forms of innovation, such as scientific discovery and engineering. Chinese companies are using a distinctly Chinese way to nimbly accelerate experimentation and learning on a large scale.[320]

Perhaps a glimpse of the future can be seen by the following observation by a graduate student from Australia who studied at Peking University. He characterized Peking University as, perhaps, China's top university. Each year, every position in the School of Management and Finance receives approximately 30,000 applicants. If you get the opportunity to study there (as he did), you are studying with some of the most ambitious, intelligent, and hard-working students on the planet. China is graduating a huge pool of well-educated, bilingual, and culturally-adept graduates. In Peking University there is a distinctly different ethos with respect to hard work and ambition. Students have 'hard-core' attitudes to study and professional ambition. International students might grab a beer on the weekend, but Chinese students study until their dorm lights flicker out at 11 p.m. Shortly afterwards they relocate to the brightly lit diners of the nearby McDonald's and Kentucky Fried Chicken. These students might represent the nerds, but in Peking University the nerds are the norm. The hunger to succeed pervades—and they are proud of it. There is no 'tall poppy' syndrome[321] there, only admiration—and, of course, envy and jealousy—for those who make it.[322]

Perhaps another indicator is in a story circulating on the Internet: A mathematician asks, "How do you write 4 in between 5?" An Indian says, "Is this a joke?" A Japanese says, "Impossible!" An American replies, "The question is all wrong!" A British person says, "It's not found on the Internet." And the Chinese writes: F(IV)E. The story concludes with, "This is the reason Chinese are everywhere in the world: in finance, business, medicine, engineering ... anything to do with using both sides of the brain."

CHAPTER 12. THE BOXER REBELLION REDUX

In 1900, a Chinese secret society called the Boxers (*Yihequan* or "Righteous and Harmonious Fists") arose and attempted to drive all foreigners from China. The resulting Boxer Rebellion, as it is known in Western histories, began as a people's movement but received official sanction as the imperial household realized that it would be a useful instrument to help rid the country of foreign influence. Prior to the rebellion, China had been subjected to humiliating military defeats by technologically superior Western and Japanese armed forces. Foreigners were living in privileged enclaves, and outsiders were thought to be destroying traditional Chinese values by spreading Christianity and importing Turkish and Indian opium. The slogan of the Boxers was "Build China, Expel Foreigners." Their chief aim was to purify and reinvigorate their nation by the utter annihilation of all foreign devils. The rebellion was brutally squelched by an eight-nation expeditionary force. In the aftermath, *Puck* magazine ran a political cartoon showing people representing the eight nations cowering around a banquet table while a sword of Damocles hung over their heads. On the sword was written the "Awakening of China" and captioned, "A disturbing possibility in the East." (See **Figure 12.1.**)

FIGURE 12.1. THE AWAKENING OF CHINA

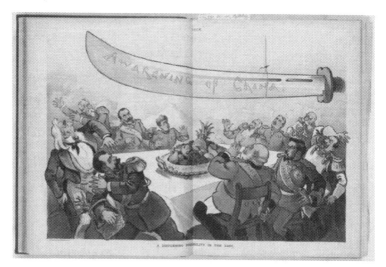

Source: By Udo Keppler / Library of Congress Prints and Photographs Collection.

The actual awakening of China did not occur at the turn of the twentieth century like a slash of the sword of Damocles, but it happened gradually over the next hundred years as the Qing dynasty was overthrown and the country was battered by war and turmoil both from external and internal forces. As the PRC welcomed the twenty-first century, the Western and Asian powers were again feasting at the banquet table, but this time they had been welcomed as foreign investors into what was rapidly developing into the second largest economy in the world.

Still there existed a conflict of interests between the desire for profits by foreign companies operating in the PRC and Chinese memories of being exploited by Western powers. Westerners making profits in China also did not fit well into the Confucian and communist ideas of social order. While Beijing recognized the contribution that the foreign investors had made to the industrialization of the country, sentiment was strong that it was time to take back the nation.

The new paradigm, as seen in the discussion of intellectual property, innovation, and government industrial policy, is to beat back foreign companies and take over industries whether by legitimate or illegitimate means. The Chinese are confident of one thing: anything you can do, particularly if you are doing it in China with Chinese workers, they can do equally as well or better. In 2012, a prominent American businessman with long experience in the PRC remarked to me that any multinational corporation that is relying on manufacturing in China for its product will be out of that line of business within a decade or so. He thought that a Chinese company will either put out a cheaper product or will compete so ruthlessly that the multinational corporation will have to withdraw at least from the Chinese market if not from other major markets of the world.

This warning serves as a word of caution to foreign business interests not to underestimate domestic competition in China. The foreign company may have superior technology, brand loyalty and name recognition now, but there is no assurance that these advantages will continue into the future. Competition is intense, and modern Boxers are ready to rise up and expel the foreigners. Although it is improbable that China will become a dominate force in all industries, the government is aiming at creating national champion companies in particular sectors.

The strategy by China to take over industries can be seen through the experience of multinationals in many sectors. This chapter briefly examines three of these industries in which competition is intense and Beijing is encouraging domestic industry and national champions to arise. The industries are high-speed rail, automobiles and passenger aircraft. These are industries in which technology is advancing rapidly and foreign companies have held a competitive advantage for a long time.

High-Speed Rail

Trains are the main method for traveling long distances in China. Trains are the most common mode of transport in China for trips between cities. In the seven-day Spring Festival holiday alone, people in China make more than 2.3 billion trips on all kinds of trains. A major goal of Beijing has been to establish a nationwide network of high-speed trains similar to those in Japan, Taiwan and Europe.

In 2003 the Chinese Ministry of Railways released its first planned network of dedicated high-speed railroads, called the Mid-to-Long-Range

Network Plan, a blueprint to outline the future development of its railway network. Aiming to make China more economically competitive, the plan called for development of fast intercity regional passenger networks in the densely populated eastern half of the country while connecting the disparate regions inland. The major decision of the plan was to separate passenger and freight services. Passenger services have been addressed by building dedicated lines operating at top speeds of 250-350 km/hour (155-217 mph).

According to a World Bank report, China invested approximately $163 billion in high-speed rail from 2007 to 2009 and another $200 billion in 2010 and 2011.[323] China now has the world's longest high-speed rail network, stretching over 8,300 km (5,150 miles) in 2010, with plans to exceed 16,000 km (9,900 miles) by 2020.[324]

High speed rail followed the Chinese model to a "T." Chinese companies first acquired the necessary technology through a joint venture and other arrangements with foreign firms. Once confident that they could proceed on their own, the Chinese firms began producing their own versions of the high speed rail systems.

Foreign manufacturers, including Germany's Siemens, France's Alstom, Japan's Kawasaki Heavy Industries, and Canada's Bombardier, provided technology and equipment to help build China's network. They entered into intense competition for this fast-growing market. As in many other sectors, technology transfer was a requirement for partnerships with state-backed Chinese companies, and those Chinese companies now are major competitors. In 2002 foreign-based companies accounted for about 70 percent of the Chinese market for rail equipment; by 2010, their combined shares were less than 20 percent.[325]

Japan's bullet trains provide a case in point. In 2005, Japan's Kawasaki Heavy Industries teamed with China's CSR Sifang (CSR Qingdao Sifang Locomotive & Rolling Stock Co., Ltd) in a joint venture to supply the country's high-speed rail market. The shares of the joint venture, called Qingdao Sifang Kawasaki Rolling Stock Co., were Kawasaki (39%), CSR Sifang (39%), CSR (China South Locomotive & Rolling Stock Corporation Limited), the parent company of CSR Sifang (11%) and Itochu, a Japanese trading company (11%). Through the joint venture, Kawasaki hoped that it would be able to sharpen its competitive edge and, by providing engineering expertise, increase its orders in the Chinese market. Over the longer term, Kawasaki also planned to use the joint venture to procure rail car parts both within China and worldwide.[326]

Now CSR is producing high-speed rail cars that Kawasaki claims are a version of its Hayate model at a price highly competitive with those of foreign firms. A Japanese executive familiar with the 2004 deal said members of the Kawasaki-led consortium realized the deal could help give China a start in the industry, but they could not imagine the catch-up would be so fast. "Of course they are angry," the executive says. "But they know well it would be a waste of time and money to fight the PRC government."[327] Complainers could be shut out of the Chinese market.

FIGURE 12.2. CHINESE HIGH-SPEED RAIL TRAIN

Photograph by D. Nanto

In the case of building the Beijing-Taijin high speed railway, in 2005, Siemens AG and China CNR Corp. Ltd. (CNR) were jointly awarded a contract to construct 60 passenger trains each capable of seating 600 passengers and traveling 300 kilometers per hour (186 mph). Siemens built the first three trains at its plant in Germany and trained more than 1,000 CNR technical staff. The project was completed in time for the 2008 Beijing Olympics. Despite subsequent success by Siemens in providing subway cars and a baggage handling system for Chinese projects, CNR rose to become a significant competitor to Siemens. In March 2009, Siemens announced that it had been awarded a $1 billion contract to provide trains for the Beijing-Shanghai high-speed railway. Following the announcement, China's Ministry of Railways denied the existence of the deal and insisted that Chinese technology would be used in the project. Ultimately, CNR was awarded the contract, although Siemens did provide considerable key components.[328]

Such transfer of foreign technology has enabled Chinese companies, such as China Southern Railway and China Northern Railway to become global competitors virtually overnight. International companies, moreover, are also assessing the growing opportunities to form partnerships with Chinese groups bidding on high-speed rail projects all over the world (what the Chinese refer to as high-speed rail diplomacy). Siemens dropped its own bid in 2010 to build and operate a high-speed rail line in Saudi Arabia so that it could join a Chinese-led consortium bidding for the same project.[329] In December 2010, CSR and General Electric announced an agreement to form a joint venture to build high-speed trains in the United States using Chinese technology.[330] The joint venture would be the first U.S.-based manufacturer ready to supply the proposed high-speed rail corridors in California and Florida.[331]

In 2014, CNR surprised the global rail industry by winning a $570 million tender to supply more than 280 subway cars to Boston's public transit system. CNR reportedly intends to invest about $1.3 billion in new rolling stock, a manufacturing site in nearby Springfield and maintenance facilities in Medford and Boston. The Chinese vision for future travel from Beijing to Boston might be to fly on a Chinese Comac C919, take a CNR subway car on the Blue Line from Logan Airport to the Government Center and there be picked up by someone driving a Volvo, a Swedish carmaker that had been acquired by Geely Holding Group. In short, Beijing hopes for a future in which long-distance travel would feature Chinese made planes, trains and automobiles.[332]

In July 2014, China and Turkey celebrated the inaugural run of a 330 mile high speed rail line that runs between Ankara and Istanbul. This line was the first to be completed overseas by a PRC high speed rail company. It had been built by a consortium consisting of the China Railway Construction Corporation, the China National Machinery Import and Export Corporation and two Turkish companies, Cengiz Construction and Ibrahim Cecen Ictas Construction.[333]

In the case of magnetic levitation trains, the story has been much different. Although there was early enthusiasm for the technology, Transrapid International, a joint venture between Siemens and ThyssenKrupp, using proprietary German technology, was able to build only a 30.5 km (20 mile) link between Shanghai's Pudong area and its international airport. Transrapid International refused to share the technology with its Chinese partner or to manufacture the cars locally. As a result, when the line was built in 2004, it turned out to be relatively expensive. In the case of maglev trains, the tracks and train cars are integral to the propulsion system, so separating out components for local manufacture was difficult and not advisable. All major components of the system had to be imported. Even though maintenance of maglev systems tends to be less costly (since there are no wheels, axles, transmissions, or tracks to wear out), without local production, when compared with high-speed rail, the maglev costs were still significantly higher.

FIGURE 12.3. SHANGHAI MAGLEV TRAIN.

Source: Photo by D. Nanto

The high-speed rail experience has followed the pattern for industries that Beijing would like to pursue. First, form a joint venture or other industrial arrangement to acquire the latest technology from the top firms in the world. Second, learn how to make the product and run a manufacturing plant in China. Third, establish a Chinese company to use the technology and underprice the foreign joint venture. Fourth, switch all future procurement to the Chinese company and away from the foreign joint venture. Fifth, partner with a different multinational company to enter foreign markets and attempt to sell abroad.

Automobile Industry

In the 1980s, imports of luxury cars were so restricted and were selling at such a premium in China that smugglers would go to extreme lengths to acquire them. According to an urban legend in Hong Kong, one method of sneaking European luxury cars past customs was to take huge sheets of plastic shrink wrap and wrap them around the car so securely that the whole package became waterproof. The car could then be sunk to the bottom of the Pearl River and a boat could tow it underwater up the river from Hong Kong to Guangzhou where it could be brought to the surface and sold.

At that time, bicycles still accounted for a high percentage of personal transportation, and private cars were out of reach for most households. Bicycle riders jammed the right lanes in the avenue in front of Tiananmen Square and everywhere else. On country roads farmers could be seen driving smoke-belching hand tractors pulling small trailers with vegetables and grains for city markets. The first private vehicles appeared in Beijing in 1984. In 1985, the Chinese media gave front page coverage of the first farmer who bought his own truck.[334]

In the late 1980s, the automobiles that could be seen on Chinese roads consisted mainly of locally-produced Soviet-style vehicles plus Volkswagen Santanas and Jeeps. The Santanas were designed for Shanghai's taxi fleet, while the Jeeps could negotiate the rough roads outside the cities. Here and there one could see a smattering of Toyota minivans and Daihatsu vehicles, as well as European and American upscale passenger cars. Fortunately for General Motors, Mao Zedong had used a Buick, so Buicks were in high demand even though they were greatly taxed and few and far between.

China's modernization of its motor vehicle transportation sector has paralleled that which has occurred in the rest of the economy. In order to meet rising demand for reliable and stylish vehicles, China either had to import them or modernize its outdated automotive industry. Given that hard currency was scarce and needed for capital rather than consumer goods, Beijing had no choice but to develop its own domestic industry. Prior to Deng Xiaoping's reforms, China's automakers had relied on Russia for technology to build vehicles primarily for industrial and military use. The time had come for the auto industry to prepare to enter the twenty-first century.

The government first designated the automotive sector a "pillar industry," a designation that brought it favorable industrial policies and government subsidies. The initial goal was to create an automotive market dominated by a limited number of internationally-competitive joint venture assemblers, supplied by local parts manufacturers, and producing to world standards. What happened was a tale of two economies.

When the push to build a modern automotive sector began, the existing industry reflected the policies of the Great Leap Forward and other misguided attempts to industrialize. Instead of a pillar industry, the emphasis on provincial self-sufficiency and reliance on domestic technology had generated what might be called a fence-post industry. It was highly fragmented with too many small producers relying on ties to local governments. They made a limited number of outdated and uncompetitive vehicles according to a central plan. In 1983, these enterprises produced about half of all vehicles made in China. By 1992, their market share had nearly disappeared and then began to recover slowly.

On the other side of the automobile industry have been the real pillars, the large, foreign-affiliated enterprises, most of them state-owned companies. As indicated previously in the discussion of investments by foreign automakers, most of the foreign-affiliated manufacturers have built vehicles with technology and designs from abroad. Beijing has kept the foreign companies from monopolizing the market by limiting their share in any joint venture to 50 percent. A few domestic automakers, however, have become major producers without relying on joint ventures with foreign brand-name automakers, although each got its start by producing knock-off versions of foreign cars or by producing vehicles for China's military.

The Chinese government hoped, initially, that joint ventures would allow Chinese car producers to tap the technological and management expertise of their international partners. In exchange, foreign automakers would gain access to the vast Chinese market. This schema has not worked all that well. Chinese automakers feel that they have not gained the market shares they should possess in their own country. In 2014, the China Association of Automobile Manufacturers lashed out at foreign competitors, claiming domestic brands will be "killed in the cradle" if the government allows U.S. and Japanese car companies free rein in the nation.[335]

In 2004, China had a total of 144 automakers. Of these, 48 were foreign affiliated (including nine affiliated with Taiwan and Hong Kong); 30 were state-owned or collective; and 65 were corporations, share holding companies, or privately owned.[336] By 2011, there were officially fewer than 40 domestic carmakers, and many of them were expected either to disappear or be consolidated with other companies. However, in 2012, China's Ministry of Industry and Information Technology found that the country still had 171 domestic automobile, truck and bus manufacturers. Many of them made only a few thousand vehicles each year.[337] Under the current Five-Year Plan, China wants to see the number of domestic automakers reduced to only a few dozen tier-one and tier-two producers.[338]

From stark backwardness as late as the 1980s, China not only has become the largest automobile producer in the world but also has the largest market for automobiles. In 1998, Chinese automakers sold only 550,000 automobiles. However, by the year 2000, production nearly reached 2 million vehicles, and by 2010 was close to 17 million—twice the level of production by Japan or the United States.[339] By 2014, production of automobiles in China reached 23.7 million units, up 7.3 percent over that in 2013.[340] This rapid growth in production stands in stark contrast to the industry's prospects in 1988. After a visit to China and its fledgling automotive sector, then-Chrysler Corporation CEO Lee Iacocca is said to have reflected that China's modernization process would be, "a long haul, a very long haul."[341] Little did Iacocca know at the time that the long haul would actually apply as much to the Chrysler Corporation as to Chinese automakers.

In 2013, an analysis by Sanford C. Bernstein & Co. described the Chinese auto industry as being just a few miles away from stepping into international competition. The analysis concluded that the Chinese have the will and money to make their auto industry world class. They already were 80 percent of the way there and just needed to invest more in development in order to step into global competition.[342] Another study, however, reported that the initial quality of Chinese domestic brands had declined in 2012 and the gap between domestic and international brands had widened.[343]

Chinese automakers have found that building passenger cars is quite different from making a television set or cellular telephone. The components of such consumer electronics are readily available, and the major problem is one of design, assembly, and marketing. For automobiles, however, consumer safety is at stake, so regulations are stricter. Foreign models cannot simply be copied, even though some Chinese companies have attempted to do so. Automobile technology is continually changing, and innovations are protected by patents and trademarks. A knock-off car may be acceptable in a poor country, but once consumers acquire income, information, and modern tastes, they want the genuine article. In addition, consumer perceptions come into play. Each car line has a history and reputation, whether actual or a product of advertising, that can be difficult to create for newer companies.

The automotive experience also is highly personal with dozens of sensory items that cannot be easily duplicated. In the 1980s when American cars were being challenged by imports from Japan, a reviewer commented that certain Japanese cars had knobs and handles with just the right touch and feel. The turn signal lever on particular Japanese cars, for example, had just the right resistance and click, while using the turn signal lever on a certain American car felt like breaking a chicken's leg. A car can have all the necessary components, but still not have the feel of integrated luxury when driven.

SAIC Motors, Changan Motors, FAW Group, and Dongfeng Motors comprise China's "Big Four" domestic automakers. SAIC Motors, headquartered in Shanghai, is the largest, with most of its sales originating from joint ventures. Of the 4.4 million vehicles it sold in 2012, 1.4 million were from the joint venture with GM and 1.3 million from its joint venture with Volkswagen. It also sold 1.5 million commercial vehicles under its own nameplates, but its sales of passenger cars under its own brand amounted to only 0.2 million vehicles.[344] This illustrates the dependence of Chinese automakers on sales of foreign branded passenger cars. However, the foreign marque seems less important in sales of commercial vehicles.

The development strategy being pursued by SAIC Motors departs somewhat from the basic Chinese model and reflects the nature of the domestic automobile market. SAIC has relied on foreign technology, design, and expertise acquired through its joint ventures, but it has not transferred that knowledge and experience to a wholly-owned subsidiary to compete with the JV company. Rather, the company is using its joint ventures to expand market share domestically and to expand abroad.

China's second largest automaker, Changan Automobile, descends from a military supply company founded in 1862 and is a pioneer of China's modern industry. A state-owned enterprise with an annual capacity of about two million vehicles, Changan has six large bases of operation centered on Chongqing in the western region of the PRC. The company makes a full line of motor vehicles including its own brand models and in 2012 ranked 13th in the world in automobile production.[345]

In 2001, Changan established a joint venture with Ford called Changan Ford Automobile and two years later renamed it Changan Ford Mazda Automobile Co. Ford and Mazda each own 15% of the JV company. The JV's Chongqing plant produces Ford vehicles, while another plant in Nanjing mainly produces small Fords and Mazda cars. In 2011, the JV sold more than a half million vehicles. Changan also has a joint venture with Suzuki of Japan.

Changan attempts to push the frontier in automotive technology with extensive R&D facilities, including the Changan European Design Center in Turin, Italy. The company claims to have produced for China the first Jeep-type, off-road vehicle and in 2007 was the first in China to mass produce a hybrid fuel vehicle. In 2012, the company began making an all-electric vehicle on a demonstration basis. Changan continues to develop its own-brand models even though Ford and Mazda have been careful not to share their core technologies and have maintained control over the JV production line, manufacturing processes, marketing channels, and parts procurement.[346]

The third largest automaker in China, the FAW Group, was formerly known as the First Automobile Works. It is a quintessential Chinese company, founded in 1953 through an agreement signed by Chairman Mao Zedong and Prime Minister Zhou Enlai with Soviet leaders. As a state-owned enterprise, it began by using Soviet technology, equipment, and training to build trucks. Located in Changchun in northern China near the border with the Soviet Union, it was part of a Soviet agreement to support industrial development in the PRC.[347]

While the initial focus of the company was on trucks and other commercial vehicles, in 1953, it built a Chinese luxury automobile called the Hongqi. Designed to provide both visibility and security, it became the vehicle of choice for Chinese leaders and for visiting foreign dignitaries—including former President Richard M. Nixon during his historic 1972 trip to China.

Growth of the company was set back considerably during the Great Leap Forward and Cultural Revolution, but as the political focus turned to reform and opening, the company resumed normal operations. In 1988, FAW signed an agreement with Volkswagen to jointly assemble Audi cars from knock-down kits. The first Audi rolled off the assembly line a year later. In 2002, FAW acquired Tainjin Automotive, a deal which brought it a joint venture with Toyota. In 2009, FAW also established a joint venture with General Motors.

In 2002, sales of FAW-built passenger cars exceeded trucks and other commercial vehicles for the first time. In 2011, FAW-VW sold 903,000 vehicles while FAW-Toyota sold 510,000 cars. Total capacity is around 2.6 million vehicles.

Rounding out the big four automakers in China is Dongfeng Motors. The Chinese government created and capitalized the company in 1969 partly to provide a mechanism to supervise smaller automobile companies at the provincial level. Dongfeng had the ill luck of being founded at the time Mao Zedong was pursuing a Third Front strategy under which it had to locate far inland in Hubei province as a precaution in case of a foreign invasion of the coastal area.[348] This meant it was far away from other automobile companies and a supply base. Until 1992, the enterprise was known as the Second Automobile Works. Traditionally, Dongfeng mainly produced commercial vehicles.

Dongfeng partnered in 1992 with the French PSA Group to make Citroën cars. By 2003, Dongfeng had also established joint ventures with Kia Motors, Honda, and Nissan. Its model lineup, therefore, has a distinct European and Japanese flair. In 2009, Dongfeng helped in further consolidating the sprawling Chinese automobile industry. In 2012, Dongfeng sold a total of 1.7 million cars and 0.4 million trucks.[349]

Among the domestic automakers not in the big four, Geely Automobile Holdings is emerging as a competitive manufacturer with advanced engine technology. It is one of the few automakers without ties to the state. The company bought Volvo from the Ford Motor Company and is manufacturing Volvo branded automobiles in China. In 2015, it began exporting a sedan from the PRC rather than from Sweden to the United States for use in its existing Volvo distribution network. The car was designed for the Chinese market and has more leg room in the back for buyers who have a driver and ride in the back seat.[350]

The Chery Automobile Company provides an interesting case of a company that lifted itself up by its own bootstraps in an entrepreneurial manner with Chinese characteristics. The government of Wuhu city in the poor eastern province of Anhui founded the company in 1997. It began by selecting a name that looks like Chevy (Chevrolet) and by purchasing an old Ford assembly line in the United Kingdom that it used to cobble together a workable vehicle. Without a license to manufacture automobiles, the company began to secretly manufacture cars in 1999 that were sold to local taxi companies. Their production, however, was overruled by the central government which had strict industry entry limits, and it was compelled to join with SAIC Motors in order to break through the red tape needed to begin production of vehicles for sale to the public. Chery borrowed further from GM by producing a knockoff version of GM's Chevrolet Spark or Matiz made in South Korea by the GM's partner Daewoo.[351]

From that humble beginning, Chery has emerged as China's largest independent vehicle maker by focusing on passenger cars and SUVs that are low in cost and eminently exportable to developing countries. The company claims to be China's largest exporter of passenger vehicles. Chery's chairman has said, "In the beginning, no one had confidence in us ... but now we are looking globally for markets."

In 2012, as Chery gained greater credibility in the auto world, it reached an agreement with Jaguar Land Rover to make and market vehicles in China.[352] A previous agreement with Chrysler to build cars for the U.S. market to be sold under the Dodge brand fell victim to the 2007-09 global financial crisis and the difficulty Chery had in building cars that would meet strict U.S. emissions standards.[353]

Chery's corporate culture mixes old communist propaganda with an entrepreneurial spirit. Posters on factory walls have exhortations such as "Know plain living and hard struggle" or "Do not wallow in luxuries and pleasures," and harken back to the era of socialist motivation. Yet the assembly lines are as organized and modern as any foreign auto plant.[354] Chery produces about 700,000 vehicles per year.

Chery, however, has benefited greatly from government subsidies. In 2009, government subsidies for Chery accounted for $93 million of $97 million in non-operating revenues. The company received $37 million in subsidies and grants in 2007 and $68 million in 2008. Government subsidies dedicated to R&D climbed from $26 million in 2007 and $41 million the following year to $65 million in 2009. Moreover, Chery received cash tax refunds of $129 million in 2008 and $42 million in 2009. The local governments also have invested considerably in Chery's R&D. Since 2003, Anhui Province has provided $10 million annually in R&D subsidies while the city of Wuhu has provided $13 million each year.[355]

The subsidies along with rising profits have enabled Chery to invest heavily in R&D and to hire foreign expertise to design and build its own brand of vehicles. A joint venture between Chery and Israel Corp. is developing the Qoros, a luxury sedan, under the direction of executive designers who previously had worked for Mini, Volkswagen, and BMW.[356]

Other domestic Chinese automakers, such as Great Wall Motors and Guangzhou Automobile Group, are also performing well.

A goal of the Chinese economic planners has been to create an automobile industry that is able to compete in world markets and generate foreign exchange for the country. As noted earlier, while Chinese built cars may not be ready for acceptance in the high income countries in Europe, North America, and northeast Asia, they have made inroads into lower and middle income countries. In 2011, Chinese automakers exported 1.3 million cars and trucks worth $7.6 billion.

In 2014, U.S. imports of new and used passenger cars from China were valued at a paltry $77.7 million. This was down from $213 million recorded in 2007.[357] In 2007, China's cars received poor safety ratings, and the PRC government announced it was cracking down on exports by automobile manufacturers too small to compete internationally.[358] China's automobile exports to the United States paled in comparison to those from South Korea in 2014 ($14.5 billion) or those from Japan ($33.9 billion).[359]

However, in automobile parts, the story is not the same. In 2014, China exported $18.4 billion in motor vehicle parts (including engines, chassis and tires) to the United States—up from $9.9 billion in 2010. The PRC is increasingly becoming a major exporter of motor vehicle parts, a development of great concern to the U.S. industry.

Passenger Aircraft Industry

In 1989 at a visit to the Shanghai Aviation Industrial Corp., I was shown the Y-10, the first Chinese produced passenger airplane. It was parked at the rear of the runway area past a long row of MIG fighter jets that appeared to have been retired from the PRC's military. With a capacity of 178 passengers, the company explained that the plane had been tested and even flown to Tibet and back. It was reminiscent of a Boeing 707 and used Pratt & Whitney turbofan engines that had originally been procured as spares for 707s that already were in service in China. After the plane was built, however, the company was confronted with reams of regulations that had to be met before the plane could be flown in foreign airspace. That, combined with the political problems of the company president, meant that not one plane ever was ordered, and it was never put into commercial production.

Airline passenger travel in China had to undergo the same reform and opening that occurred in other parts of the economy. In the late 1980s, I experienced a flight right out of a Marxist playbook when traveling from Beijing to Guangzhou on a domestic Chinese carrier. The plane was a no-frills Russian Ilyushin with a pilot who seemed to be a former military hotshot. The flight attendants efficiently herded us up the airstairs and down the cramped aisles of the plane. As we took off, the tail end of the plane began to swerve back and forth, and I hit my head on the window. This was the only time I ever feared getting whiplash on an airplane. The Chinese passengers seemed to take it all in stride, but as Americans we thought that the CAAC, the Civil Aviation Authority of China, might live up to its nickname: CAAC—Chinese Airlines Always Crash. Fortunately, we made it into the air. A while later, the flight attendants served the meal. It consisted of a box lunch that the attendants almost tossed at you as if they were dealing cards. After reaching our destination, our emotions were similar to those after an amusement park ride—relief at making it down safely but with lingering feelings of exhilaration and terror.

We were glad that our pilots had stayed in the cockpit because we had heard the possibly apocryphal story of Chinese pilots who put their plane on autopilot and came back to greet the passengers. Unfortunately, when they shut the cockpit door it locked behind them. They had to use the emergency axe to break the lock and get back into the cockpit.

Over the ensuing years, there has been somewhat of a reversal between U.S. and Chinese airline service. The level of service and amount of complimentary food by U.S. air carriers has declined while that in the PRC has improved remarkably. The opening of China's airlines to more international travel and travelers seems to have compelled China's flight attendants to take cues from the gracious attendants on airlines from Japan, Taiwan, or Singapore. The larger comfort factor for travelers, however, has been the dominance of passenger planes built by Boeing and Airbus flying on Chinese routes.

Boeing began sales to the PRC after former President Nixon's trip to China in 1972. By 2013, Boeing had delivered 1,000 airplanes to China and was holding onto a 51 percent market share in passenger aircraft with more than 100 seats.[360] Airbus accounted for the rest of the Chinese aircraft fleet with 891 planes in service.[361]

Even though both Boeing and Airbus have invested in suppliers, training facilities, and, in the case of Airbus, an assembly plant in the PRC, the high cost of foreign aircraft has become a concern among Beijing's economic planners. China has made the development of its state-owned aerospace industry a top priority. The long-term goal has been to lessen dependence on Boeing and Airbus and to develop a globally competitive passenger aircraft industry.[362] In 2008, the government created the Commercial Aircraft Corporation of China Ltd. (COMAC) and charged it with the mission of producing passenger jet planes. For China, this goal was as significant as the nation's development of nuclear weapons or the launch of the country's first satellite.

COMAC has two passenger jets in the works. The first is the AR J-21, a medium-sized regional jet seating between 90 and 105 passengers and designed for short-haul flights of less than three hours. Begun in 2002, during the Tenth Five-Year Plan (2001–05), the AR J-21 is intended first and foremost to meet China's burgeoning demand for internal air transport.

COMAC's second aircraft under development is the C919 passenger jet. The baseline version of the plane would have 156 to 168 seats. The company received design approval in 2010 and expects to begin deliveries in 2016.[363] Since only the United States, Europe and Russia have been able to produce passenger aircraft with more than 150-seat capacity, building the C919 is a matter of national pride for the PRC.

As has been the case with other high-technology industries, China aspires to climb the technology ladder with the help of foreign partners. In the corporate competition for contracts on the C919, Mark Howes, president of Honeywell Aerospace Asia Pacific, stated that the Chinese government made it clear to Western companies that they should be "willing to share technology and know-how."[364]

The technology for the C919 aircraft is a mixture of foreign black box, domestic Chinese components and technology acquired through joint ventures. The engines are to be imported. CFM International, a 50-50 joint company between France's Snecma S.A. (Safran group) and General Electric, is to supply LEAP-1C engines. This is the same engine that is to power the Boeing 737 MAX aircraft.[365]

Other technology is to come through joint ventures or cooperative agreements. For example, Ryanair, the low-cost European airline, has agreed to provide its expertise and experience to COMAC in developing the C919 aircraft. Ryanair also is considering augmenting its fleet of Boeing aircraft with those from COMAC.[366]

In November 2009, GE-Aviation and Aviation Industry Corporation of China (AVIC), a Chinese state-owned enterprise, announced plans to form a 50-50 joint venture to develop and market globally advanced integrated avionics systems for commercial aircraft. In July 2010, GE Aviation announced that COMAC had chosen GE and AVIC to provide the avionics core processing system, display system, and on-board maintenance system for the C919 aircraft.

Some U.S. analysts have raised concerns about this partnership. A January 17, 2011, article in the *New York Times* reported that the GE joint venture would result in its "sharing its most sophisticated airplane electronics, including some of the same technology used in Boeing's new state-of-the-art 787 Dreamliner." *Washington Post* columnist Steven Pearlstein wrote on January 18, 2011, that GE's agreement with China sounded "as if one of America's leading technology companies has decided to sell some of this country's crown jewels to ensure access to China's rigged market, potentially jeopardizing the competitive advantage enjoyed by this country's leading export industry." An AVIC official was reported by the *South China Morning Post* as stating: "It is a milestone for AVIC to tap into the most advanced technology for integrated avionics systems."[367]

In view of concerns over the transfer of technology with such significant commercial and military applications, GE has provided the following assurances:[368]

- The joint venture is to create and market commercial integrated avionics systems around the world, although the initial focus is to be on providing an integrated avionics system for the C919 aircraft and building a global customer and product support infrastructure.

- The venture is to create new technologies. The two companies have agreed to ensure that it will establish a robust compliance plan to guard the technology and use it solely for civilian applications. Only approved personnel will be employed by the JV and there are strict security measures outlined in the technology control plan, such as physically separating both the joint venture itself and its information technology from the respective parent companies. Third-party compliance audits are to be conducted at least annually.

- No AVIC personnel or person in China who retains military-related responsibilities is to be given access to technical data from GE or the joint venture. No cross-employment will be allowed with military or intelligence departments or with their suppliers. AVIC personnel are not allowed to work for the military or be put on a military assignment for two years after leaving the joint venture.

General Electric concedes that eventually China will become a potent player in the commercial jetliner market, and GE wants to be a major supplier to the emerging Chinese producers. John G. Rice, vice chairman of GE stated, "They are committed for the long term and they have every probability of being successful. We can participate in that or sit on the sidelines. We're not about sitting on the sidelines." He also pointed out that AVIC has supplied GE with some parts for jet engines for years and said, "This venture is a strategic move that we made after some thought and consideration, with a company we know." He also claimed that the deal was not something they were forced into by the Chinese government.[369]

Among the companies that have placed orders for C919s is GE Capital Aviation Service (a GE subsidiary). By the end of 2012, a total of 380 orders for the plane had been placed, mostly by Chinese carriers such as Air China, China Eastern, and China Southern.[370]

Some analysts contend that the Chinese government's promotion of a domestic aircraft industry will undercut Boeing's future aircraft sales, especially since Beijing must approve commercial aircraft purchases by Chinese airlines. Also, if China is able to market the C919 and other passenger aircraft abroad, this could displace Boeing's sales in third-country markets and in the United States, although the extra competition could push down the price of new aircraft for U.S. airlines.

Boeing also recognizes the potential competitive threat from China's aircraft industry. For its own 737 airliner, Boeing transferred technology and allowed China to supply parts as a strategy to gain sales there. The C919 is expected to use some of the same or similar parts and to compete directly with the Boeing 737. The C919 could cost as much as 20 percent less than the Boeing 737 and not be faced with China's 23 percent import duty on airplanes.[371]

Boeing has forecast that over the 20-year period 2011-30, China will buy 5,000 new commercial airplanes valued at more than $600 billion and will be Boeing's largest foreign customer for commercial airplanes.[372] Boeing also contends that the long-term ability of U.S. firms to compete against Chinese firms (and globally) will largely depend on their ability to innovate vis-à-vis their competition. When asked about potential competition from China's domestic passenger aircraft industry, one Boeing official reportedly stated: "Boeing must make sure that we are building tomorrow's plane while they are building today's ... we have to maintain that edge."[373]

In 2014, the United States exported $13,925 million worth of civilian aircraft, spacecraft and parts to China. During that same year, the United States imported $504 million worth of aircraft, spacecraft and parts from the PRC. This large favorable balance in trade occurs in one of the few industries in which the United States still holds competitive advantage over China. If the PRC planners have their way, this is due for a change.

The Boxer Rebellion II

The Boxer Rebellion also has been called the Boxer Uprising. Neither term quite describes what is happening in China today. The original rebellion was quelled by 20,000 troops from Austria-Hungary, France, Germany, Italy, Japan, Russia, Britain and the United States who came in with superior weaponry, took Peking, burned the Summer Palace and rescued the foreigners under siege. This humiliating defeat so weakened the Qing (Ch'ing) rulers that following a domestic uprising eleven years later, the dynasty ended.

This time, Beijing's efforts to expel the foreign investors are more subtle and revolve around industrial policies, the long arm of government and effort by domestic competitors. Ironically, the contributions of the foreign devils to Chinese industrialization have strengthened, not only the Chinese enterprises that the PRC would like to see become national champions but the government itself. Three decades of rapid economic growth have given the government credibility, legitimacy, resources, and the experience needed to tilt the playing field against foreign companies without gross violations of its international commitments.

The PRC's strategy has several components. First is to rely on state-owned enterprises to combat the foreign investors. Second is to strengthen both state-owned and other domestically-owned enterprises through subsidies, regulations, government procurement, and other favorable treatment. Third is to thwart the activities of foreign enterprises through licensing, accusations of misdeeds (such as food contamination), intervening in court deliberations, or using any other tool of government against them when needed.

In this strategy, a wide gap exists between China's central and local governments. While Beijing has dreams of restoring China to its past glory and reclaiming the Chinese economy from foreign investors, provincial and local governments are focused on creating local GDP growth and well-paying jobs for their people. They want investments of any kind whether foreign or domestic. To them the results are essentially the same.

Irrespective of the efforts of the PRC government to promote stronger domestic enterprises, the companies, themselves, are quickly learning how to compete in the cut-throat world of international business. For example, COFCO (China National Cereals, Oils and Foodstuffs Corporation), China's largest food processing holding company, is a profitable state-owned enterprise. In order to stay competitive in global markets, the company has adopted efficiency and innovation measures as well as management carrots and sticks. Although COFCO isn't publicly traded, seven of its subsidiaries are. In 2012, it spent $3 billion on R&D and hired 400 PhDs. It recently began a gross profit sharing bonus program for all employees. Managers get incentives but are also held accountable through what it calls its replacement on evaluation plan. Every year the lowest scoring 5 percent of COFCO's top 100 managers must be replaced. "The effect is like 100 people running from a tiger. Nobody wants to be caught."[374]

As a settlement of the original Boxer Rebellion, China was forced to pay $330 million to the foreign nations, remove its forts protecting Peking (Beijing) and allow foreign legations to station troops in Peking for their own defense. With the rebellion today, there can be no comprehensive settlement, only dispute settlement actions at the World Trade Organization, negotiations, unfair trade practice cases, and close monitoring of Beijing's proposed regulations and their implementation. The main burden remains with the foreign investors to protect their proprietary technology, to remain competitive, and to continue to innovate while keeping in mind the situation as described by a Westerner in China who prefers to go unnamed: Beijing will not throw a foreign enterprise out of the country but will make it suffer death by a thousand cuts until the foreign investor departs on his own.

CHAPTER 13. CHINA'S OUTWARD DIRECT INVESTMENT

In the late 1980s, I met with an executive with CITIC (China International Trust and Investment Corporation) in Shanghai to discuss China's economic development. CITIC is a state-owned investment company that was established in 1979 and has a variety of investments both in the PRC and abroad. They had financed the huge bridge connecting Shanghai and Pudong. At that time, CITIC had made a few investments in the United States, including a steel mill in New Jersey and timber land in Oregon. The executive said that their main purpose for those investments was to learn about U.S. labor relations from the steel mill, which was in decline, and about environmental regulations from the timber land. As it turned out, they learned plenty from the steelworker unions, and the executive said that he would not care if he never heard a hoot from a northern spotted owl again in his entire life. The company did not harvest a single tree from the timber land because the owl nested in old growth forests that came under environmental protection to provide a home for the owl as the species became threatened.

This chapter addresses the opposite side of foreign investment in the PRC—Chinese investment abroad. For foreign firms competing in the PRC, it not only is essential to know their competition in the Chinese market, but also to be aware of what Chinese firms are doing on their flanks. Perhaps Chinese companies are following the advice of Sun Tzu, the ancient Chinese war strategist. He said, "Place your army in deadly peril, and it will survive; plunge it into desperate straits, and it will come off in safety. For it is precisely when a force has fallen into harm's way that it is capable of striking a blow for victory. Success in warfare is gained by carefully accommodating ourselves to the enemy's purpose. By persistently hanging on the enemy's flank, we shall succeed in the long run....."[375] By investing overseas, Chinese companies are entering the homeland of their competitors. It is there that they will be tested and savor the chance of victory.

Much has changed since those early Chinese outward investments that went under the radar screen of most American and other officials. China now is a major investor in assets around the world. Chinese companies are buying into or acquiring foreign companies to gain access to technology, increase market share, provide jobs at home, capture more of their supply chain and to take a short cut to establishing a presence abroad. In 2014, the PRC had outward investments of $116.0 billion and a cumulative outward investment stock of $729.6 billion.[376] In 2012, an estimated 30% of global capital inflows in emerging markets came from China.[377]

The Chinese government calls the wave of overseas investments "going global," and this trend is raising concerns in businesses and government circles in other countries. According to some, this could be a new Cold War, a battle to be waged, not with threats of mutually assured destruction, but in the interplay of companies within the crucible of capitalism. The battle is not about great power confrontation, but often it is between Western, market-based corporations and Chinese state-owned enterprises.[378]

In this competitive struggle, some claim that the Chinese companies have a basic structural advantage because of Beijing's industrial policy. In the same manner that Beijing has promoted its national champion companies at home, they now are doing so abroad. These companies operate from a home base with an undervalued yuan that allows them to sell at low prices and generate an export surplus and excess foreign exchange. State-owned banks then harvest that foreign exchange and loan it to state-backed enterprises that are able to go abroad and acquire assets and forge market shares partly because of their ease of access to financing.

While this Cold War characterization might be somewhat overstated, the reality is that Chinese companies have become a new force in international markets. Most economic friction still centers on problems created by China's exports and lack of complete access to the Chinese market, but the PRC's outward direct investment flows are rapidly becoming another source of contention.

For Beijing, the exhortation for Chinese companies to go global fits well into China's dream of reclaiming its position as the center of the world. But for many Chinese companies, going global is a natural next step in their becoming world-class enterprises.

Much of the foreign investment is being done by China's large state-owned enterprises. Between 2002 and 2012, State-owned enterprises on average initiated 98.7 percent of all completed outbound investment deals.[379] These state-owned enterprises, moreover, are backed by state-owned banks. For example, in 2009, China National Petroleum Corp., parent of the state-run oil and natural gas giant PetroChina, announced that it had received a low-interest $30 billion loan from the China Development Bank to finance overseas acquisitions.[380]

Motivations

The reasons that PRC companies have invested abroad are analogous to the reasons that they have teamed up in partnerships and joint ventures in the Chinese market with foreign companies. The difference is that in the case of overseas investments, the Chinese company is the one with the cash and looking either to buy into an existing foreign company or to establish a presence in the foreign company's home market. However, investing in foreign countries has not been easy for companies that are only a generation away from the massive political turmoil and great distrust of Westerners that existed during the rule of Chairman Mao. Even though Chinese managers are graduating from foreign universities in ever rising numbers and company personnel are being exposed to international best practices, all but the most experienced enterprises find it difficult to succeed in foreign markets without some assistance.

The routes into international markets are as varied as the companies that have taken them. They are both pushed and pulled into investing abroad. One major reason to go abroad is to secure sources of supplies for raw materials in these uncertain times. In this world of unstable markets and economic sanctions, China is not confident that it will always have access to the raw materials and energy needed to fuel its economic boom.

Much of China's investment, particularly in emerging markets, has been based on its enormous appetite for energy, food, and metals needed for its industries and growing consumer sector. China's socialist thinkers tend to distrust open markets. They would prefer not to have to compete with other countries for supplies of essential products knowing that competition for food, energy, and other critical commodities will only intensify as population increases and incomes rise. They would rather that they own the sources of supply themselves. Beijing also looks with horror at the economic sanctions placed on countries such as Iran and previously on South Africa to induce or hasten political change. Beijing also recalls the Tiananmen Square sanctions by the United States in 1990 that included a suspension of export licensing for articles being shipped to the PRC related to defense, crime control, satellites and nuclear production.[38]I If a democracy movement should occur in China and be brutally crushed, China could face severe economic sanctions that could impede its access to raw materials and energy. Owning production assets in supplier countries could give the PRC a voice in whether or not a country participates in any proposed international sanctions.

Vertical integration also is a natural step in global expansion. A steel maker in China naturally wants to gain more control over international prices and sources of iron ore and other raw materials, particularly if the buyer perceives that the sellers have some monopoly pricing power. China's investments in iron ore mines in Australia are a case in point. Vertical integration can go both upstream toward inputs and downstream toward distribution.

Heretofore, most Chinese companies have relied on low prices for their products backed by low costs of production to gain market shares in foreign countries. Most of China's export sales, however, have been of products with foreign brands and which have had only the manufacturing and packaging outsourced to China. The goal for many Chinese companies is to win market share under their own brand names. However, the leap from assembling a product, such as a computer, to competing directly with international computer companies in their home markets is not an easy task. One way to short-cut the process is to purchase market share by buying into existing companies. Lenovo went this route with its acquisition of IBM's personal computer division.

Other Chinese companies attempt to buy both market share and technology by snapping up distressed or not-so-distressed assets. This process is common among companies all over the world. Yet other Chinese companies may be establishing an international presence to become more competitive at home. As Chinese incomes have risen, so has demand for Western goods. Foreign brands not only provide a sought-after cachet, but they also provide a certain level of quality and purity of product. A fake luxury watch is of limited value if it does not tell time accurately or has a watch band made of brittle plastic. A knock-off pair of designer jeans likewise is of little use if the zipper is shoddily made and comes unzipped all the time.

Another way that Chinese companies are seeking to improve their competitive standing is to invest overseas in order to acquire specific new methods and expertise. Many of the corporate acquisitions include highly advanced technology, such as deep water drilling for oil or fracking of oil shale. The acquisition of technology also is one reason that so many international high-technology companies have a presence in Silicon Valley, and one of the reasons that the Chinese automaker SAIC recently opened an office in Detroit despite its joint ventures with GM. In some cases, cyber spying is replacing opening branches in foreign industrial clusters whose major function is to gather intelligence. Still, nothing can substitute for friendly conversations in coffee shops and having a place to hire workers from competing firms who would not accept employment if they had to move their families to China.

Considerable outbound investment is occurring by large Chinese companies with name-brand products to sell that require a specialized distribution system also capable of providing after-sales service. China's automobile makers need local dealerships. China's makers of automobile parts also have located closer to assembly plants abroad. For example, Chery Automobile Company has made two major investments in Brazil, one in Turkey and one in Venezuela. Chinese automobile companies have invested $1.4 billion in Brazil and a similar amount in the United States.

China also has sovereign wealth funds that invest excess foreign exchange reserves. China Investment Corporation (CIC) is one of the PRC's main sovereign wealth funds. The CIC operates differently from other direct investors. As a sovereign wealth fund, the goal of the CIC is to invest Chinese government assets in order to preserve and increase the wealth of the country. It was established in 2007 with an initial war chest of $200 billion. According to the International Monetary Fund, countries should hold foreign exchange reserves sufficient to cover three months of short-term imports and to meet debt obligations for nine months. These reserves must be held in instruments that are highly liquid and low in risk, two conditions which imply low returns. For the PRC, this contingency foreign exchange reserve would amount to about $1 trillion. Given China's foreign exchange reserves in excess of $3.8 trillion, the country has more than $2.5 trillion that it can put into investments with higher returns than U.S., European, and Japanese government securities.

The CIC operates on three basic principles: (1) to operate commercially, (2) to make independent financial decisions and (3) to increase the rate of return on assets. Its fundamental approach is act as a long-term passive investor and to hold, manage, and invest its mandated assets to maximize shareholder's value. The fund usually does not take a controlling role or seek to influence operations in the companies in which it invests. The CIC relies on firms such as Cambridge Associates in Boston for investment advice and BlackRock for risk management. It has directed a sizable share of its funds toward companies in the financial sector, investments which also can provide the CIC with expertise in managing large asset portfolios.[382]

The Chinese State Administration of Foreign Exchange (SAFE) is the administrative agency tasked with drafting rules and regulations governing foreign exchange market activities and managing the PRC's foreign exchange reserves. It has invested most of the reserves in high grade U.S.-dollar-denominated debt, such as U.S. Treasury securities, and in Euro or other government issued securities. In 1997, it created a sovereign wealth fund called SAFE Investment Company incorporated in Hong Kong with an initial endowment of $20 billion. The company's portfolio of corporate equities has included holdings in financial institutions and large energy companies.

Dick K. Nanto

Bilateral Investment Treaties

The PRC has added more access and security for its outbound investors by concluding nearly 90 bilateral investment treaties (BITs). These treaties help to protect private investment, encourage the adoption of market-oriented policies that treat private investment in an open, transparent, and non-discriminatory way, and promote the promulgation of laws in signatory countries consistent with the objectives of the BITs. China's BITs have included a guarantee of most-favored-nation treatment and, in recent treaties, have incorporated a mechanism for resolving disputes. The BITs have been particularly important for the PRC in opening the way for investment in countries with which it does not have other agreements that protect investor rights and assure most-favored-nation treatment.

The first BIT for China that went into force was with Sweden in 1982. This was followed in 1985-86 by similar treaties with a number of countries including Germany, United Kingdom, France, Denmark, Norway, Austria, Belgium-Luxemburg and Finland in Europe as well as Singapore and Thailand in Asia. The BIT with Japan went into force in 1989, while that with Russia in 2009. China's recent BITs were with Nigeria in 2010 and with Uzbekistan in 2011.[383] The United States and the PRC have been negotiating on but have not yet signed a BIT.

The Scope of Outward Investment

As shown in **Figure 13.1**, in 2014, according to the PRC's official figures reported to the United Nations, net outward direct investment flows totaled $116.0 billion, up from $87.8 billion in 2012. Flows of outbound direct investment for the post-WWII period began in 1982 from virtually zero and exceeded a billion dollars a decade later. In the 1990s, as the PRC accumulated foreign exchange reserves and companies engaged in overseas activities, investment flows remained at about $2 billion per year. The great surge in overseas investments began in the first decade of the twenty-first century as the flows increased to $12 billion in 2005, to $69 billion in 2010 and exceeded $100 billion for the first time in 2013. The stock of China's outward direct investment likewise rose from essentially

250

zero in 1980 to $57 billion in 2005, to $317 billion in 2010 and to $730 billion in 2014.

FIGURE 13.1. CHINA'S OUTWARD DIRECT INVESTMENT

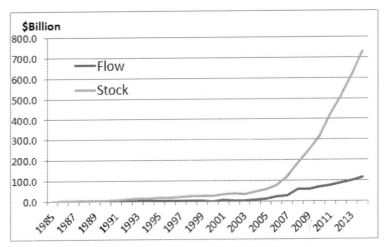

Note: Valued at current prices and current exchange rates
Source: United Nations Conference on Trade and Development, UNCTADstat

The major sectors receiving PRC outward investment include leasing and business services, financial intermediation (banking), mining, wholesale and retail trades, manufacturing and transportation/storage/post. Much of the leasing and business services as well as transportation investments have been in support of Chinese businesses and logistics. A significant share of the investment in financial institutions has been by China's sovereign wealth funds and state-owned banks.

The Heritage Foundation in Washington, DC, maintains a dataset of Chinese outbound direct investments that are valued at more than $100 million per case. The dataset excludes aid, loans, and bond purchases. These data list China's outbound investments by date, investor, value, partner and share size, sector, and destination country.[384] These data do not include reinvested earnings. Any troubled investments that were rejected on the basis of security or antitrust considerations are included on a separate data sheet. The dataset is useful in determining specific target sectors, corporate sources and trends in such investments.

Between 2005 and June 2013, according to the Heritage Foundation dataset, China had a total of $430 billion in major outward direct investments. This dataset confirms that much of Chinese overseas investment has been a story of a quest for secure sources of energy, raw materials, metals, food, and chemicals to meet demand by its industrial and consumer sectors. The PRC also has invested in infrastructure to ease shipping raw materials and energy and in technology. The major industrial companies that have invested abroad to distribute their products or operate businesses have been in automobiles, finance, and real estate.

TABLE 13.1. PRC OUTWARD INVESTMENTS BY TOP TWELVE SECTORS

Millions of U.S. Dollars

Sector	2012 Flow	End of 2012 Stock
Total	87,803.5	531,940.6
Leasing and Business Services	26,740.8	175,698.0
Financial Intermediation	10,070.8	96,453.4
Mining	13,543.8	74,784.2
Wholesale and Retail Trades	13,048.5	68,211.9
Manufacturing	8,667.4	34,140.1
Transport, Storage and Post	2,988.1	29,226.5
Construction	3,245.4	12,856.0
Real Estate	2,018.1	9,581.4
Electricity, Heat, Gas and Water	1,935.3	8,992.1
Scientific Res. and Tech. Scvs.	1,478.5	6,792.8
Agriculture, Forestry, Fishery	1,461.4	4,964.4
Software, Information Tech.	1,240.1	4,819.7

Source: China Statistical Yearbook, 2013, Table 6-19.

Destination Countries and Economies

In 2012, the recipient countries or economies for the PRC's official data on its stock of outbound direct investment of $531 billion were topped by Hong Kong at $306 billion, the United States at $17 billion and Australia at $14 billion. (See **Table $13.2**) The PRC also reported investments in the Virgin and Cayman Islands at $61 billion. Most of the investments in these tax havens as well as some of the investments in Hong Kong have to be discounted for funds that originated in China but were round tripped back to the PRC in order to qualify as foreign investment so that the investing enterprise could take advantage of special incentives and protections accorded foreign investors. A considerable portion of these outbound investments was merely the first leg of this circuitous route. For Hong Kong, separating out the funds that were "round tripped" from those that were legitimate direct investments would be very difficult.

The PRC data in **Table 13.2** also show that the flows of net outward direct investments in 2012 went to Asia ($64.8 billion) of which Hong Kong received $51.2 billion, to Europe ($7.0 billion), to Latin America ($6.2 billion) of which $3.1 billion went to the Cayman and Virgin Islands, to North America ($4.9 billion), to Africa ($2.5 billion) and to Oceania ($2.4 billion). After Hong Kong and the Cayman/Virgin Islands, the largest destination countries were Australia at $2.2 billion, Singapore at $1.5 billion and Indonesia at $1.4 billion.

Dick K. Nanto

TABLE 13.2. PRC's OUTWARD DIRECT INVESTMENTS BY COUNTRY/ECONOMY

Millions of U.S. Dollars

Country or Region	Official PRC Data		Heritage F.
	2012 Flows	End of 2012 Stock	2005-June 2013
Total	87,803.5	531,940.6	430,430
Asia	64,784.9	364,407.1	75,410
Hong Kong	51,238.4	306,372.5	0
Indonesia	1,361.3	3,098.0	14,050
Japan	210.7	1,619.9	1,520
Singapore	1,518.8	12,383.3	7,510
Republic of Korea	942.4	3,081.9	2,120
Thailand	478.6	2,126.9	2,740
Vietnam	349.4	1,604.4	460
Africa	2,516.7	21,729.7	57,110
Nigeria	333.1	1,949.9	8,000
South Africa	-814.9	4,775.1	8,740
Europe	7,035.1	36,975.1	92,300
United Kingdom	2,774.7	8,934.3	17,840
Germany	799.3	3,104.4	4,910
France	153.9	3,950.8	9,230
Russia	784.6	4,888.5	15,630
Latin America	6,169.7	68,211.6	57,270
Cayman/Virgin Is.	3,066.7	60,923.0	0
Brazil	n.a.	n.a.	25,810
Argentina	n.a.	n.a.	9,200
North America	4,882.0	25,503.0	91,240
Canada	795.2	5,050.7	37,430
United States	4,047.9	17,079.8	53,810
Oceania	2,415.1	15,114.1	57,100
Australia	2,173.0	13,873.1	55,900

Sources: *China Statistical Yearbook* 2013, Table 6-18. Heritage Foundation data include only those projects valued at more than $100 million. <http://www.heritage.org/research/projects/china-global -investment-tracker-interactive-map>

254

According to the Heritage Foundation dataset of major investments by project, the leading recipients of Chinese outward investment between 2005 and June 2013 were Australia and the United States. Other major recipients were Canada, Brazil, Britain, Indonesia, and Singapore. In 2012, the China National Offshore Oil Corporation's (CNOOC) $15.1 billion acquisition of Nexen of Canada, pushed Canada to the top of the list of recipient countries in that year. The United States also received a record $14 billion in Chinese investments which made North America the top destination for Chinese outward investments for that year.

The prominence of North America as a destination for outward investments in 2012 extends a pattern. Chinese enterprises have shown a clear tendency to move in packs. Large-scale investment started in Australia in the middle of the first decade of the twenty-first century. Sub-Saharan Africa received a rush of investment at the end of the decade. Then it was South America's turn in 2010-11. The focus then turned to North America. Now it appears that Europe and the oil-producing countries in the Middle East are to take their turn as destinations for the pack.[385]

One reason for the pack mentality is in the nature of state-owned enterprises. A senior director involved with outbound investment at a PRC financial institution explained the problem as follows. He said that the people expect large and politically powerful SOEs to lead Chinese outbound investment. He noted, however, that the managers of many of the SOEs are basically party politicians, not experienced business managers. They do not know what they want, have no strategy and change their ideas all the time. Their decision-making process is unclear, and there constantly are new people emerging in the decision-making process. He also noted that very few SOEs have structures or formal processes for international investment. At times, this leads to total improvisation with sudden changes. Without formal procedures, companies often revert to going with the pack. Chinese managers also tend to have unrealistic expectations: at the beginning they are very aggressive and want the sky, but in the end they want guarantees and no downside risk. The SOE system does not reward individuals for success, but punishes mistakes very aggressively.[386] For politically-motivated managers, there is less risk in investing overseas when the government says to go global, and they follow the pack in doing so.

Although most of the early investments overseas were by Chinese state-owned enterprises and the PRC's sovereign wealth funds, recently more private firms have also gone global. One reason is that many privately-held firms have become public and through sales of stock now have ample reserves of cash to deploy. Also, even though the rapidly-growing Chinese economy generates rising revenues and profits and is a stable home base, competition is intense and market position at home is not secure. Companies need to expand, and where else to go but abroad. For their own well-being, moreover, privately-held companies also give heed to government advice and look to SOEs for direction.

Investments in Australia

Over the 2005-June 2013 period, China invested $58.2 billion in Australia in major projects according to the Heritage Foundation data. The main attraction of Australia for China, in addition to proximity, has been in metals and energy. Of the 60 major investments in Australia, 25 ($29.7 billion) were in metals; 25 ($24.4 billion) were in energy, 4 ($1.5 billion) in agriculture, 2 each in finance and real estate, and 1 each in shipping and chemicals. Some of the notable investments were the 2006 investment by CITIC of $2.9 billion in Mineralogy, a mining and steel production company and the 2009 investment by Yanzhou Coal of $2.9 billion in Felix Resources Energy in coal production. However, the largest and most controversial has been the attempt by Chinalco (Aluminum Corporation of China) to acquire part of Rio Tinto, a maker of aluminum and exporter of iron ore.

In 2008, Chinalco invested $14.0 billion for a nine percent share of Rio Tinto. This followed Rio Tinto's acquisition of Alcan (Aluminium Company of Canada) in 2007 that had left Rio with $34 billion in debt. There also was a failed attempt to take over Rio Tinto by BHP Billiton a British-Australian resources company. In February 2009 in the depths of the global recession, Chinalco offered to double its stake in Rio Tinto and gain two seats on its board for $19.5 billion. Chinalco's bid was financed partly by loans from state-owned banks that were 3 percentage points below market interest rates and amounted to an implicit subsidy of $538 million annually.[387] At the time, Rio's share price had dropped so much that the offer looked promising. As the review by the Australian government dragged on, however, stock prices began to recover and the offer became less and less attractive. Other issues, such as ownership of key natural resources by China, the low interest rate being charged by Chinese state-owned banks to finance the investment, and the role played by the Chinese government in pushing the deal raised several red flags on the Australian side. On June 5, 2009, shareholders rejected Chinalco's offer even though the company had to pay a $195 million escape fine.[388] In what was seen as more than a coincidence, a month later on July 5, 2009, the PRC arrested four staff members of Rio Tinto's Shanghai office on charges of espionage and bribery. They were sentenced in 2010 to prison time, but this incident raised questions over whether the arrests were a form of retribution for the rejected bid.

Shutting the prison doors on the Rio Tinto executives, however, did not shutter the Chinalco-Rio Tinto relationship. In 2011, the two entered into a joint venture to explore for mineral deposits in the PRC, and in 2012, they formed a joint venture to develop and operate the Simandou iron ore project in West Africa.[389] The African joint venture represented a line of strategy followed by several Chinese companies. For PRC enterprises attempting to go global, partnering with a foreign transnational corporation with wide experience in global markets, such as Rio Tinto, provides a better mapped path for entering unfamiliar ground. It not only gives them access to experience and expertise, but it helps to avoid quicksand traps and other obstacles made worse by the weight of the baggage that China's national champion companies carry.

Investment in the United States

As for the United States, between 2005 and June 2013, according to the Heritage Foundation dataset, China had invested $53.8 billion in the U.S. economy despite the political pressure in 2005 that compelled the China National Offshore Oil Corporation (CNOOC) to withdraw its $18.5 billion bid to acquire the American oil company, Unocal. The Heritage Foundation included the $4.7 billion acquisition by Shuanghui International Holdings of Smithfield Foods that was under review in 2013 and eventually approved.

According to official U.S. data, in 2011, the total asset value of majority-owned U.S. affiliates in which China was the beneficial owner[390] totaled $52.6 billion. In order to be counted as foreign direct investment, U.S. data collection rules require control of companies and do not include smaller investments by Chinese companies in which they do not gain control even though the relationship might provide other benefits to the investing company. According to U.S. data, these majority-owned affiliates employed 13,200 people in 2011 and generated losses of $214 million for the owners.[391]

However, according to U.S. data, the foreign direct investment position (net total investment) for the PRC in the U.S. economy was considerably smaller than either the total asset value of Chinese majority-owned U.S. affiliates, the figures reported by China or those compiled by the Heritage Foundation. Official U.S. data show that China's foreign direct investment position in the United States was $3.6 billion in 2011 and $9.5 billion in 2015.[392] This $9.5 billion was considerably less than the $17.1 billion for 2012 reported by China or the $53.8 billion for 2013 compiled by the Heritage Foundation. It also was much lower than the $36.0 billion reported in U.S. statistics for South Korea or $372.8 billion for Japan. It seems to be far below what would be expected given the many large investments by Chinese companies in the United States. Why the official numbers from the Department of Commerce are so low is a mystery even to professionals in the field.

According to the Heritage Foundation dataset, nearly half of China's investments in the United States were in finance ($20.3 billion). Most of these investments, however, were made by China Investment Corporation, one of the PRC's sovereign wealth funds. Among the CIC's investments were $6.2 billion in Morgan Stanley, $3.2 billion in Blackstone, and $3.2 billion in the J.C. Flowers Fund managed by J.C. Flowers, a private equity investment firm focused on investments in the financial services sector.

The PRC's other sovereign wealth fund, SAFE Investment Company, also has invested in the U.S. financial sector. It had $2.5 billion in the private equity group TPG and had invested $1.5 billion to purchase some private equity positions in General Motors' pension plan. Purely financial investments, however, are not counted as foreign direct investment.

China also has invested $12.5 billion in U.S. energy companies, including a $2.4 billion investment by Sinopec (China Petrochemical Corporation) in Devon Energy, $2.4 billion by CNOOC in Chesapeake Energy, and $1.6 billion by CIC in the AES Corporation. In addition, PRC investors have put $5.8 billion in U.S. real estate, $3.0 billion in technology (including the $1.7 billion purchase in 2005 by Lenovo of IMB's personal computer business) and $4.3 billion in other sectors (such as Dalian Wanda's $2.6 billion purchase of AMC Entertainment).

The more visible Chinese investments in the United States have been met with a firestorm of criticism and political opposition. The attempted lease in 1996 by the China Ocean Shipping Company (Cosco) of port facilities at a former U.S. naval base in Long Beach, California, raised questions of U.S. national security, gun smuggling, weapons proliferation, and the general issue of Chinese control over critical U.S. infrastructure. Proponents of the deal pointed out that Cosco had been using the port since 1981 and its ships were welcomed at other U.S. ports, even in Norfolk, Virginia, home to a large U.S. naval base.[393] The proposed lease eventually was cancelled, although Cosco continued its quest and in 2001 formed Pacific Maritime Services with joint venture partner Stevedoring Services of America to operate the largest specialized container terminal in North America. Located in Long Beach and complete with 15 gantry cranes and 5 berths, the terminal serves container vessels owned primarily by Cosco but also by other parties.[394]

The 2005 bid by the China National Offshore Oil Corporation (CNOOC) to acquire the U.S. energy company Unocal for $18.5 billion generated a blizzard of criticism from the public and policymakers. At issue was Chinese ownership of critical U.S. energy resources, the backing of CNOOC by the PRC government and its banks and various security issues. A review by the Committee on Foreign Investment in the United States (CFIUS) presumably centered on whether a company that is majority-owned by the PRC—a country some viewed as a potential military threat—should be allowed to acquire American assets that include vital energy supplies, dual use technology, and access to sensitive geographical locations. The withdrawal of the bid by CNOOC stopped formal action against the proposed acquisition, but it left unanswered most of the questions raised by the bid.[395]

The U.S. government has placed the Chinese maker of electronic communications equipment Huawei Technologies under close watch and has confronted it in several ways. In 2007, Huawei and Bain Capital (a U.S. private-equity firm) attempted to acquire 3Com, a U.S. telecommunications company, for $2.2 billion. Although Huawei would have held a passive 16.5% stake in 3Com, with Bain holding the rest, the deal collapsed a year later after doubts that CFIUS would approve the acquisition. In Congress, Representative Duncan Hunter in welcoming the decision to scuttle the merger stated that the proposed transaction "was a bad deal for American security," but also a harbinger of challenges facing the government, as China, awash in capital, continues to look to the United States for acquisition opportunities.[396]

In 2011, Huawei dropped its attempt to acquire the remaining assets of 3Leaf, a failing Silicon Valley virtualization and cloud computing company, after receiving negative signals from CFIUS.[397] In essence, Huawei has effectively been banned on national security grounds from acquiring any U.S. telecommunications company or even supplying major pieces of equipment to them. U.S. companies have to think twice about importing equipment from Huawei.

Investments in Canada

In Canada, Chinese investments pose little threat to Canadian national security but are important for the PRC's energy security. According to the Heritage Foundation, from 2005 to June 2013, China's investments in Canada totaled $37.5 billion. This included the CNOOC acquisition of Nexen in 2012-13 for $15.1 billion. Through the deal, CNOOC gained control of Nexen's Long Lake oil sands project in Alberta province as well as production in the North Sea, the Gulf of Mexico, western Africa, the Middle East, and other places in Canada. The Canadian government approved the takeover even though some members of the ruling Conservative Party had misgivings about it. The government indicated that the CNOOC-Nexen deal was the last of its kind and that it would not approve any more state-controlled companies taking majority stakes in the oil sands.[398]

Of China's 28 major investments in Canada, 14 have been in energy, particularly petroleum. Other investments include $3.3 billion in metals and $0.4 billion in agriculture.

Investments in Europe

With respect to Europe, Chinese consumers love European luxury brand goods, and Chinese companies with money to invest are seeing Europe not just as the greatest outdoor museum in the world but also a great place to make money. Early investments were in offices to procure goods and collect market intelligence, but PRC businesses are now looking to buy into companies that provide synergism at home and earning opportunities abroad. Major PRC investments in Europe (including Eastern Europe) totaled $92.3 billion over the 2005-June 2013 period and were spread across the continent. The recipient countries with the largest amounts were the U.K. with $17.8 billion, France with $9.2 billion, Switzerland with $8.2 billion, Germany with $4.9 billion and Portugal with $4.0 billion. In Eastern Europe, Russia received $17.0 billion and Kazakhstan $10.0 billion.

Great Britain once ruled a quarter of the world with an empire far flung and upon which investors could set even if the sun could not. British investments followed in the wake of the British navy. Now the United Kingdom is as much a recipient of foreign investment as it is a provider. The Chinese once saw British foreign devils off their shores; now Chinese have arrived in the Britain. About 500 Chinese companies are operating in the United Kingdom. Since 2005, major Chinese investments have totaled $17.8 billion. Still, the Chinese presence is relatively small. Official British government statistics show that in 2011, out of a total of $1,200 billion in foreign direct investment in the U.K., the PRC plus Hong Kong accounted for $33.3 billion, or less than 3 percent. Foreign investment in the U.K. is dominated by that from the United States, other European countries and Canada. Some notable Chinese investments include $3.0 billion by the China Development Bank in Barclays Bank, $2.0 billion by SAFE in British Petroleum and $1.5 billion by Sinopec in Talisman Energy.

The British citizenry, however, became somewhat exercised over several Chinese investments, such as Dalian Wanda's purchase of Sunseeker, the upscale yacht maker, and its investment of $1 billion to build a luxury hotel in London. Dalian Wanda is a conglomerate company with activities in real estate, tourism, hotels and entertainment. These investments came on the heels of the $0.9 billion purchase by CIC, the sovereign wealth fund, of Thames Water (London's largest water utility) and a $0.7 billion purchase of a 10 percent interest in Heathrow Airport—two critical components of London's infrastructure. The $1.9 billion purchase by China's Bright Foods of Weetabix in 2012 was ironic, since Weetabix's slogan has been "Real British Wheat, Real British Farmers, Real British Values." Are they to add a fourth line of "Real Chinese Owners"?

France has traditionally been suspicious of Chinese investment in the country. The attitude has been to say no first and then perhaps to reconsider. Recently, however, the attitude has shifted somewhat. France still will look carefully at acquisitions of French companies by Chinese investors in order to keep some strategic interests in French hands, but in the end, the French government's view ostensibly is that Chinese investments are welcome.[399] Chinese companies seem to be investing to seek access to the French and European markets, although strategic asset-seeking motivations also prevail. A major fear is that Chinese firms will attempt to reduce costs rather than to create jobs in France, but, in some cases, the Chinese investment has helped to revive an ailing French firm and has saved jobs.[400]

Of the $9.2 billion invested in France, the largest have been by China's sovereign wealth funds. The CIC invested $3.2 billion in GDF Suez (utilities), and SAFE invested $2.8 billion in Total (oil and gas). Chinese companies also have invested in French agriculture and chemicals. A leading investor has been China National Chemical Corporation through its subsidiary China National Bluestar Group. In 2006, it acquired the Adisseo Group, a global leader in animal nutrition feed, for $0.48 billion and Rhodia's organic silicon business, including its patents, manufacturing equipment, and distribution channels, as well as the company's sulphide business, for $0.7 billion.

Some recent investments in French providers of luxury goods have caught the public's attention. These include Fosun's purchase of Club Med and Chinese purchases of parts of Bordeaux vineyards. China has become Bordeaux's largest export market, and accordingly, Chinese (including some from Hong Kong) have bought about 20 Bordeau châteaux. Actress Zhao Wei bought a St. Emilion chateau while Shanghai Sugar Cigarette and Wine bought 70 percent of Diva Bordeaux, a wine trading company. The Chinese jewelry chain TESiRO purchased Château Laulan Ducos in Bordeaux in 2011 and sent the domain's entire production to China rather than preserving existing distribution deals.

One problem is that French vineyards seem relatively inexpensive to the growing number of Chinese wine connoisseurs. For example, in 2012, Hong Kong gambling tycoon Louis Ng of SJM Holdings purchased Château de Gevrey-Chambertin in Burgundy for €8 million (about $10 million). The acquisition included a 12th century château and five acres of vines. It stirred a backlash against foreign investments by some residents in Burgundy, as well as in greater France, partly because Ng's bid far exceeded the €5 million bid by group of local vintners and much more than the run-down property was considered to be worth. In addition to the property passing to outsiders, a fear was that the inflated price would raise inheritance taxes on all vineyards in an area where properties are passed from generation to generation. The president of the local union of wine producers said of Ng's acquisition, "It is a despoliation. Our heritage is going out of the window.... How would the Chinese feel if a French investor bought 10 meters, or 50 meters, of the Great Wall of China?"[401]

In Germany, China's $4.9 billion in major investments include the Chinese company Sany's acquisition of the German mid-sized company Putzmeister, a leading manufacturer of concrete pumps; Lenovo's takeover of the electronics company Medion; and Weichai Power's purchase of a stake in Kion, one of the world's largest forklift truck manufacturers. A study by the Technische Universität München and the Munich Innovation Group found that Chinese companies investing in Germany are being driven by a desire to gain access to state-of-the-art technology, but contrary to initial expectations, most of the new owners were not interested in draining their newly acquired companies of knowledge. Instead, the study found that the German affiliates and Chinese investing companies were collaborating in research and development. They also found that Chinese companies saw their investments as a way to expand their product portfolios, strengthen their position in China and gain a lasting foothold in Europe.[402]

In 1950, Switzerland was among the first Western nations to establish diplomatic relations with the PRC, and in 1980 the Swiss company Shiler Elevators was among the first to establish an industrial joint venture there. China has reciprocated by investing $8.2 billion in major projects in Switzerland. About 60 Chinese companies are reported to operate in the Swiss economy. They are primarily interested in energy, luxury goods (such as wristwatches and high-end hotels), metals, and commodities.[403] Major investments include Sinopec's acquisition of Addax Petroleum for $7.2 billion, and the Jinsheng Group's purchase of machine toolmaker Oerlikon for $0.7 billion.

As for Russia, no longer does Beijing look to that country for technology, trade and direction on how to grow a communist economy. In the economic calculus, Moscow is almost irrelevant, but the part of Russia that is directly north of the PRC beckons bountifully. For China, eastern Russia appears to be a cavernous caldron nearly bereft of people but packed with sources of power and space to live. Since military clashes over the Russo-Chinese border seem to be problems of the past, it seems almost natural that Chinese should be drawn into the great void that is eastern Russia. China also has traditional claims to parts of Siberia. The ethnic Russian population in this region is declining while the infrastructure to extract energy and natural resources is improving. China's economic power now dwarfs that of Russia, and many suspect that large-scale illegal Chinese immigration across the border into the Russian Far East already is occurring.[404] The PRC has more than a half billion people still crowded into its countryside. A good portion of the aspiring peasants plan to move to urban areas, but others long for their piece of the good earth, perhaps it could be a hectare or two up north that has been warmed enough, partly by China's CO_2 emissions, to enable farming.

Setting aside the questions of sovereignty and illegal immigration, Chinese oil companies have actively sought investment opportunities in Russian energy. Since 2005, of the $17 billion PRC companies have invested in Russia, $10.3 billion has been in energy. In 2006, Sinopec acquired Udmurtneft for $3.5 billion. Udmurtneft was a subsidiary of the energy company Rosneft and is the largest oil-producing enterprise in the Udmurt Republic. Sinopec and Rosneft also are partners in drilling for oil in the Sakhalin-3 project, an oil and gas development near Sakhalin Island. In 2010, China Yangtze Power Co., the country's largest listed hydropower corporation and operator of the Three Gorges Dam, invested $2.4 billion in an agreement with EuroSibEnergo, the largest privately-owned power company in Russia, to build power plants in eastern Siberia. In 2013, the State Grid Corporation of China, the largest electric utility company in the world, agreed with the Sintez Group, a privately held Russian company with diversified holdings in power, oil, and gas, to invest up to $1.1 billion to upgrade and build electricity power plants in Russia and to supply electricity to China. In 2014, Russia's Gazprom and the China National Petroleum Corporation signed a $400 billion contract for Russia to sell natural gas to the PRC. This was the largest natural gas deal Russia has sealed since the collapse of the Soviet Union. The contract runs for 30 years and calls for the construction of pipelines and other infrastructure that will require tens of billions of dollars in investment.[405] China also has invested in Russia's metals, automobile, transport, and finance industries.

It is ironic that Chinese complaints about investing in Russia echo those by foreign companies investing in the PRC. In Russia, Chinese companies have faced popular backlash and political hurdles. They also have been deterred by inefficient and corrupt Russian institutions and a lack of transparency. Instability in Russia and the increased risks it generates also have contributed to the lack of Chinese investment there.[406]

Chinese companies also are looking to the smaller European countries for technology, expertise, and opportunities for partnerships. The advantage of firms in such nations is that they have been compelled to find markets outside of their small domestic economies. They have been going global for a long time. In Sweden, for example, while Geeley Automobile's acquisition of Volvo has generated the most publicity, dozens of smaller investments have gone largely unnoticed. For example, in 2006, the Chinese medical giant Dongbai Biopharmaceutical set up manufacturing operations at Ferring Pharmaceuticals' old factory in Limhamn and took the name Rechon Life Science. Rechon now produces advanced medicines primarily for the European market. In 2011, DingLi Communications (a leading authority in wireless network diagnostics) acquired the Swedish company AmanziTel. DingLi then transferred its research and development resources to AmanziTel and is using the company to sell products, services, and solutions throughout the world for a range of data networks. The communications technology giant Huawei has established R&D centers in Stockholm, Gothenburg, and in the university town of Lund. Its goal there is to build up world-leading competence in modern technology for cellular systems. The Lund region is well known for its skill in the consumer side of telecommunications and takes advantage of talent and research activity in universities in Lund, Malmö and Denmark.

Some European countries actively court Chinese investment. Those with the largest investment promotion authorities have been France, Germany and the U.K., and each has successfully facilitated investments from the PRC. In addition, relatively smaller countries with correspondingly smaller budgets for investment promotion, such as Sweden, also have been successful.[407] Sweden's government has established a Sino-Swedish innovation fund aimed at promoting Chinese direct investment into what is called Future Position X, a cluster of some 200 innovative technology companies in Gävle. The fund also provides resources for Swedish companies to expand into the China market. The Future Position X technology cluster was incubated and funded through a mixture of Swedish federal government grants and Swedish high-net-worth investors. The Sino-Swedish innovation fund focuses on commercialization and cross-border market expansion of geographic data management systems and knowledge-enabling technologies. The intent is to invest in sectors critical to sustainable urbanization, including healthcare and wellness, knowledge infrastructure and data management of smart cities, and environmentally-friendly and energy efficient technologies.[408]

Other Countries

China's quest for supplies of energy has taken its investors to oil- and coal-rich countries. Since 2005, PRC companies have spent $202.0 billion in 152 direct investments in energy. Of these, 52 were in oil, 24 in gas, 20 in coal, and 17 in alternative energy. In Indonesia, of the 17 major investments worth $14.0 billion, eight were in energy, particularly coal and petroleum. Kazakhstan has received $10.0 billion for six Chinese investments, of which five were in energy. The largest among these were China National

Petroleum Corporation's $4.2 billion acquisition of PetroKazakhstan and $2.6 billion investment in Central Asia Petroleum. Nigeria received $8.0 billion in investments in energy including a $2.2 billion investment by CNOOC in South African Petroleum and a $2.5 billion purchase by Sinopec from Total of an oil exploration project.

Brazil's more diversified economy has attracted a wider variety of Chinese investments, but energy also has been a major draw. Most Chinese investment in Brazil began in 2010, when Brazil received an unprecedented $13.09 billion from PRC companies. In 2010, six of China's national champion companies, including Sinopec, Sinochem, and Wuhan Iron and Steel Group, entered Brazil with the aim to expand and facilitate commodity exports. Most of the investment was concentrated in extractive industries, sources of critical natural resources. Since then, Brazil adopted a stricter mining code and reinterpreted a land-purchasing law that restricts foreign land acquisition. This action has turned Chinese investors away from natural resource extraction toward market-seeking investments in Brazil's industrial and service sectors.[409]

Of the $25.8 billion in Chinese investments in Brazil during the 2005-June 2013 period, $16.8 billion was in energy, including electrical power transmission. Of these, Sinopec's $7.0 billion in Repsol and $4.8 billion investment in Galp Energia were notable. China's State Grid also invested $0.9 billion in Brazil's Plena Transmissoras and for $1.0 billion bought seven power transmission lines in Brazil from ACS (Actividades de Construccion & Servicios SA), a Spanish construction company. The Sinochem Group also invested $3.1 billion in Statoil.

For Singapore, a nation that received $8 billion in Chinese investments, the attraction for China has been two-fold. The first has been the favorable business climate and the majority population of ethnic Chinese already dominating the economy there. The second has been the PRC-Singapore Free Trade Agreement. Among its provisions, the free-trade agreement provides for greater access for each country into the banking system of the other. In 2012, Singapore granted full banking licenses to two Chinese banks, the Bank of China and the Industrial and Commercial Bank of China. Each is permitted to open as many as 25 branches and offer services, including accepting retail deposits in Singapore. Of the 116 foreign banks operating in Singapore, only 8 previously had attained the status of being a qualified full bank.[410]

In addition, many wealthy Chinese are diversifying their assets overseas by moving accounts to Singapore. In 2010, Singapore held an estimated $512 billion of private-banking assets, the largest pool of such cash in Asia. Singapore's banks also are becoming sources of finance for wealthy Chinese who are buying private airplanes and yachts as well as speculating in stock markets. Aircraft usually cost between $20 million and $40 million while luxury yachts can cost up to $100 million.[411]

One of the reasons for financing private aircraft by banks in countries, such as Singapore, is that Beijing is just opening its airspace to civil aviation. The skies over the PRC have heretofore been the private domain of the military. Commercial airlines fly only with permission from the military. Private aircraft have had to be based in places such as Hong Kong and Singapore. Some even have had to be flown periodically to the United States for maintenance. China has approached the establishment of civil aviation by hiring consulting companies from the United States to provide training, operating manuals, and other instruction for Chinese authorities.

The PRC so far has invested relatively little in Japan or South Korea. From 2005-June 2013, China had invested $1.5 billion in Japan, of which nearly $1 billion was by the CIC, China's sovereign wealth fund. The PRC had invested $2.1 billion in South Korea, of which $1.8 billion was in real estate.

The rising costs of manufacturing in China is causing even China's companies to look at establishing new manufacturing facilities in countries, such as Vietnam, Indonesia, Bangladesh, Mexico and Brazil. However, according to a business acquaintance in Hong Kong, trying to cut costs by manufacturing in a less developed Asian country, such as Vietnam, Indonesia or Bangladesh poses its own problems. Labor usually is cheaper, but parts and components often are not available locally and have to be imported from China. One Japanese company with a garment factory in Vietnam found that even if it buys packing cartons from Bangladesh or sewing thread from Indonesia, much of the raw material for those inputs still comes from China. The lesser-developed Asian countries also lack industrial clusters, quality control methods and transportation networks.

Workers also tend to be less productive. A Chinese seamstress can sew about 180 T-shirts in a 12 hour shift. In Vietnam, Bangladesh and Indonesia, productivity is about 60 percent of that in China and about 40 percent of that in the Philippines.

Country Responses to Chinese Outbound Investments

The world reaction to the Chinese presence in local economies has been mixed. Some countries are facilitating that investment, some are passive bystanders and letting it happen, and some are actively resisting it through the political process. Since the PRC is a member of the World Trade Organization, outright discrimination against Chinese investment would violate the WTO rules, but countries are able to block certain types of investments, particularly if they are subsidized by state-owned banks, and they can deny potential investments that threaten national security. At times, public opinion and political backlash has deterred investments even without official government action.

The treatment some PRC investors receive is like the experience of one of my college history professors who had visited China during the 1960s. He had taken the Trans-Siberian Railroad across Russia before traveling south by bus to Beijing. In northern China, the bus stopped in a small village. The professor needed to use the toilet but could not find one, so he asked where he could do his business. A villager told him to go to a nearby empty lot, make a pile of stones, and accomplish the task while squatting behind the stones. He wondered what the stones were for, but thought they must be related to some local custom. The pile certainly was not enough to shield him from view. So he found a good handful of small stones, put them in front of him and began to defecate. As soon as the odor wafted through the air, a hungry pig came running to where he was squatting. The pig was intent on having dinner. Then the professor realized what the stones were for. He tossed them at the pig and kept it at bay long enough to finish his business.

Chinese investors certainly are not pigs, but sometimes they are treated as though they are hogging some of the best investments with the advantage provided by financial backing from state-controlled banks. Others may resent their sniffing around and swooping in on damaged or sensitive assets.

As a result, some countries have developed piles of stones to toss at PRC investors to keep them at bay.

According to the Heritage Foundation database of China's troubled investments, since 2005 there have been 110 potential investments that ran into problems because of commercial considerations or difficulties obtaining approvals. As might be expected, most have been in the sectors in which the PRC has invested most heavily. Of the 110 troubled transactions, 33 were in metals, 29 in energy, 14 in transportation (including autos), 11 in finance, 10 in real estate, 8 in technology, and 5 in agriculture. By country, Chinese investors encountered the most resistance in Australia with 20 cases and in the United States with 19 cases.

Australian Resistance

In Australia, the problem with Chinese investments can be summarized by the results of a 2013 Lowy Institute poll.[412] According to the poll, Australians view the PRC through a strategic lens as one point of the Australia-United States-China triangle. Seventy-six percent of those polled saw China as the most important economy to Australia. This was far more than the 16 percent who saw the U.S. economy as the most important. Australians, however, considered their relationship with the United States as being more valuable than that with the PRC. When they see the prospect of strategic competition between the United States and a rising China, they wonder if it is possible to maintain good relations with both nations. Australians seem to understand that if these two giants get into a fight, some innocent bystanders will get trampled. They do not want to be one of the little guys who gets stomped on by the giants.

The majority of poll respondents (61%) agreed that China will eventually replace the United States as the world's leading superpower. Fifty-seven percent of Australians considered that their government was allowing too much investment from China, and a significant minority (41%) thought it likely that China would become a military threat to Australia in the ensuing 20 years.

Underlying the strategic aspect are problems with Chinese perceptions of a lack of trust and even discrimination against them in Australia. This has arisen partly from the additional Australian government scrutiny of

Chinese government-related investment through its Foreign Investment Review Board (FIRB). Under Australian law, all foreign government investors must notify the Australian government and obtain prior approval before making a direct investment in the country, regardless of the value of the investment. The same holds for starting a new business or acquiring an interest in land, including any interest in a prospecting, exploration, mining or production company. This poses a problem for the PRC's state-owned enterprises, companies that are considered to be foreign government investors. Also, privately-owned foreign businesses must notify the government and receive prior approval before acquiring a substantial interest in a corporation or control of an Australian business that is valued above $230 million. (For Americans and Australians, the threshold is $1,002 million). Australia also restricts foreign investments in media, airlines, airports, banks, the telecommunications company Telstra and real estate.[13] Among the general public, there has been particular resistance to Chinese purchases of Australian natural resources and farmland.

Beginning in 2008, a number of high-profile Chinese investment proposals were either blocked or were substantially modified by the Australian government following FIRB advice. The government also has established additional criteria for the FIRB to consider when assessing applications from state-owned enterprises and sovereign wealth funds. These include the investor's independence from government; whether the investor has clear commercial objectives; corporate governance practices; and whether an investment may hinder competition or lead to undue concentration and control.

Among the 20 troubled cases of Chinese investment in Australia, 16 were in metals (of which 6 were in steel and 3 in aluminum), 2 were in agriculture, and 2 in energy. In addition to the failed $19.5 billion Chinalco bid for Rio Tinto (a metals and mining company) were a $5.4 billion bid by CITIC in metals; a $2.0 billion attempt by Sinosteel in steel; a $1.5 billion attempt by Bright Foods to acquire CSR's Sugar and Renewable Energy business, Sucrogen; and a $1.3 billion bid by China National Chemical Corporation (ChemChina) for Nufarm, Australia's leading producer of crop protection chemicals (herbicides and pesticides).

Of course, even after investments are approved, they have not always gone well for the Chinese owners. Investment plans are like battle plans. They are good only until the first encounter. Both the project itself and the government can destroy even the most realistic cost estimates. For example, CITIC Pacific, a Hong Kong subsidiary of the CITIC Group (formerly China International Trust and Investment Corporation), committed $3.5 billion for the Sino Iron mine project to build a greenfield plant in Pilbara, a sparsely inhabited wasteland in northwest Australia. The area is so barren and remote that it is used by the U.S. space agency NASA to simulate surface conditions on Mars. The project ran into huge cost overruns as CITIC not only had to build facilities to process and ship ore to its steel mills in China but also had to build electricity generating and desalination plants. The remote location also required that CITIC fly skilled labor in to work on constructing the mine facilities. Australian immigration refused to approve work visas for Chinese to labor in the mine as is had been done in projects elsewhere, particularly in Africa. The cost for as many as 4,000 fly-in-fly-out Australian workers averaged $230,000 per person per year. Even Australian janitors there earned a base pay of $75,000 plus the cost of housing and transportation.[414]

Huawei has come under special scrutiny by the FIRB. Citing security concerns, in 2012 the Australian government blocked Huawei from bidding on contracts in the $38 billion Australian National Broadband Network being planned. This network was intended to connect 93 percent of homes and workplaces with fiber-optic cable, thereby providing broadband service in rural as well as urban areas.[415]

U.S. Resistance

In the United States, certain Chinese investments also have been blocked primarily because of national security concerns. Of the 19 troubled transactions, 7 were in finance, 5 in technology, and 4 in energy. The largest was the proposed $18.0 billion acquisition of the U.S. oil company Unocal by CNOOC, the China National Offshore Oil Corporation. Four of the five attempted investments in technology were by Huawei, including the $5 billion bid by Huawei and ZTE for Sprint.

Official assessments of national security risk are done by the Committee on Foreign Investment in the United States (CFIUS), a multi-member board headed by the Secretary of the Treasury. It has discretionary authority to review any merger, acquisition, or takeover of an American company by or with a foreign entity which could have an impact upon U.S. national security. CFIUS considers factors such as domestic production needed for national defense requirements and the control of domestic industries and commercial activity by foreign citizens as it affects the capability and capacity of the U.S. to meet the requirements of national security. It also considers the potential effects of the proposed transaction on U.S. international technological leadership in areas affecting national security. CFIUS makes recommendations to the President, who has the authority to block the merger, acquisition, or takeover. Often proposed transactions will be dropped during the initial 30-day period of review or later during the formal CFIUS investigation. After being informed of national security concerns, the acquiring company may enter into mitigation agreements with CFIUS, such as divesting sensitive parts of a company to be acquired, in order for the transaction to receive approval.

CFIUS was established in 1975 by an Executive Order by President Gerald R. Ford out of concern over the rapid increase in investments by the Organization of the Petroleum Exporting Countries (OPEC) in American portfolio assets (Treasury securities, corporate stocks and bonds), and to respond to concerns of some that many of the OPEC investments were being driven by political rather than by economic purposes. Over the ensuing five years, however, CIFIUS met only 10 times and could not decide whether political or economic criteria should bear sway in determining whether a particular investment posed a threat to U.S. national security.[416]

In the 1980s, several disputes erupted over acquisitions of U.S. companies and properties by investors from Japan. One case that drew particular attention was the proposed sale in 1987 of Fairchild Semiconductor Co. by Schlumberger Ltd. of France to Fujitsu Ltd. of Japan. The proposed acquisition came at a time of high tensions in U.S.-Japan trade relations and a dour mood among many Americans who feared that such purchases of companies were evidence that the United States was declining as an international economic power. The book, *Japan as Number One,* by Ezra Vogel, had been published in 1979, and Japanese management and quality control were the rage among the business cognoscenti. Even though Fairchild Semiconductor already was owned by a European company, the Defense Department opposed the deal because some officials believed that the acquisition would give Japan control over a major supplier of computer chips for the military and would make U.S. defense industries more dependent on foreign suppliers for sophisticated high-technology products.

In 1988, after intense debate, Congress passed and President Ronald Reagan signed the Omnibus Trade and Competitiveness Act of 1988, which contained the so-called Exon-Florio provision. The provision arose out of concern that foreign takeovers of firms could not be stopped unless the President declared a national emergency or regulators invoked federal antitrust, environmental or securities laws. Through Exon-Florio, Congress attempted to strengthen the President's hand in conducting foreign investment policy while limiting its own role as a means of emphasizing that, as much as possible, the commercial nature of investment transactions should be free the from political considerations. CFIUS, however, was not able to establish an independent approach to reviewing foreign investment transactions, since it operates under the authority of the President and reflects his policy guidance.

In 1990, President George H.W. Bush, using the authority granted under the Exon-Florio provision, directed the China National Aero-Technology Import and Export Corporation (CATIC, a company owned by the PRC's Ministry of Aerospace Industry) to divest its acquisition of MAMCO Manufacturing, a Seattle-based firm producing metal parts and assemblies for aircraft. The main concern was that CATIC might gain access to technology that could be used by the Chinese military.[417]

After the terrorist attacks of September 11, 2001, Congress again strengthened CFIUS and broadened its mandate to include U.S. critical infrastructure in considerations of national security. In 2007, the Foreign Investment and National Security Act of 2007 (FINSA) was signed into law. It maintained the narrow scope (genuine national security concerns, not broader policy interests) and timeline of CFIUS's review process, broadened membership in the committee, increased senior-level accountability and added to the illustrative list of national security factors for CFIUS and the President to consider.[418]

Currently, CFIUS applies a three-part national security analysis to each transaction that it reviews: (i) threat analysis: does the acquirer have the ability or intent to exploit or cause harm; (ii) vulnerability analysis: does the target U.S. business have a relationship to any weakness or shortcoming in the U.S. national defense or any susceptibility to impairment of U.S. national security; and (iii) risk analysis: what are the consequences if threat and vulnerability interact as the result of a particular transaction? As a result of this risk analysis, if CFIUS concludes the transaction threatens national security, CFIUS may enter into so-called mitigation agreements with the parties to the transaction. Mitigation agreements provide conditions on the transaction to address the national security risks and may include a mix of governance measures, security requirements, or monitoring and verification mechanisms. From 2009 through 2011, roughly eight percent of all cases reviewed by CFIUS resulted in the use of legally binding mitigation measures.[419]

As shown in **Table 13.3**, over the period from 2008 to 2013, CFIUS received a total of 480 notices of foreign investment transactions. During the review stage, 17 of these were withdrawn and 193 investigations were conducted. During the investigations, 38 more notices were withdrawn. There was one transaction by the Ralls Corporation that resulted in a Presidential decision during the period. The President ordered this deal to be undone.

In most cases, discussions between the companies involved in a transaction that probably will result in a negative assessment by CFIUS are sufficient to induce the companies to abandon or restructure the transaction. In recent cases, the potential of a future military conflict with China looms so large in considerations of U.S. national security that if a Chinese company sought to acquire a property within 50 miles of a U.S. military facility in which weapons or other testing can be seen from outside the facility, the transaction could be blocked. For example, in December 2009, Northwest Ferrous International Investment Company, a Chinese government-controlled company, abandoned its acquisition of a 51 percent interest in the Firstgold Corporation and its Nevada gold mine after

CFIUS recommended blocking the transaction because it involved assets located within 50 miles of the Naval Air Station Fallon in Nevada. This Navy site is a major training facility where pilots test laser-guided weapons.

TABLE 13.3. FOREIGN INVESTMENT TRANSACTIONS REVIEWED BY CFIUS, 2008-13

Year	Number of Notices	Notices Withdrawn during Review	Number of Investigations	Notices Withdrawn during Investigations	Presidential Decisions
2008	155	18	23	5	0
2009	65	5	25	2	0
2010	93	6	35	6	0
2011	111	1	40	5	0
2012	114	2	45	20	1
2013	97	3	48	5	0
Total	635	35	216	43	1

Source: Committee on Foreign Investment in the United States, *Annual Report to Congress,* Report Period: CY 2013, Issued: February 2015, Public/ Unclassified Version, p. 3.

In May 2012, a CFIUS review forced Far East Golden Resources Group Ltd., a subsidiary of Chinese company Hybrid Kinetic, to divest its majority interest in Nevada Gold Holdings, Inc., a U.S. mining company also located near Naval Air Station Fallon. This action occurred nearly two years after the investment was made.

In June 2013, a CFIUS review compelled China's Procon Mining and Tunnelling, Ltd., along with its affiliate, the Chinese state-owned enterprise China National Machinery Industry Corporation, to sell its entire investment in Canada-based Lincoln Mining Corporation. Lincoln Mining's core mining operations were in Nevada near the Fallon Naval Air Station and in California near the Marine Corps Air Station Yuma.

In September 2012, the President blocked a bid by Ralls Corporation, which is owned by two executives of China's SANY Group, to build wind farms in Oregon. The Ralls Corporation is affiliated with a Chinese construction equipment company that manufactures wind turbines. In June 2012, CFIUS had contacted Ralls and requested that the firm file a voluntary notification to have its investment retroactively reviewed. After reviewing the acquisition, CFIUS recommended that Ralls stop operations until a complete investigation could be completed as a result of objections by the U.S. Navy over the placement of wind turbines near or within restricted Naval Weapons Systems Training Facility airspace where drones are tested. After a full investigation, CFIUS recommended that President Obama block the investment and imposed other requirements on Ralls to remove equipment it had installed.[420]

In some cases, U.S. national security concerns were mitigated by excluding key assets from being acquired by the Chinese or other foreign firm. In December 2012, a U.S. subsidiary of Chinese automotive parts manufacturer Wanxiang Group attempted to acquire the insolvent U.S. lithium ion battery manufacturer A123 Systems for roughly $257 million. A123 possessed U.S. government and military contracts and had developed new battery technologies, including new chemistries for battery packs used by U.S. soldiers. The company also had used a grant from the Department of Energy to build two manufacturing facilities in Michigan. Several members of Congress voiced opposition to the acquisition because it allegedly resulted in the transfer of taxpayer-funded sensitive technologies to a Chinese company. However, despite significant political opposition, CFIUS cleared the transaction in January 2013 after Wanxiang divested its military contracts to a small Illinois battery company, Navitas Systems, and took other mitigation measures.[421]

Even though investors from the PRC have received considerable scrutiny, other countries also have had to file their investments with CFIUS. Over the 2011-13 period, however, the greatest number of filings were from China. Of the total 322 covered transactions considered by CFIUS, 54 were from China, 49 were from the U.K. and 34 each from Canada and Japan. The number of covered transactions from China has been rising.

They increased from 4 in 2009, to 6 in 2010, to 10 in 2011, 23 in 2012 and 21 in 2013.[422]

In addition to CFIUS reviews, foreign investors are constrained by legislation that bars foreign direct investment in the United States in such industries as maritime, aircraft, banking, resources and power. Such restrictions are common in regulated sectors in other countries, including in the PRC.

Resistance to Chinese Investments

Chinese investments affect not only the individual companies involved but, in many cases, the nation as a whole. At first, there may be doubt and mistrust as to intentions. There also may be surprise that Chinese, traditionally thought of as poor laborers or small-time laundry and restaurant owners, should have the resources to take over major companies with long histories as bulwarks of economies. Still, Chinese investment may create or help retain much needed jobs in communities. In many cases, the companies are managed by local citizens and ownership becomes a non-issue.

At times, resistance to Chinese investment appears to be outright discrimination, particularly when similar investments from European companies are welcomed. In the United States, such cases may harken back to the Chinese Exclusion Act of 1882, the first significant law restricting immigration into the country. Congress passed the exclusion act to placate American workers who attributed unemployment and declining wages to Chinese laborers whom they also viewed as racially inferior.[423] In 1943 when China was an ally of the United States, Congress lifted the ban on Chinese immigration and citizenship and voted to allow up to 105 Chinese immigrants each year. From the Chinese point of view, therefore, it first was resistance to inflows of Chinese people and now it is opposition to inflows of Chinese capital.

In a survey of Chinese overseas investments by the Economist Intelligence Unit, one of the Chinese interviewees described problem in this way: "We do see an anti-Chinese sentiment developing in certain markets. As China becomes economically stronger, there is bound to be a sense of fear among countries that are current and former economic powers."

Another interviewee singled out the United States as one country it would avoid because of perceived prejudice there against Chinese investors. In the survey, 49 of the 110 respondents selected the United States as the hardest country in which to make acquisitions. Still, 39 percent of respondents said they would focus their outbound investment on North America, just behind the number (42%) saying they would focus on Asia. Africa was viewed as the easiest country in which to conduct mergers and acquisitions.[424]

Every society, however, tends to view newcomers with some suspicion, and xenophobia can also apply to those from other parts of the country. Even when trying to be hospitable, sometimes the words just do not come out right. In the 1980s in a public hearing on Japanese investment in the southern state of Georgia in the United States, one southern gentleman in trying to express his welcome to the Japanese automaker and conjuring up remembrances of the Northern carpetbaggers who came into the South after the Civil War exclaimed, "Well, I would rather have yellow than Yankee!"

More Going Global?

Chinese firms are becoming more mature and are gaining more experience in operating in different cultural and business environments. They definitely are going global. Some of their proposed investments have been burned by public resistance and national security concerns, but PRC enterprises are being pushed as well as pulled abroad. The Chinese economy is maturing, competition at home is intense, and the PRC government sees economic assets abroad as both means to build power in the international arena and to contribute to their own national security, particularly in securing stable supplies of energy and natural resources. Some investments have been opportunistic as the industrialized world dropped into recession in 2007-09 and Europe faced economic turmoil in 2011-12. During these periods, American and European companies became relatively cheap takeover targets badly in need of infusions of capital. Meanwhile the thriving PRC economy continued to generate profits for enterprises, and China's huge trade surplus continued to provide foreign exchange that needed to be invested somewhere.

National security concerns and public criticism of proposed deals remain critical factors in future Chinese investments. In the United States, investments that provide access by Chinese companies to critical U.S. infrastructure, particularly in ports and telecommunications systems as well as in high-technology industries have diverted some Chinese investors toward deals in Europe and in the developing world. Still, the United States remains a favorable destination for Chinese outward investments. PRC companies also are looking for deals that will fly under the political radar but still provide access to technology, expertise, and markets. These include buying into companies at lower levels of ownership that do not imply gaining control and joining with established multinational corporations to invest in other countries. Many cash-strapped corporations welcome Chinese infusions of capital, so governments often face a trade-off between national security considerations and providing jobs by allowing Chinese investors to revive zombie companies.

The political risk for Chinese buyers can be expected to further increase. As the number of Chinese transactions continues to rise, governments will have to adapt their review criteria and mechanisms to account for technological change and new security assessments. The issue of state-owned enterprises backed by state-owned banks being able to outbid private sector companies also remains unresolved. Recent debates over state-sponsored cyber espionage, accounting frauds, quality control, and food safety also are spilling over into the cross-border investment arena. This will further increase the risk of politicization outside of the formal government screening process.[425]

Still, Chinese investors are likely to find ways around both public and private resistance. By 2015, the end of the PRC's previous five-year plan, the government expected outbound investment to reach a cumulative total of $560 billion.[426] By 2012, it had already reached $532 billion. Other estimates see such investment to rise to $1 trillion by 2020.[427] By then, cumulative Chinese outward investments will be about the same as foreign direct investments in China. The PRC then will have joined the club of advanced industrial nations that are able to both provide and receive international capital.

CHAPTER 14. CHINA'S ROCKY PATH FORWARD

As illustrated in this study, foreign direct investment in China was the key that unlocked economic growth and triggered changes in government policy that enabled the country to modernize. Under Mao, the PRC lacked investment capital, modern technology, efficient management methods, worker incentives and foreign exchange. After the Great Leap Forward and Cultural Revolution, the socialized system for producing both agricultural and industrial goods was in shambles. The country had been shackled by decades of misguided economic policy and had missed the economic miracles that had occurred in Japan, South Korea, Singapore, Hong Kong and Taiwan.

Like nature abhorring a vacuum, opportunities for foreign companies abounded. Gaps were everywhere just begging to be exploited—gaps between the foreign standard and what was available in the Chinese economy. There were gaps in product quality and design, technology, capital and labor productivity, wages, work habits, land costs, tax levels, standards of living, funding sources, and just about every other aspect of economic life. The main issues were access and control.

Beijing chose to close these gaps by relying on foreign direct investors and by nurturing domestic enterprises, both state-owned and privately held, to help them compete with the foreign companies. Beijing warily chose to dance with the foreign devils, even though the early investors were not really so foreign after all. They came mainly from Hong Kong, Taiwan, and Singapore and were more like homing pigeons who were returning to their homeland.

Initially, foreign investors and modern domestic companies were kept caged in clusters within special economic zones. But the success of these SEZs not only triggered policy easing by Beijing but competition among cities for similar economic clusters and rising expectations among consumers who were getting a taste of the accoutrements of contemporary high society. The modern PRC economy began to emerge, and more and more Chinese discovered that indeed, to get rich is glorious.

The crucial role that foreign direct investment has played in providing the economic foundation for China's rise has been argued in several chapters of this book. On one hand, China's integration into the world economy has enabled greater inflows of information and exposure to ideals and the development of values more consistent with those of the non-communist world. Market-based economic activity and decision making, individual rights, a rising standard of living and greater communication all have contributed to the development of institutions and attitudes in the PRC that are more attuned to individualism, democracy and other values that at times have been anathema to the ruling Communist Party. On the other hand, technological advances and growth in Chinese industries have enabled Beijing to engage more effectively in suppressing information, quell nascent opposition movements and build a modern military.

The way ahead may be as difficult for Beijing to negotiate as was the way behind. Any country that has hurtled into the twenty-first century with the speed at which the PRC has traveled is bound to face major adjustments and growing pains. China has built too much production capacity, still has too few leading multinational companies, faces problems with the quality of production, suffers from excessive competition—both licit and illicit—and has to cope with rising Chinese nationalism. In addition, the PRC faces internal dissent and possible political instability. Each of these will affect the calculus of investors as they assess their position in the Chinese marketplace.

Overcapacity

Once China opened to the world, its economic growth was miraculous. In 1980, China's GDP at $0.3 trillion was one tenth the size of that of the United States and a quarter the size of Japan's. Twenty years later in 2010,

China's GDP ($5.9 trillion) had surpassed that of Japan ($5.5 trillion) and was more than a third as large as that of the United States ($15.0 trillion). By 2019, the International Monetary Fund projects that if China's growth rate continues at between 6 and 7 percent per year, its GDP at about $14.8 trillion would be at about the same level that the United States GDP was in 2010.[428]

Of course, as a variation of a Danish adage states, forecasting is very difficult, especially about the future, and also past performance is not a sure predictor of the future. The PRC is pushing hard to keep economic growth at a high level and to ensure that its economy does not grow old before it grows rich. China's rate of economic growth is slowing and likely will continue to decline in the near term. Growth rates could fall to around 4 percent or even into negative territory.[429] Still, the country is growing fast enough to provide huge opportunities for businesses and consumers alike. Albert Einstein once said that insanity is doing the same thing over and over again and expecting different results. In China's case, economic insanity is doing the same thing over and over again and expecting the same economic results. Approaches will have to change because underlying economic conditions are changing.

Once the high growth rate in the PRC begins to decline, the drop can be abrupt. The problem lies in overcapacity. Much of Chinese growth has been a result of building capacity in industries, housing, and infrastructure. As long as the economy and exports are growing at high rates, excess capacity will take care of itself. In a rapidly expanding economy, the greater mistake is to have undercapacity, not overcapacity. Companies must have sufficient manufacturing equipment and personnel to meet rising demand or risk losing market share. Rather than face supply shortages and lost market opportunities, companies race to build more production lines. But when economic growth and exports began to lag, excess capacity eats into profits. Bank loans may not be met, and soon the economy suffers from an overhang of nonperforming loans and idle assembly lines. Inventory accumulates that has to be sold at lower and lower prices. Growth slows further, and, before long, the country is in a growth recession. It may be still expanding but at a much lower pace.

Zhang Ping, former head of the National Development and Reform Commission, said the overcapacity problem is especially serious in traditional sectors like steel, cement, electrolytic aluminum, sheet glass and hard coke. He stated that some firms will either have to fail or be merged with more profitable ones.[430] In industries with overcapacity, each enterprise hopes that other enterprises in its sector, rather than themselves, will suffer in a softer market. Local governments, in particular, refuse to see their prize enterprises go under and continue to provide subsidies in the hope that their technically bankrupt companies will recover. Some even promote building new production capacity clinging to the hope that their new and efficient capacity will out-compete older enterprises in the sector. Banks also have been pushing troubled enterprises to stay in the market so that they do not have to face default on loans extended.[431] A major question is how much longer can Chinese firms which are surviving on state subsidies and bank loans remain in business—much less keep on expanding? At some point such zombie companies have to meet their inevitable fate.

Fostering Growth

In 2013, China's new leadership seemed committed to economic reforms to foster growth rather than provide for more stimulus spending. Chinese President Xi Jinping has taken charge of drawing up ambitious reform plans to revitalize the economy to include addressing the problem of overcapacity. Premier Li Keqiang has written that the government will implement a new wave of pro-market restructuring aimed at reducing the state-owned sector and enforcing productivity increases. He said that Beijing will make an all-around effort to deepen market-oriented reform, unleash the dividends of change and grow the economy thereby improving the people's livelihood and promoting social equity.[432] Time will tell whether this is more rhetoric or will result in actual pro-market policies.

Heretofore, the PRC has been playing catch-up in the global game of economic development. It has been relatively straight-forward for companies and government to pick the low hanging fruit. Now that gaps are closing, the path forward becomes more difficult. Catching up is one thing, but keeping up and possibly overtaking competitors is another. China now is at a critical stage of its development. Beijing wants to avoid the middle-income trap in which growth and wealth creation stagnates as exports and market share are taken by lower-cost competitors in other nations but the economy as a whole has yet to attain high-income status.

As indicated in the chapters in this book dealing with PRC industrial policy, the drive for indigenous innovation and attempts to create national champion companies and take back industries dominated by foreigners appears to be two recent themes in Beijing's economic policy. Is it possible for China to generate innovation and to create its own multinational corporations able to compete without government subsidies? The PRC is determined to climb the high-technology ladder. So far, it has succeeded in increasing the number of patents granted to Chinese inventors and in training more students in science, engineering and technology. The jury is still out, however, on whether this will translate into innovative products that will win in the marketplace.

National champion companies may be emerging from China, but government attempts to create them can lead to consummate failures. In most other economies, national champions develop through the competitive process. They have been forged in the crucible of competitive markets. In China's case, the potential national champions are chosen and supported by the government. Subsidized success may last for a while, but eventually the market will dictate the winners and losers.

Take the example of Wuxi Suntech, once the world's largest supplier of solar panels. The company effectively went bankrupt in 2013. Wuxi Suntech had been part of a huge Chinese government effort to dominate renewable energy industries. As prices for solar panels dropped by 75 percent, even this darling of Beijing could not stay afloat. In December 2012, China's State Council signaled that it would stop funding unprofitable domestic solar-panel makers and instead encourage mergers among healthy companies. The council also indicated it would not allow local governments to support struggling companies in an industry that was losing as much as $1 for every $3 in sales.[433]

Quality Control

World consumers also are beginning to doubt that Chinese companies, particularly those without foreigners overseeing quality control, will be able to maintain quality under relentless pressure to reduce costs. Among construction workers in the United States a new swearword is emerging. Often when a nail head pops off or a screw head strips, the carpenter will yell "Chinese." Some claim that as much as 20 percent of the construction nails from China have heads that are too thin and will break off when pounded. Chinese quality control often leaves much to be desired.

The book *Poorly Made In China*[434] gives accounts of the trouble with products made in the PRC. Whether the problem be bacterial contamination in shampoo, workers spitting on the factory floor and not washing their hands after using the restroom, rampant counterfeiting of products, or substitution of ingredients, all have occurred with products labeled "Made in China." It often is said that success has many fathers, but failure is an orphan. In the case of Chinese manufacturing, success often comes only in the first shipment, and subsequent failures have no fathers. No one wants to take responsibility for defective products. It is the fault of suppliers, of a worker (who already has been fired), of a machine or of the shipping company. A typical Chinese response to a quality problem is that the product was fine when it was shipped. Many foreign investors have been compelled to take control over their own production processes in order to assure product quality.

For small businesses, however, hiring their own people in the PRC to monitor quality, let alone establishing a manufacturing plant in China, is surprisingly difficult. The Chinese government does not allow foreign companies to operate or to hire locally-based employees without a legal establishment in China. And expatriate employees cannot obtain the necessary permits to live and work in the PRC unless there is a local entity available to act as sponsor. For local hires, foreign companies without a Chinese presence cannot make mandatory social welfare contributions for their employees. Most qualified potential hires are unwilling to work under such conditions.[435]

In one case, Sleek Audio, a small U.S. company, gave up on manufacturing its earphones in China. The company found that the Chinese manufacturer would take great care to satisfy them when they were there to oversee the operation. The Chinese company would make the product perfectly, but when Sleek Audio gave the green light to make thousands of pieces and their representative returned home, the problems began. One ruined shipment of 10,000 sets of earphones that cost millions of dollars nearly brought the company to its knees. The company owners concluded that "even though there is a tremendous cost savings when you go to China, in the end it really is not that much. It is the hidden costs—the delays, the shipping costs—you pick all that up on a learning curve."[436]

Even large manufacturers have difficulty monitoring the quality of parts coming out of China. In February 2014, The British luxury sports carmaker, Aston Martin, recalled most of its sports cars built since late 2007 after finding that Shenzhen Kexiang Mould Tool Co., a Chinese subcontractor that molded the affected accelerator pedal arms, was using counterfeit DuPont plastic material.[437]

Quality, moreover, not only applies to the manufacturing process itself, but to finances and recordkeeping. I once spoke with an American forensic auditor whose work it was to determine whether appropriate royalties were being paid by Chinese companies to the foreign holders of intellectual property. Since the amount of the royalty paid was according to the number of units produced, the auditor would go into Chinese factories and try to determine the number of units manufactured using the intellectual property in question. In one case, when he went into a factory and asked to see the production records, he was given a set of books kept by hand. Taken aback by the primitive accounting being used, he asked why the company did not use computers for their accounting. The factory manager said that the company did not have computers, so the records were kept by hand. When the auditor looked around the factory, however, he found a different story. Indeed, the factory did have computers, not only for use in manufacturing, but for keeping financial and production records. The books he was shown were used only when outsiders inquired about confidential matters. The data in them were totally fabricated. He said that it was not unusual for companies to keep two or three different sets of books, one for real, one for the taxing authorities and another for foreigners.

After Caterpillar acquired the Chinese equipment manufacturer ERA Mining Machinery and its subsidiary Siwei for $800 million, the company had to take a $580 million accounting charge in 2012 because of accounting fraud at Siwei. The bookkeeping irregularities had been done in order to increase the value of the company on paper and were discovered by Caterpillar after it conducted a physical count of inventory and investigated the causes of the discrepancy between the count and the accounting records. According to Caterpillar, several Siwei senior managers had engaged in deliberate misconduct beginning several years prior to the acquisition. The company had engaged in improper cost allocation and revenue recognition that resulted in overstated profit.[438]

A U.S. law firm indicated to me that it is working with a client to sue a Chinese company because a container of products received in the United States was completely defective. The Chinese company insisted on full payment before the container could be opened for inspection. When the U.S. buyer balked at buying a pig in a poke, the Chinese company threatened to sell the shipment to a competitor. After making the payment and discovering the defective products, the American company demanded a refund. The Chinese company refused and even sent death threats by e-mail to the U.S. buyer.

In a similar case, an American acquaintance of mine worked as a consultant with a U.S. company that had established an enterprise in the PRC to distribute automobile parts. After several years of successful operation, the U.S. side discovered that the Chinese manager had been skimming off funds from the enterprise and using the money for himself and for certain Communist Party members. When the U.S. headquarters tried to have the manager arrested and prosecuted, the American consultant working on the case in China received death threats.

The blame for poor quality, however, cannot be laid solely at the feet of Chinese manufacturers. Factories in China make products for buyers all over the world. Each country has different standards. The factory managers in China say, "You tell me what standards you want." The U.S. government blames China for not imposing standards, but actually the importer of record may be as much to blame if it does not verify the quality of the products ordered. Some importers look the other way when, for example, the thread count in cloth is lower than the label indicates if the wholesale price is also lower.

Most major buyers of products manufactured in China have learned how to ensure quality, but it takes extra effort and resources. One company from Japan that has garments assembled in the PRC has found that training factory workers how to sew properly and to use only fabrics and accessories that meet Japanese quality standards is possible, but it is a long and strenuous process often requiring years of hard work and dedication. Even then, the company from Japan has a team of more than 20 Japanese technicians who visit each factory every day to check on the production process.

Are problems with quality only growing pains or are they endemic to China? Japan also encountered severe quality problems when it began industrializing. In the 1960s, a town in Japan called Usa was notorious for making cheap products that could be labeled "Made in USA." Likewise, South Korea had a period when it produced many knockoff products of questionable quality. Itaewon in Seoul used to be a favorite shopping spot for tourists and American soldiers because they could pick up Gucci watches, name-brand luggage, designer clothes, and other items of questionable provenance at bargain prices. High quality products of all kinds now originate from both Japan and South Korea.

Excess Competition

China differs from most countries of the world because of its population of 1.3 billion people. China's population is equivalent to the number of people in both North and South America (942 million in 2011) with another South America thrown in for good measure. Think of how much competition for business there would be if all the people in the Americas with their current living standards were squeezed into an area the size of the United States. That is the situation in China. Competition not only is cut-throat, it is cut-arms, -hands, -feet, and -toes. Every day, hundreds of millions of people are looking for another way to make money. If there have been 144 makers of automobiles and trucks, think how many companies are making clothing, toys, or consumer electronics.

With such a huge domestic market and hundreds of millions of people emerging from poverty, there is almost insatiable demand for modern products at an affordable price. Not everyone can afford genuine, high-quality consumer goods, but Oil of Olan (not Oil of Olay), Adadis (not Adidas) athletic shoes, SQNY (not Sony) electronics, Calvim Klain (not Calvin Klein) clothing, Wrlgleys Doubiemlnt (not Wrigley's Doublemint) chewing gum or Pizza Huh (instead of Pizza Hut) are good enough for them, particularly when the names are combined with real-looking logos and customers who may not speak English very well. The danger for the makers of the genuine product is that the bottom feeders will eventually become proficient enough at making a knockoff product that they will begin to move upscale, establish their own brands, and begin to compete head to head with the genuine product.

In a visit to ZN Animation, a Chinese company that makes children's cartoons, the group I was with was met by a former Disney manager who had worked in California on products with tie-ins to famous Disney characters. His company was a leading maker of cartoons for both Chinese and American television (including Nickelodeon). At his Chinese company, he showed a display room full of stuffed animals, children's athletic shoes, school bags, pens, hats, and T-shirts all carrying the names and images of the company's popular cartoon characters. He said that each time they came out with a new stuffed animal or other product, an identical knockoff would appear within days. They could scarcely keep ahead of the copy-cat companies. Competition is ruthless, even for Chinese enterprises.

The innovator's dilemma, as described by Clayton Christensen, is being played out with a vengeance in China.[439] Virtually any consumer product being made today, no matter how complicated, likely has a competitor in China with a version that might do less but also costs a lot less. The product also might be in the target sights of the government's industrial policy that has the intention to replace the foreign manufacturer with a domestic Chinese company. Every company has to decide, do I keep above the competition with innovation and higher quality or do I drop down and compete head on with those coming up from the bottom and try to prevent them from encroaching on the market?

FIGURE 14.1. POPULAR ZN ANIMATION CARTOON CHARACTERS

Photograph by D. Nanto.

Promises and Pitfalls

For international investors in the PRC, the road ahead is full of promise and pitfalls. The easy pickings are rapidly disappearing, but opportunities still exist. In the *Catalogue of Industries for Guiding Foreign Investment* that took effect on January 30, 2012, there were 354 sectors in the encouraged category and only 80 restricted sectors and 39 sectors prohibited.[440] However, the first question the Chinese regulator will ask the prospective foreign investor is, "What are you going to bring that is not here already?"

China still remains a destination of choice for foreign investment. Operating there may be hell, but as Winston Churchill once said, "If you are going through hell, keep going." Now hardly is the time to withdraw, because in many ways the Chinese market has just begun. In 2013, a U.S. Embassy trade official in Beijing remarked that there is a huge gap between the potential market in China and what actually is happening. The market may be open, but U.S. companies are not taking advantage of it. As an American lawyer in Beijing told me in 2010, companies that come to China have more obstacles to overcome than they thought, but they also can make more money than they thought possible.

Mark Hutchinson, president and CEO of GE China since 2011 had this advice for those entering the Chinese market:

> When one of our customers thinks about coming to the Chinese market, I say, look, don't do it alone. Talk to people who have been here a while. It could be the U.S. Embassy; it could be agencies like the Export-Import Bank; it could be us or other multinationals. Most people are willing to talk about the pitfalls. We'll give you some ideas of who you should be partnering with or where you might locate. Also, you have to breathe China. I would encourage newcomers to send someone for a year to really get a feel for the place, and maybe not to Shanghai or Beijing but to other big cities undergoing major growth. GE has been in China 100 years but we've become more of a local company in the last 10 years. Of our 20,000 employees, 99 percent are local.[441]

In a 2015 survey by the McKinsey & Company of company heads of multinational corporations in China, the vast majority of respondents said that China remained a top-priority growth engine for their companies and that experience as the China head was a rocket to advance their own careers. On the whole, however, most did not see the business environment in China as getting any easier. Most also feared that the policy environment for multinationals in the country would become more challenging.[442]

How did China go from poverty to prosperity and onto a trajectory to become the largest economy in the world? Much can be traced to the foreign investors who came with their technology, capital, managerial ability, product designs and links to international supply chains. The miracle of China has been the miracle of foreign direct investment. This inflow was the key to China's industrial revolution, and Beijing was pragmatic enough to alter its policies and allow a transition from the shambles of a socialist economy to a mixed market economy that has functioned remarkably well.

As the title of this book suggests, the international investors were the foreign devils, and Beijing has danced with them. Even the overseas Chinese investors who in many respects were merely coming home, brought with them the methods and attitudes that were devilishly foreign. At first the two sides approached each other with wariness and caution. Then, particularly at the local level, there was a warm embrace and the building of long-term relationships.

Currently, however, something akin to the seven-year itch has entered the scene. PRC policymakers would like nothing better than to replace the foreign enterprises with their own national champion companies. Some foreign investors may be squeezed by China's regulatory authorities and suffer something like what the Imperial Chinese referred to as slow slicing or *lingchi* a form of torture involving the repeated slicing of a prisoner's skin. Alternatively, an investor may be the victim of one slash of the regulatory sword. Some companies may find themselves facing a growing government-backed competitor—either a state-owned enterprise or a state-backed technology. For these companies, the tables have turned. Beijing no longer wants to dance with foreign devils, and they are left to cope with whatever the government throws their way.

However, there are some indications that the slowdown in growth in China is causing Beijing to rethink its unequal treatment of the foreign devils. In 2015, China unveiled some draft proposals that could ease its restrictions on foreign investment that would, for example, lift the requirement that in industries deemed strategic, a foreign investors must invest only through a joint venture and must transfer technology. Foreign firms would supposedly be treated the same way as national ones.[443]

Still, no company can ignore the China market. In a 2016 television interview Travis Kalanick, the Co-founder and CEO of Uber, indicated that Uber was able to sustainably invest a billion dollars or more per year into China. He said, "When you go to China, you cannot go there half-hearted. You have to go in all in. The opportunity for Uber is to say, if you have a chance to be Amazon and Alibaba at the same time, you should most definitely try. And if you try, you do it full heartedly; you do it all the way. You give it a shot. The expected outcome is there. The return on investment is there, so let's go."[444]

Despite the iron fist of government, many foreign investors are finding that China is developing into more of a partner than just a cheap platform to manufacture things. The PRC has become a source of talent and innovation, a place to locate regional headquarters and a massive consumer market that has been the stuff of dreams for over a century. For hundreds of foreign companies, the dance has led to marriage, and the enterprises are becoming less foreign and more part of the warp and weft of the modern Chinese economy.

INDEX

ENDNOTES

1   For convenience in this study, the People's Republic of China is referred to as China, and the Republic of China is referred to as Taiwan.

2   UNCTADSTAT database, http://unctadstat.unctad.org.

3   United Nations Conference on Trade and Development, *World Investment Report 2013*; Figure I.25, p. 22.

4   United Nations Conference on Trade and Development, *World Investment Report 2014*; Figure I.28, p. 28.

5   "Sectors: Rankings—By the Numbers—China Has It Made," *Foreign Direct Investment*, (August 1, 2011).

6   Interview by Andy Van Vleck, Shanghai, 2011.

7   Credit Suisse Research Institute, *Global Wealth Report 2014*, https://publications. credit-suisse.com/tasks/render/file/?fileID=60931FDE-A2D2-F568-B04IB58C5EA59IA4 (Accessed October 22, 2014)

8   People's Republic of China, National Bureau of Statistics, *China Statistical Yearbook 2010* (China Statistics Press, 2013). United Nations Conference on Trade and Development Statistics database.

9   UN Conference on Trade and Development, *World Investment Report 2013*; Country Fact Sheet: China, http://unctad.org/wir

10 UNCTAD, *World Investment Report 2013*; Annex Tables 19 and 22.

11 US-China Business Council, *Foreign Direct Investment in China, Top 10 Origins of Non-Financial FDI*, https://www.uschina.org/statistics/fdi_cumulative.html.

12 National Bureau of Statistics, *China Statistical Yearbook 2013*.

13 "Rubber to the Road: Ford Is Betting That a Renewed Global Strategy Will Help It Close the Gap in China, Says Joseph Hinrichs, Chairman and CEO of Ford China," *China Economic Review* (Mar 2011).

14 PriceWaterhouseCoopers, "Automotive/China Growth," http://www.pwc. com/gx/en/automotive/issues-trends/china-growth.jhtml. Craig Trudell, "Henry Ford's Century-Old Line Finds $15 Billion in China," *Bloomberg*, September 25, 2013.

15 Hong Kong Trade and Development Council, *Economic and Trade Information on Hong Kong*, February 2012.

16 Republic of China, Ministry of Economic Affairs, Investment Commission, "Monthly Report," http://www.moeaic.gov.tw/system_external/ctlr?PRO=PublicationLoad&lang=1&id=183 (Accessed October 11, 2014)

17 Jia-ke Hung and Chen-yuan Tung, "Contributions of Taiwan Businesspeople towards the Economic Development of China," (in Chinese) Report by the Chung-hua Institution for Economic Research, c. 2011.

18 Henry Wai-chung Yeung, "The Political Economy of Singaporean Investments in China," East Asia Institute, National University of Singapore, EAI Working Paper No.22, 1999, p. 12.

19 Barry Naughton, "SASAC and Rising Corporate Power in China," *China Leadership Monitor*, No. 24, March 12, 2008, p. 4.

20 U.S. Bureau of Economic Analysis, "U.S. Direct Investment Position Abroad on a Historical-Cost Basis," Interactive Data/International Data/Direct Investment and Multinational Companies-Comprehensive Data//U.S. Direct Investment Abroad. Accessed February 20, 2014.

21 Japan, Ministry of Economy, Trade and Industry, "Summary of the Japan-China-Korea Trilateral Investment Agreement" (provisional translation), May 2012.

22 Rawski, Thomas G. "The Rise of China's Economy," *Foreign Policy Research Institute Footnotes*, Vol. 16, No. 06, June 2011, p. 5.

23 "Report to the Second Plenary Session of the Seventh Central Committee of the Communist Party of China (March 5, 1949)" in *Selected Works of Mao Zedong*, vol. IV, p. 374.

24 Robert Miller, "China Learns from the Soviet Union, 1949-Present," *The China Journal*, vol. 65 (January 2011), p. 261. Book review of *China Learns from the Soviet Union, 1949-Present*.

25 Mao Zedong, "Speech at a Conference of Cadres in the Shansi-Suiyuan Liberated Area," *Selected Works of Mao Zedong*, English, IV, 1948, p. 232.

26 Y.Y. Kuth, "Mao and Agriculture in China's Industrialization: Three Antitheses in a 50-year Perspective," *The China Quarterly*, 187 (September 2006) 700-723.

27 James S. Kung and Louis Putterman, "China's Collectivization Puzzle: A New Resolution," *The Journal of Development Studies*, vol. 33, no. 6 (August 1997), pp. 741-63.

28 Yixin Chen, "Cold War Competition and Food Production in China, 1957-62," *Agricultural History*, vol. 83, no. 1 (winter 2009), pp. 51-78.

29 For a detailed account of hardships during the Great Leap Forward, see: Dikötter, Frank, *Mao's Great Famine: The History of China's Most Devastating Catastrophe, 1958-1962* (New York, Walker Publishing Company, 2010) 421p.

30 Dikotter, Frank, *Mao's Great Famine, op. cit.,* Kindle location 99..

31 John Sunyer, "Frank Dikotter, The Books Interview," *New Statesman*, July 25, 2011, p. 42.

32 Presentation by Frank Dikotter at the Asia Society, October 13, 2010.

33 See Aam Wing Chan and Will Buckingham, "Is China Abolishing the *Hukou* System? *The China Quarterly*, 195, September 2008, pp. 582-606.

34 Presentation by Frank Dikotter, op. cit.

35 John Leicester, "Footsteps of a Revolution," Associated Press, *Tulsa World*, November 26, 2006, p. H4.

36 Ma Jisen, The Cultural Revolution in the Foreign Ministry of China (Chinese University Press, 2004) 466 p.

37 "Ignoring the Past, China," *The Economist (US)*, May 20, 2006, p. 43.

38 Joseph Sobran, "After the Nightmare," *National Review*, vol. 38 (July 18, 1986), p. 48. Book review of *After the Nightmare* by Liang Heng.

39 John Pomfret, *Chinese Lessons* (New York, Holt, Henry, and Company, 2007), 312 p.

40 Harry Harding, "Reappraising the Cultural Revolution," *The Wilson Quarterly*, vol. 4, no. 4 (Autumn 1980), p. 137.

41 Source List and Detailed Death Tolls for the Primary Megadeaths of the Twentieth Century, http://necrometrics.com/20c5m.htm.

42 Robert Ash, Squeezing the Peasants: Grain Extraction, Food Consumption and Rural Living Standards in Mao's China," *The China Quarterly*, 2006, p. 966.

43 *2008 China's Industrial Development Report* (Executive Summary in English), p. 659.

44 Quoted in Gregory C. Chow, *China's Economic Transformation*, 2nd ed. (Malden, MA, Blackwell Publishing, 2007), Kindle location 311.

45 The World Bank Group, World Development Indicators. Taiwan's annual per capita national income is from Republic of China, Taiwan National Statistics database.

46 Christian Ploberger, "China's Reform and Opening Process—A Fundamental Political Project," *Asian Social Science*, Vol. 6, No. 11, November 2010, p. 28-41.

47 Y. Y. Kueh, "Mao and Agriculture in China's Industrialization: Three Antitheses in a 50-Year Perspective," *The China Quarterly*, 2006, pp. 713, 721.

48 Wu Nanian, "The Xiaogang Village Story," China.org.cn, March 6, 2008.

49 Min Ye, "Policy Learning or Diffusion: How China Opened to Foreign Investment," *Journal of East Asian Studies*, vol. 9, issue 3, September-October 2009, pp. 405-408.

50 Ibid.

51 A.D. Barnett and R.N. Clough (eds.), *Modernizing China: Post-Mao Reform and Development* (Boulder, CO, Westview Press, 1986), quoted in Sheying Chen, "Economic Reform and Social Change in China: Past, Present, and Future of the Economic State," *International Journal of Politics, Culture and Society*, Vol. 15, No. 4, Summer 2002. p. 572.

52 Unlike Japan and South Korea, Hong Kong was a free port with no import tariffs or investment barriers.

53 Adapted from: Min Ye, "Policy Learning or Diffusion: How China Opened to Foreign Investment," op.cit.

54 Opening Speech at the Twelfth National Congress of the Communist Party of China, September 1, 1982, in *Selected Works of Deng Xiaoping*, Volume III, 1982-1992. For a review of Deng's accomplishments, see Jiang Zemin, "Our Beloved Leader: Speech Given at Deng Xiaoping's Memorial Meeting," reviewed in *Asian Affairs*, Vol. 24, No. 2, Symposium on China after Deng Xiaoping (Summer 1997), pp. 113-124.

55 Yue-man Yeung, Joanna Lee, and Gordon Kee, "China's Special Economic Zones at 30," *Eurasian Geography and Economics*, Vol. 50, No. 2, 2009, p. 224-225.

56 Data are from the Bank for International Settlements, Consolidated Banking Statistics.

57 Yuqing Xing, "Facts about and Impacts of FDI on China and the World Economy," *China: An International Journal*. Vol. 8, No. 2, September 2010, p. 309.

58 Patrick Chovanec, "Step In, Then Step Back," *China Economic Review*, October 2010.

59 "The Last Shall Come First," *China Economic Quarterly*, Second Quarter, 2000.

60 Kevin Daly and Xiaoxi Zhang, "The Determinants of Foreign Direct Investment in China," *Journal of International Finance and Economics*, Vol. 10, No. 3, 2010, p. 123.

61 Global Business Council and A.T. Kearney, *FDI Confidence Index*, Vol. 5, September 2002, p. 24.

62 U.S. Government Accountability Office, "World Trade Organization: Analysis of China's Commitments to Other Members," Report No. GAO-03-4, Oct. 3, 2002.

63 PriceWaterhouseCoopers, "Establishing a business presence in China: A guide for private companies," 2007, p. 20.

64 See, for example, Tian, X., Lin, S. and Lo, V.I. "Foreign Direct Investment And Economic Performance In Transition Economies: Evidence From China," *Post-Communist Economies*, Vol. 16, No. 4, 2004, 497-510; Jiang, Xiaojuan. (2003) *FDI in China: Contributions to Growth, Restructuring and Competitiveness in China in the 21ˢᵗ Century* (New York, Nova Science Publishers, 2003), 243 pp.

65 Ziling Xing, Qianqiu Gongzui Mao Zedong (Mao Zedong: Merits and Crimes of the Century) (Hong Kong, Shuzuofang Chubanshek, 2007) p. 739, cited in Carl E. Walter and Fraser J.T. Howie, Red Capitalism, *The Fragile Foundation of China's Extraordinary Rise* (Singapore, John Wiley & Sons (Asia), 2011), p. 24.

66 See Gregory Chow, *China's Economic Transformation*, 2ⁿᵈ ed. (Malden, MA, Blackwell Publishing, 2007), Kindle location 1534ff.

67 Data from China Data Online.

68 The totals for the stock of foreign investment in China reported by the United Nations Conference on Trade and Development (UNCTADSTATS, http://www.unctad.org) also has apparent errors in the running total. For several years beginning in 1994, the corresponding stock number is less than the previous year's stock number plus net inflows. The accumulation of these apparent errors made the FDI stock in China at $832.9 billion reported by the U.N. for 2012 considerably less than the total of the annual net inflows of FDI at $1,353.9 billion.

69 Income Tax Law of the People's Republic of China.

70 Clyde Prestowitz, "The $64 Trillion Question (Part I)," *The New Republic*, June 22, 2010. Intel Corp., "Intel China Describes Long-Range Strategy." *Industry Updates*, August 24, 2009. PriceWaterhouseCoopers, "Global Reach, China's Impact on the Semiconductor Industry, 2010 Update," November 2010, p. 5.

71 ET today.com, April 15, 2003, http://www.ettoday.com, as cited in Tse-Kang Leng, "State And Business in the Era of Globalization: The Case of Cross-Strait Linkages in the Computer Industry," *The China Journal*, Issue 53, January 2005, p. 21.

72 Off-the-record interview, February 2012.

73 A business cluster is a geographic concentration of interconnected businesses, suppliers, and associated institutions in a particular field. Clusters are considered to increase the productivity with which companies can compete, nationally and globally.

74 Michael E. Marti, *China and the Legacy of Deng Xiaoping* (Dulles, VA, Brassey's Inc, 2002), p. 7.

75   Michael E. Porter, *The Competitive Advantage Of Nations* (London, Macmillan, 1990) p. 90.

76   "FIEs Industrial Clusters in Dongguan's Electronic Industry," *China & World Economy*, January/February 2003.

77   Douglas Zhihua Zeng, "How Do Special Economic Zones and Industrial Clusters Drive China's Rapid Development?" World Bank Policy Research Working Paper No. 5583, March 1, 2011. P. 1.

78   Michael E. Porter, "Location, Clusters, and the 'New' Microeconomics of Competition," *Business Economics*, January 1998, Vol. 33, No. 1, p. 7-17.

79   Min Ye, "Policy Learning or Diffusion: How China Opened to Foreign Investment," *Journal of East Asian Studies*, vol. 9, issue 3, September-October 2009, p. 410-411.

80   Data from Statistical Yearbook of Shenzhen (1994) cited in Zai Liang, "Foreign Investment, Economic Growth, and Temporary Migration: The Case of Shenzhen Special Economic Zone, China," *Development and Society*, Vol. 28, No. 1, June 1999, p. 119.

81   Shenzhen government, "Investment Environment," available at: http://english.sz.gov.cn/ftz/.

82   Nadeem M. Firoz and H. Amy Murray, "Foreign Investment Opportunities and Customs Laws in China's Special Economic Zones," *International Journal of Management*, Vol. 20, No. 1, March 2003, p. 109.

83   World Shipping Council, "Top 50 World Container Ports."

84   Barry Naughton, The China Circle, Economics and Technology in the PRC, Taiwan, and Hong Kong (Washington, Brookings Institution Press, 1997), p. 94.

85   The American Chamber of Commerce in South China, *2011 Special Report on the State of Business in South China*, a *South China Business Journal* Special Report, February 22, 2010. p. 18.

86   "Taiwan Food Company to Build New Factory in E. China," *Business Daily Update*, January 31, 2012.

87   Ching-Mu Chen, Konstantinos A. Melachroinos and Kang-Tsung Chang, "FDI and Local Economic Development: The Case of Taiwanese Investment in Kunshan," *European Planning Studies*, Vol. 18, No. 2, February 2010, p. 227-228.

88   Jon Blankfield, "Risk Assessment: Taiwanese Semiconductor Investment in China," Xiphias Consulting, c. 2010, p. 13.

89   Chien, S. "Institutional Innovations, Asymmetric Decentralization, and Local Economic Development: A Case Study of Kunshan in Post-Mao

China," *Environment and Planning C: Government and Policy*, 2007, 25(2), pp. 269–290.

90 Chun Yang, "Strategic Coupling of Regional Development in Global Production Networks: Redistribution of Taiwanese Personal Computer Investment from the Pearl River Delta to the Yangtze River Delta, China," *Regional Studies*, Vol. 43.3, April 2009, p. 401.

91 Tain-Jy Chen, "The Creation of Kunshan ICT Cluster," The International Centre for the Study of East Asian Development, Kitakyushu, Working Paper Series Vol. 2008-07, April 2008, pp. 2-3.

92 Yen Tzung-ta, "Retrospection and Refection on the Impact of Cross-Straits Economic Relations," in *Cross Straits Relations and the Future of China* (Taipei: Democracy Foundation, 1991), 59, cited in Tse-Kang Leng, "The State and Taiwan's Mainland Economic Policy," *Asian Affairs*, Vol. 23, No. 1, Symposium on Taiwan (Spring, 1996), p. 21.

93 Ching-Chang Chen, "Understanding the Political Economy of Cross-Strait Security: A Missing Link," *Journal of Chinese Political Science*, Vol. 15, No. 4, December 2010, pp. 391–412.

94 Chen-yuan Tung, "Cross-strait Economic Relations," UNISCI discussion papers, Madrid: Unidad de Investigacion sobre Seguridad y Cooperacion Internacional, January 2004, cited in Murray Scott Tanner, *Chinese Economic Coercion against Taiwan, a Tricky Weapon to Use*, Santa Monica, CA, Rand, National Defense Research Institute, 2007, p. 41.

95 Collected Regulations of Investing on Mainland China (Taipei: Ministry of Economic Affairs, 1993).

96 *Lien Ho Pao*, October 12, 1993, cited in Tse-Kang Leng, "The State and Taiwan's Mainland Economic Policy," *Asian Affairs*, Vol. 23, No. 1, Symposium on Taiwan (Spring, 1996), p. 24.

97 "A Huge Power Play on the Mainland," *Business Week* (International Edition), March 31, 1997, Internet edition.

98 Ching-Chang Chen, "Understanding the Political Economy of Cross-Strait Security: A Missing Link," *Journal of Chinese Political Science*, Vol. 15, No. 4, December 2010, pp. 391–412.

99 For details, see: Alan Romberg, *Across the Taiwan Strait: From Confrontation to Cooperation 2006-2012*, Vols. I, II, and III, Stimson Center, 2012.

100 Trade data accessed via Global Trade Network.

101 Interview by Dick Nanto at the Chung-Hua Institution for Economic Research, March 11, 2006.

102 Peggy Pei-chen Chang and Tun-jen Cheng, "The Rise of the Information Technology Industry in China: A Formidable Challenge to Taiwan's Economy," *American Asian Review*, Vol. 20, No. 3, Fall 2002, p. 125-174.

103 Cheng-chao Wang and Min-sheng Huang, "A Research on Taiwan's Investment in Mainland China and Its Spatial Spread," *Human Geography*, Vol. 23, No. 6, December 2008, p. 71 (in Chinese).

104 Mainland Affairs Council, Economic Statistics, "Table 7. Taiwan Investment in Mainland China." http://www.mac.gov.tw/public/Attachment/422017182737.pdf

105 The data shown in **Figure 7.3** exclude retroactive approvals in 1993, 1997, 1998, 2003, and 2004. These were for previously unregistered investments (probably before 1991) that were later registered in those years. Their total was 28,925 cases worth $11.2 billion. These retroactive approvals are included in the cumulative totals.

106 Hejian Technology web site. "About Us." http://www.hjtc.com.cn/aboutHJ/aboutUs.asp.

107 "The Taiwan Connection," *China Economic Quarterly*, Fourth Quarter, 2003. ProQuest document ID 210795298.

108 8 U.S. Embassy Beijing cable, "UMC Announces Deal with PRC's He Jian," March 25, 2005.

109 8 Josephine Lien, Taipei; Jessie Shen, "UMC Approved to Raise Stake in HeJian," *Digitimes*, December 21, 2012.

110 "Taiwan Approves TSMC China Chip Plant Upgrade," *International Business Times: Companies*, September 30, 2010, Internet edition.

111 Tse-Kang, Leng, "State and Business in the Era of Globalization: The Case of Cross-Strait Linkages in the Computer Industry," *The China Journal*, Issue 53, January 2005, 63-79.

112 Semiconductor Manufacturing International Corporation, Securities and Exchange Commission, Form F-1 Registration Statement, filed February 11, 2004.

113 Bruce Einhorn, TSMC's "Next Move in China," *Bloomberg Business Week*, November 10, 2009, Internet edition.

114 *Economic Cooperation Framework Agreement (ECFA)*, translation provided by Taiwan's Mainland Affairs Council.

115 Interview in Taipei by Dick Nanto with a Foxconn manager, January 2012.

116 Frederik Balfour and Tim Culpan, "Everything Is Made by Foxconn in Future Evoked by Gou's Empire," *Bloomberg News*, September 9, 2010.

117 Interview in Taipei by Dick Nanto with a Foxconn manager, January 2012.

118 118 Charles Duhigg and Nick Wingfield, "Apple Opens Factory Doors to Inspection of Conditions," *International Herald Tribune*, February 12, 2012. Internet edition.

119 Fair Labor Association, "Independent Investigation of Apple Supplier, Foxconn, Report Highlights," March 2012.

120 Jia-ke Hung and Chen-yuan Tung, "台商對中國經濟發展的貢獻 : 1988-2008 年" (Contributions of Taiwan Businesspeople towards the Economic Development of China: 1988-2008), Graduate Institute of Development Studies, National Chengchi University report, c2010, Taipei, Taiwan.

121 Bill Gertz, "China's High-Tech Military Threat," *Commentary*, April 2012.

122 See, for example, the YouTube video that went viral by Vince Wade, "General Motors Is Becoming China Motors." May 4, 2012.

123 Interview by Dick Nanto with a business executive in Hong Kong, February 28, 2011.

124 Off-the-record exchange by Andy Van Vleck.

125 See the American Chamber of Commerce in Shanghai's web site at < http://www.amcham-shanghai.org/AmchamPortal/portaldefault.aspx>

126 For a partial list of U.S. and other foreign companies that either own factories or have contract factories producing their products in China, see: "American & International Corporations In China," *Jie's World* (Internet edition).

127 Demko, Caroline. "100 Years of AmCham: Singer Revolutionizes Shanghai Fashion," *Insight*, November 11, 2014.

128 The U.S. Department of Commerce calculates the direct investment position or stock to be the net book value of U.S. parent companies' equity in, and outstanding loans to, their affiliates abroad. A change in the position consists of increases or decreases in equity, reinvested earnings of incorporated affiliates, and changes in intercompany debt.

129 The dip in 2005 reflected the one-time tax provision provided to U.S. parent firms to reduce the amount of reinvested earnings going to their foreign affiliates under the American Jobs Creation Act of 2004.

130 Karel De Gucht, "Speech, EU-China: A New Growth Equation," European Commission, SPEECH/12/890, November 30, 2012.

131 "China's Biggest Banks Post Record Profits as BofA, RBS Stumble," *Bloomberg Business Report*, August 24, 2011.

132 "China Falls Out Of Love With Cash," *Financial Times* (Internet edition), February 28, 2014.

133 He Ping, "Chinese Household Savings Surge to 50 Percent, *Epoch Times*, February 19, 2013.

134 PriceWaterhouseCoopers, *Foreign Banks in China*, January 2014, p. 13, 35.

135 HSBC, "HSBC A Brief History," May 2012. p. 35. Dora Cheok, "Foreign Banks in China," *Bloomberg Business*, June 6, 2012.

136 Prudence Ho, Yvonne Lee, and Justin Baer, "Goldman Sachs Selling ICBC Stake," *Wall Street Journal*, May 20, 2013.

137 M. Rochan, "Bank of America Sells Remaining Stake in China's CCB for $1.47bn," *International Business Times* (Internet edition), September 4, 2013.

138 Prudence Ho, et al., "Goldman Sachs Selling ICBC Stake," op. cit.

139 J.P. Morgan, "About J.P. Morgan's Business in China," https://www.jpmorgan.com/pages/jpmorgan/china90/about.

140 For a detailed account of problems in the joint venture, see: James McGregor, *One Billion Customers: Lessons from the Front Lines of Doing Business in China* (New York, Free Press, 2005) Chapter 2.

141 Cathy Chan and Katrina Nicholas, "Morgan Stanley Said to Sell Its 34.3% CICC Stake to TPG, Singapore's GIC," *Bloomberg*, December 1, 2010. "'Princeling' Levin Zhu Steps out of Father's Shadow," *Want China Times*, April 3, 2012. Lee Han Shih, "Levin Zhu Yunlai and Morgan Stanley," *The Asia Magazine*, December 12, 2008. Gregory White, "China Just Swung the Door Wide Open for Two American Banks," Clusterstock *Business Insider*, January 7, 2011.

142 Kazunori Takada, "UBS Launches China Unit, Eyes Wealth Management Business," *Reuters*, January 16, 2013.

143 "UBS Success in the China Market," CNBC television report, September 12, 2012.

144 PriceWaterhouseCoopers, China Banking 2013, op. cit., p. 24ff.

145 Alisa Priddle, "Ford says it will need more expansion in China after 2015 goal," *Detroit Free Press*, October 9, 2013.

146 For details, see Rachel Tang, *The Rise of China's Auto Industry and Its Impact on the U.S. Motor Vehicle Industry*, Congressional Research Service Report R40924, November 16, 2009.

147 Michael J. Dunne, *American Wheels, Chinese Roads* (Singapore, John Wiley & Sons (Asia), 2011), Kindle Edition, location 423.

148 "Letting BAIC bid for Opel reflects a major government policy shift," Automotive News China, July 8, 2009.

149 Bentley Motors, "Bentley Motors China Full Speed Ahead In 2013," Press Release, January 11, 2013.

150 Michael Dunne, op. cit.

151 Tim Higgins, "Jeeps Sell for $189,750 as China Demand Offsets Tariffs," *Bloomberg*, May 21, 2012.

152 Michael Dunne, op. cit., Kindle locations 938-942.

153 Michael Dunne, op. cit., Kindle locations 910-913.

154 "Strong China Sales Spur Automakers' Success," http://China.org.cn.

155 TUSIAD, "Analysis of European Union Foreign Direct Investment (FDI) in China," *China Business Insight*, January 2012.

156 "BMW Expects Slower Sales Growth in China," *Market Watch (Wall Street Journal)*, April 21, 2013.

157 GM China. "General Motors in China," Backgrounder for the media. c. 2014..

158 Paula M. Miller, "General Motors Races Ahead in the China Market," *China Business Review (online)*, April-June 2011.

159 Michael Wayland, "Buick Sales Top 3 Million in China Since 1999," *Michigan Automotive News*, April 26, 2011, Mlive.com.

160 Keith Bradsher, "After Nearly 90 Years, Ford Wants China to Give It a Second Chance," *New York Times*, October 20, 2013, p. B7.

161 Ford Motor Company. *2014 Annual Report*, c. 2015. p. 22.

162 Kenneth Rapoza, "China Island Dispute Whacks Japanese Auto Sales," *Forbes*, October 9, 2012.

163 Li Fangfang, "Japanese Carmakers Report Sept Sales as 'Disastrous,'" *China Daily*, October 10, 2012.

164 "Forget Anti-Japan Protests—Here's the REAL Reason Toyota Flopped in China," *Reuters*, October 29, 2012.

165 Ma Jie and Yuki Hagiwara, "Nissan Says China Sales to Rise as Anti-Japan Sentiment Wanes," *Bloomberg*, April 20, 2013.

166 Ken Kuwahara, "Nissan lines up 50 billion yuan wager aimed at doubling China production," *The Nikkei Weekly*, August 1, 2011. "Nissan Celebrates 40th Anniversary In China," Nissan Press Release, September 14, 2013.

167 Honda web site, http://world.honda.com/group/manufacturing-facilities/China/.

168 The main Taiwanese companies are Foxconn Electronics (Hon Hai), Quanta Computer, Wistron, Inventec, and Mitac International.

169 Fahmida Y. Rashid, "Intel Opens $2.5 Billion Fab Plant in China," *eWeek*, October 26, 2010.

170 Willy Shih, Kamen Bliznashki, and Fan Zhao, "IBM China Development Lab Shanghai: Capability by Design," Harvard Business School case 9-611-055, June 23, 2011. IBM China, "China Research Laboratory," access on IBM home page, March 12, 2012.

171 Micron Technology, "Micron Technology Opens New Manufacturing Facility in China," press release, March 20, 2007. Ma Lie, "Micron

Technology Injects $300m in Xi'an Hi-tech Zone," *China Daily*, February 4, 2010.

172 Dell Computer. "Dell to Build Flagship Manufacturing and Customer Support Center in Chengdu to Support Western China Growth; Expands Xiamen Operations," press release, September 16, 2010. Tereza Pultarova, "Dell Chengdu Facility 'A Milestone' in Company's Strategy," *Engineering and Technology Magazine*, June 6, 2013.

172 LM Ericsson Telephone Company, "Sony Ericsson Takes Majority Stake in Chinese Factory and Creates New Development Unit in China—Strengthens Commitment and Focus in China," news release, June 30, 2004.

174 James Hillmeyer, "Siemens' China Footprint," *Seeking Alpha*, February 1, 2013.

175 Siemens, *Company Report 2012*, p. 225-230.

176 Paul Elias, "Economic Spying Case over DuPont's Chemical Grows," Associated Press, March 10, 2012. The case in U.S. District Court, Northern District of California is United States of America vs. Walter Liew and Christina Liew, 11-cr-573. "Two Individuals and Company Found Guilty of Conspiracy to Sell Trade Secrets to Chinese Companies," U.S. Department of Justice Press Release, March 5, 2014.

177 Methylene diphenyl diisocyanate (MDI) reacts with polyols in the manufacture of polyurethane.

178 China Knowledge, "China Chemicals Industry," accessed March 11, 2012. Bayer, "Bayer Plans to Significantly Expand Capacities in China," Bayer press release, December 2010.

179 For details, see Anita Chan, ed., *Walmart in China* (Ithaca, NY, ILR Press, 2011).

180 "Walmart Plans More Stores and E-Commerce in China," *The New York Times*, October 24, 2013. Walmart in China, *Walmart China Factsheet*, and "Walmart Global Ecommerce Announces Increased Investment in Yihaodian," News Release, February 20, 2012.

181 Walter Loeb, "How Walmart Will Fight to Be Successful in China, *Forbes*, June 11, 2013.

182 For more examples, see Ana Douglas, "These Hilariously Bad Knock-Offs Are on Sale in China," *Business Insider*, August 1, 2012.

183 Atsushi Okudera, "Japanese Retailers Start Resuming Operations in China," *Asahi Shimbun*, October 28, 2012.

184 Phillip Kendall, "Luxury Restroom in Chinese Department Store the Envy of Japanese Shopaholics," *Rocket News 24*, July 13, 2013.

185 Balis, Ryan, et. al., *China Business Report 2013-2014*, The American Chamber of Commerce in Shanghai, 2014, p. 6-7.

186 Todd Woody, "What Solyndra's Bankruptcy Means For Silicon Valley Solar Startups," *Forbes*, August 31, 2011.

187 U.S. Congress, House Committee on Energy and Commerce, Subcommittee on Oversight and Investigations, *Testimony of Jonathan Silver, Executive Director Loan Programs Office, U.S. Department of Energy*, 112th Cong., 1st sess., September 14, 2011. Federal government subsidies to the solar energy industry were $247 million in 2010. World Trade Organization, *New and Full Notification Pursuant to Article XVI:1 of the GATT 1994 and Article 25 of the Agreement on Subsidies and Countervailing Measures, United States*, G/SCM/N/220/USA, October 5, 2011, p. 15. U.S. Department of Commerce, Fact Sheet, "Commerce Preliminarily Finds Countervailable Subsidization of Crystalline Silicon Photovoltaic Cells, Whether or Not Assembled into Modules from the People's Republic of China," May 20, 2012.

188 "China Doubles Solar Power Target to 10 GW by 2015—Paper," *Reuters Africa*, May 6, 2011, http://af.reuters.com. Keith Bradsher, "China Charges Protectionism in Call for Solar Panel Tariffs," *The New York Times*, October 21, 2011.

189 "Why Is the Sun Setting on China's Solar Power Industry?" *Knowledge@ Wharton*, June 12, 2013.

190 APCO Worldwide, *China's 12th Five-Year Plan*, Beijing, China, December 10, 2010, p. 3.

191 For a discussion of the regulation of strategic industries, see: Roselyn Hsueh, *China's Regulatory State: A New Strategy for Globalization* (Ithaca, Cornell University Press, 2011), 320 p.

192 Judith Banister, "China's Manufacturing Employment And Hourly Labor Compensation, 2002-2009," U.S. Bureau of Labor Statistics website, last modified June 7, 2013. *International Comparisons of Hourly Compensation Costs in Manufacturing, 2009*, U.S. Bureau of Labor Statistics, News release USDL-11-0303, March 18, 2011.

193 Barboza, David, "Supply Chain for iPhone Highlights Costs in China, *The New York Times*, July 5, 2010, (Internet edition). Kingsley-Hughes, Adrian, "Apple Makes Big Bucks Profit Per iPhone 3G S, *Hardware 2.0*, June 25, 2009.

194 An operational definition of industrial policy is government policies that stimulate specific economic activities and promote structural change.

195 For further discussion, see Alan W. Wolff, "China's Industrial Policy and Its Impact on U.S. Companies, Workers,and the American Economy," Prepared Statement of Mr. Alan Wm. Wolff Partner, Dewey & Leboeuf LLP, Hearing Before the U.S.-China Economic and Security Review Commission, 111th Congress, 1st Session, March 24, 2009, p. 18.

196 Reuters, "China Flexing New Anti-monopoly Muscle," *Sidney Morning Herald (Internet edition)*, May 3, 2013.

197 "Chinese Government Raids Microsoft Offices in Four Cities," *The Wall Street Journal*, July 30, 2014. Bruce Einhorn, "What to Expect When You're Targeted by China's Antitrust Cops," *Bloomberg BusinessWeek* (Internet edition), August 8, 2014. Keith Bradsher, "China Fines Japanese Auto Parts and Bearings Makers in Price Rigging," *The New York Times* (Internet edition), August. 20, 2014.

198 Elizabeth Williamson and Tom Barkley, "U.S. Wins China-Tire Fight, Resolving Major Trade Spat, World Trade Organization Backs White House Tariff," *The Wall Street Journal*, December 14, 2010.

199 Doug Young, "China Plays Security Card with Cisco Freeze Out," *Seeking Alpha*, November 15, 2013.

200 Paul Mozur, "Jitters in Tech World Over New Chinese Security Law," *The New York Times* (Internet edition), July 2, 2015.

201 Lauren Dodillet, "IBM to Share its Technology with Chinese Firms," *China Business Review*, April 6, 2015.

202 Jane Perlez and Paul Mozur, "China, Technology and Suspicion," *The New York Times*, February 28, 2015, p.BI.

203 Project-syndicate.org, "China's Turning Point," *eWallstreeter*, February 24, 2011.

204 Mei Junjie, "How Europe should view China's industrial policy," *Europe's World*, October 1, 2013.

205 Dan Steinbock, "China's New Grand Strategy," China-U.S. Focus, November 14, 2013.

206 Minxin Pei, "Think Again: Asia's Rise," *Foreign Policy* (Internet Edition), July/August 2009.

207 Ben Blanchard, "China Says 11 'Terrorists' Killed in New Xinjiang Unrest," *Reuters*, February 14, 2014.

208 Martin Patience, "Making Sense of the Unrest from China's Xinjiang," *BBC News*, March 3, 2014.

209 Ian Johnson, "Chinese Activists Continue Calls for Protests," *New York Times*, February 25, 2011.

210 Paul Carsten. "New Beijing Curbs Leave Apple Book, Film Services in the Dark," *The Washington Post*, April 22, 2016, p. A18.

211 Michael E. Porter, *The Competitive Advantage of Nations* (New York, The Free Press, 1990), p. 682.

212 Dani Rodrik, *Normalizing Industrial Policy*, World Bank, Commission on Growth and Development, Working Paper No. 3, 2008, p. 9.

213 For example, many contend that China's annual expenditures on fixed investment will produce diminishing returns over time, especially because they have tended to cause overcapacity in a number of industries.

214 Standard and Poor's, "Asia-Pacific Economies Face Stiff Test If Another Global Financial Crisis Erupts, Says Reports," September 14, 2011.

215 See Ezra F. Vogel, *Japan as Number One: Lessons for America* (Cambridge, Mass.: Harvard University Press, 1979), 272 p. or Clyde V. Prestowitz, Jr., *Trading Places: How We Are Giving Our Future to Japan and How to Reclaim It* (New York: Basic Books, 1988) 365 p,

216 The data point for one year is the average of the previous, current, and following year.

217 "Tinker, Tailor, Economists Reconsider the Merits of Industrial Policy, but Some Flaws Are Hard to Fix," *The Economist (London)*, October 1, 2011.

218 P. Aghion, M. Dewatripont, L. Du, A. Harrison, and P. Legros, *Industrial Policy and Competition*, World Bank Commission on Growth and Development, June 28, 2011, p. 17.

219 Dani Rodrik, *Normalizing Industrial Policy*, World Bank, Commission on Growth and Development, Working Paper No.3, 2008, p. 8, 17, http://www.growthcommission.org/storage/cgdev/documents/gc-wp-003_web.pdf.

220 For details on state-owned enterprises, see Andrew Szamosszegi and Cole Kyle, *An Analysis of State-Owned Enterprises and State Capitalism in China*, U.S.-China Economic and Security Review Commission, October 26, 2011, http://www.uscc.gov/researchpapers/2011/10_26_11_CapitalTradeSOEStudy.pdf.

221 *China Statistical Yearbook 2013*, Table 14-1.

222 "China's Population to Peak at 1.4 Billion Around 2026," U.S. Census Bureau news release, December 15, 2009.

223 For details, see the NDRC website at http://en.ndrc.gov.cn/.

224 Bruce Einhorn, "What to Expect When You're Targeted by China's Antitrust Cops," *Bloomberg BusinessWeek* (Internet edition), August 8, 2014.

225 "Report on China's Economic, Social Development Plan" (Parts 1-22), *Xinhua* (in English), March 17, 2011.

226 W. Michael Cox and Richard Alm, "Creative Destruction," *The Concise Encyclopedia of Economics*, 2nd edition, The Library of Economics and Liberty.

227 Zhang Ping, *Industrial Restructuring Catalog* (2011 version, in Chinese), National Development and Reform Commission, Decree No. 9, 2011, Beijng, China, April 26, 2011. Matt Velker, "NDRC Publishes New Industry Restructuring Plan," http://China.org.cn, April 26, 2011.

228 "Interim Regulations on Supervision and Management of State-owned Assets of Enterprises," Decree of the State Council of the People's Republic of China, No. 378, May 27, 2003.

229 Hao Yan, "China to Cut Central SOEs to 30-50 in 5 Yrs," *China Daily*, November 1, 2010.

230 "Global 500, the World's Largest Corporations," available at <http://money.cnn.com/magazines/fortune/global500/2013/full_list/>

231 In the United States, foreign direct investment is defined as ownership or control of 10% or more of an enterprise's voting securities. The 10% is considered evidence of a lasting interest or degree of influence over management. The government does not have to own 51% of a company for it to have de facto control of management.

232 Richard McGregor, *The Party: The Secret World of China's Communist Rulers* (Harper Perennial, 2010), p. 204.

233 According to Lenovo's web site, 41.5% of its shares are owned by Legend Holdings; 35% of Legend Holding's shares are held by the Chinese Academy of Sciences. This implies that the Chinese Academy of Sciences holds 14.5% of Lenovo's shares.

234 Derek Scissors, "The Costs of Halting Market Reforms in China," *Foreign Affairs*, May/June 2009, p. 28.

235 Ibid., and Ronald Kirk, *2011 National Trade Estimate Report on Foreign Trade Barriers*, Office of the U.S. Trade Representative, March 2011, p. 85.

236 Barry Naughton, "SASAC and Rising Corporate Power in China," *China Leadership Monitor*, No. 24, Spring 2008, p. 7.

237 World Trade Organization, *Report of the Working Party on the Accession of China*, WT/MIN(01)/3[1], November 1, 2001.

238 Organisation for Economic Co-operation and Development, *State Owned Enterprises and the Principle of Competitive Neutrality, 2009*, Policy Roundtable, DAF/COMP(2009)37, September 20, 2010.

239 "Beijing Pushes State Sector at Expense of private," *The Nikkei Weekly*, July 18, 2011, p. 17.

240 World Trade Organization, "United States—Definitive Anti-Dumping and Countervailing Duties on Certain Products from China," Dispute Settlement: Dispute DS379.

241 Stephen Canner, *U.S. Ramps Up Multilateral Attention on State-Owned Enterprises*, The United States Council for International Business, August 9, 2011.

242 Facts and Details, "China/Local Government in China."

243 American Chamber of Commerce in Shanghai, "China's 12th Five-Year Plan: How it Works & What's in Store," Presentation by Kenneth Jarrett, Chairman for Greater China of APCO Worldwide, March 3, 2011.

244 APCO Worldwide, *China's 12th Five-Year Plan*, Beijing, China, December 10, 2010, p. 3.

245 "Highlights of China's Draft 12th Five-Year Plan," *Xinhua*, March 5, 2011.

246 "Key Targets of China's 12th Five-Year Plan," *Xinhua*, March 5, 2011.

247 Kai Guo and Papa N'Diaye, "Is China's Export-Oriented Growth Sustainable?", IMF Working Paper, August 2009.

248 Pettis estimates that this policy has transferred 5%-10% of China's GDP from households to producers.

249 Peter Thomson, "China Does a '180' on Air Pollution Policy to Combat Its Deadly Smog," Public Radio International, PRI's The World (broadcast), November 11, 2013.

250 Rich, D.Q., Kipen, H.M., Huang, W., Wang, G., Wang., Y., Zhu, P., Ohman-Strickland, P., Hu, M., Philipp, C., Diehl, S.R., Lu, S., Tong, J., Gong, J., Thomas, D., Zhu, T., and Zhang, J., "Association between Changes in Air Pollution Levels during the Beijing Olympics and Biomarkers of Inflammation and Thrombosis in Healthy Young Adults," *Journal of the American Medical Association*, 307(19), 2068-2078, published online, May 15, 2012.

251 Zhang Shuangguang and Zhang Chi, "Chinese Economy and Reform after the 18th CCP National Congress: A Macroeconomic Analysis," *Quarterly Economic Brief*, January 22, 2013.

252 "Profile: Bo Xilai," *BBC News/ China* (online edition), September 21, 2013.

253 Organization for Economic Cooperation and Development, "OECD Convention on Combating Bribery of Foreign Public Officials in International Business Transactions." Entered into force on February 15, 1999.

254 "On China: Beijing's Crackdown on Corruption," *CNN*, October 15, 2013.

255 Chris Buckley, "Chinese Company Shares Details of a Corruption Investigation," *The New York Times*, September 19, 2013.

256 An Baijie, "Corruption will have 'nowhere to hide,'" *China Daily* (online version), March 14, 2014.

257 Ben Hirschler, "Bribery Scandal Slashes GlaxoSmithKline's Chinese Drug Sales," *Reuters*, October 23, 2013. Mark Jenkins, Sunny Chu, and Christopher Meadors, "FCPA Compliance in China," *Lexology*, October 14, 2013.

259 Justin Tan, Shaomin Li and Jun Xia, "When Iron Fist, Visible Hand, and Invisible Hand meet: Firm-level Effects of Varying Institutional Environments in China," *Journal of Business Research* 60 (2007) pp. 786-87.

259 "Summary of the Diamond Model (Porter)," *Value Based Management.net*, accessed November 13, 2013.

260 Richard P. Suttmeier and Xiangkui Yao, "China's IP Transition: Rethinking Intellectual Property Rights in a Rising China," National Bureau of Asian Research Special Report #29, July 2011, pp. 3-4.

261 Austin Ramzy, "A Maker of Bikes Now Makes a Point of Riding Them," New York Times, August 31, 2013, p. A6.

262 Polo, Marco and Rustichello of Pisa, *The Travels of Marco Polo*, Volume 2, Edited Henry Yule and Henri Cordier, The Complete Yule-Cordier Edition, 1903, 1920, The Project Gutenburg Ebook, Kindle location 3761.

263 Cong Cao, Richard P. Suttmeier, and Dennis Fred Simon, "China's 15-Year Science and Technology Plan, *Physics Today*, December 2006, pp. 38.

264 Scott Kennedy, "Indigenous Innovation, Not as Scary as It Sounds," *China Economic Quarterly*, September 2012, p. 15ff.

265 WTO Committee on Government Procurement, "China Announces Next Step in Joining Government Procurement Agreement," WTO: 2012 News Items, July 18, 2012. Frank Ching, "China Revises WTO Procurement Bid," *The China Post*, January 15, 2014.

266 "China Issues Draft Rules on National Indigenous Innovation Product," *International Regulatory Bulletin*, vol. 465 (April 19, 2010).

267 The White House, Office of the Press Secretary, U.S. - China Joint Statement, January 19, 2011. U.S. Department of Commerce, 21st U.S.-China Joint Commission on Commerce and Trade Fact Sheet, December 15, 2010.

268 Ding Qingfen and Lan Lan, "Discriminatory' Govt Procurement Rules Scrapped," *China Daily Online*, BizChina, July 1, 2011, http://www.chinadaily.com.cn/business/2011-07/01/content_12816108.htm.

269 Ronald Kirk, *2012 Special 301 Report*, Office of the United States Trade Representative, April 2012, Section on China, p. 34.

270 U.S. Commercial Service China, "Protecting Your Intellectual Property Rights (IPR) in China," August 15, 2012.

271 U.S. International Trade Commission, "China: Effects of Intellectual Property Infringement and Indigenous Innovation Policies on the U.S. Economy," USITC Publication 4226, May 2011, p. xiv.

272 Business Software Alliance, *Shadow Market, 2011 BSA Global Software Piracy Study*, 9th edition, May 2012, pp. 3-4.

273 Simon Hooper, "The Machine That Can Copy Anything," http://CNN.com, June 2, 2005.

274 Tim Bradshaw and Sarah Mishkin, "Apple Watch Faces Attack of the Clones at CES," *Financial Times*, January 8, 2015.

275 Semiconductor Industry Association, SIA Anti-Counterfeiting Task Force, "Winning the Battle Against Counterfeit Semiconductor Products," August 2013, p. 4-5.

276 Right of a claimant to file a subsequent application in another country for the same invention, design, or trademark effective as of the date of filing the first application.

277 Dan Harris, "Timing Your China Trademark. Not Too Soon and Not Too Late," *China Law Blog*, November 12, 2013.

278 Economist Intelligence Unit, "China, Intellectual Property Law," March 11, 2013.

279 "Chinese Disneyland Rip-off Cleaning Up Copyright Violations?" *Japan Probe*, May 10, 2007.

280 Jiwen Chen, "Intellectual Property: The Amended PRC Patent Law," *The China Business Review*, July-August 2001.

281 "Chinese Patent Litigation: Tips for US Companies," *Law360*, New York, June 19, 2009.

282 *China Statistical Yearbook 2013*, Table 20-54.

283 U.S. Patent Office, "Patent Counts By Origin And Type, Calendar Year 2013."

284 European Patent Office, *Annual Report 2012, Statistics*, <http://www.epo.org/about-us/annual-reports-statistics/annual-report/2012/statistics-trends/granted-patents.html#>

285 Interview by Dick Nanto in Hong Kong, 2011.

286 MWI China Law Offices (McDermott Will & Emery), "Top Ten Chinese Intellectual Property Cases of 2009," August 10, 2010.

287 Virginia L. Carron and Mark Sommers, "Managing Counterfeiting in China," *IP Litigator*, March/April 2004.

288 Kirk, 2012 Special 301 Report, op.cit.

289 Brad Williams and Danielle Mihalkanin, "China's Special Campaign to Combat IPR Infringement," *The China Business Review*, 38.4 (Oct-Dec 2011): pp. 42-45.

290 Sharon Kahn, "Advice on Foiling Chinese Counterfeiters," *Chazen Global Insights*, May 3, 2012.

291 Douglas Clark, "Fighting Counterfeiting in Asia," Lovells, Shanghai memorandum, http://www.jurisdiction.com, undated.

292 Adam Segal, "Curbing Chinese Cyber Espionage." *CNN*, May 9, 2011.

293 Mike McConnell, Michael Chertoff, and William Lynn, "China's Cyber Thievery Is National Policy—And Must Be Challenged," *The Wall Street Journal* (Internet edition), January 27, 2012.

294 Darlene Storm, "America Is Losing the Cybersecurity War; China Hacked Every Major US Company," *Computerworld*, March 28, 2012.

295 The Commission on the Theft of American Intellectual Property, *The IP Commission Report*, Seattle, The National Bureau of Asian Research, 2013,, p. 2.

296 Office of the United States Trade Representative, *2013 Special 301 Report*, May 2013, p. 33. Mandiant, APT1, Exposing One of China's Cyber Espionage Units," c. 2013, pp. 20, 24ff.

297 Daniel R. Russel, "Remarks at 'China's Growing Pains' Conference," The University of Southern California Los Angeles, CA, April 22, 2016.

298 World Trade Organization, *Report of the Working Party on the Accession of China*, WT/MIN(01)/3[1], November 1, 2001.

299 "Geithner Slams China's Intellectual Property Policies," *Reuters*, September 23, 2011.

300 "Data Theft Case May Test U.S. China Ties," *Boston Globe* (Internet edition), September 19, 2011.

301 "China's Price for Market Entry: Give Us Your Technology, Too," *The Wall Street Journal*, February 26, 2004.

302 Kenneth Jarrett and Amy Wendholt. "Transferring Technology to China—Is it Worth It?" *The China Business Review* 37. 2 (Mar/Apr 2010): 20-23,35. "Ten of the Biggest and the Best Manufacturers," *Wind Power Monthly*, June 30, 2015 (Internet Edition).

303 Millward, Steven, "The China R&D Dilemma for Foreign Tech Companies," *TECHINASIA*, August 24,2012.

304 *R&D Magazine*, December 2009, p. 48.

305 "China's R&D Spending Surges 21.9%," *Xinhua* as carried in *ChinaDaily.com. cn*, February 22, 2012.

306 U.S. National Science Board, *Science and Engineering Indicators 2014*, Chapter 4, <http://www.nsf.gov/statistics/seind14/index.cfm/chapter-4/c4s2.htm>

307 Interview by Dick Nanto with Huawei Technology manager, December 2011.

308 Microsoft Research, "About Microsoft Research Asia," and "Bill Gates Congratulates Microsoft Research Asia on Turning 10" (video), accessed November 1, 2012.

309 "Research & Development, Bringing R&D to China," *China Business Review*, March 2008.

310 "China Home to 1,200 Foreign R&D Centers," *People's Daily Online*, March 16, 2010.

311 For an early examination of foreign R&D, see Kathleen Walsh. "Foreign High-Tech R&D in China, Risks, Rewards, and Implications for U.S.-China Relations," The Henry L. Stimson Center, 2003, 142 p.

312 "Management Training, Fancied Up," *China Economic Quarterly*, Fourth Quarter 2003.

313 The amounts in 2005 and 2007 were $636 million and $1,146 million for China, $574 million and $547 million for Singapore, $531 million and $563 million for Italy, and $393 million and $598 million for Brazil, respectively.

314 U.S. National Science Foundation, *Science and Engineering Indicators 2014*, Appendix Table 4-26.

315 Chen Zhao, "IBM Research in China," *Interactions*, March – April 2006, pp. 20-21.

316 IBM, "A Look Inside Research, China Research Lab," http://www.research.ibm.com/about/crl.shtml.

317 Pfizer, "About China R&D Center," Pfizer web site, accessed November 3, 2012, http://www.pfizer.com.cn/research/about_china_rd_center_en.aspx.

318 Li Fangfang, "ABB sets sights on 'designed in China,'" *China Daily*, July 19, 2012 and "Challenges key to ABB's China success," *China Daily*, August 19, 2011.

319 Leslie Hook, "China Wakes Up to Innovation," *Financial Times*, February 11, 2013.

320 Jonathan Woetzel, et.al., "The China Effect on Global Innovation," McKinsey Global Institute, October 2015. 123 p.

321 'Tall poppy' syndrome is when people of genuine merit are resented, attacked, or criticized because their talents or achievements elevate them above or distinguish them from their peers.

322 Henry Makeham, "Beijing and the Reality of International Competition," *East Asia Forum*, May 22, 2009.

323 Facing the global financial crisis in 2008, the Chinese government turned the high-speed rail project into part of its economic stimulus plan.

324 World Bank, *High-Speed Rail: The Fast Track to Economic Development?* July 2010; "China Ousts Rail Minister amid 'Violations' Probe," *Financial Times*, February 14, 2011.

325 "China: A Future on Track," *Financial Times*, September 23, 2010.

326 Kawasaki Heavy Industries, "Joint Venture for Rolling Stock Engineering Company in China," press release, Feb. 22, 2005.

327 "Train Makers Rail against China's High-Speed Designs," *Wall Street Journal*, November 18, 2010; Mure Dickie, "Japan Shoots Itself in Foot on Bullet Train," *Financial Times*, July 8, 2010, FT.com Internet edition.

328 Kenneth Jarrett and Amy Wendholt. "Transferring Technology to China—Is it Worth It?", *The China Business Review* 37. 2 (Mar/Apr 2010): 20-23,35.

329 Jamil Anderlini, "Siemens Boards Chinese Rail Bid," *Financial Times*, March 17, 2010, FT.com Internet edition.

330 "GE, Chinese Railways Ministry Ink Deals Worth $1.4 Billion," BBC Worldwide, January 21, 2011.

331 In February 2011, the Florida governor rejected plans for a high-speed rail project and turned down federal funds.

332 Tom Mitchell, "Planes, Trains and Automobiles — the Chinese Way," *The Financial Times*, Jan 20, 2015.

333 Amy Qin, "China Exports High-Speed Rail Technology to Turkey," *New York Times* (Internet edition), July 28, 2014.

334 "Automobile Industry in China," *Facts and Details*, accessed March 5, 2013, http://factsanddetails.com/china.php?itemid=361.

335 "The End of the Car Is Coming," *Market Watch Update*, February 27, 2014.

336 Deqiang Liu and Yanyun Zhao, "Ownership, Foreign Investment, and Productivity—A Case Study of the Automotive Industry in China," Japan Center for Economic Research Discussion Paper No. 104, August 2006, p. 18.

337 Thomas Hemphill, "China's Dysfunctional Industrial Policy," *Real Clear Markets* (Internet version), May 9, 2013.

338 "12th Five-Year Plan for China's Auto Industry to Make New-Energy Vehicles Priority," *Green Car Congress*, October 29, 2010.

339 "Automobile Industry in China," *Facts and Details*, accessed March 5, 2013, http://factsanddetails.com/china.php?itemid=361.

340 "The Sales and Production of Automobiles Kept a Steady Growth," China Association of Automobile Manufacturers news release, January 14, 2015.

341 Quoted in Jim Mann, *Beijing Jeep: A Case Study of Western Business in China* (Boulder, CO: Westview Press, 1977), p. 296.

342 Alexandra Ho, "China Decade from Having Global Carmaker, Bernstein Says," *Bloomberg News* (Internet edition), February 21, 2013.

343 Mack Chrysler, "Domestic Chinese Auto Makers' Ranks Face Thinning," *WardsAuto* (online edition), December 6, 2011.

344 SAIC Motor website, "Investor Relations/Sales Volume of Vehicles," accessed March 12, 2013, http://www.saicgroup.com/english/tzzgx/jbqk/index.shtml.

345 Information from Changan's web site at http://www.globalchangan.com, accessed in March 2013.

346 Research Group of the Economic Editorial Department, "The Centuries of Painstaking Evolution of Chang'an Automobile—a report from the front line

of the movement 'Go to the Grassroots Level, Transform the Work Style and Change the News Style,'" *Seeking Truth*, online version, July 3, 2012.

347 Information from the FAW Group website and various articles, http://www.faw.com.

348 Wenxian Zhang and Ilan Alon, *A Guide to the Top 100 Companies in China* (Singapore, World Scientific Publishing, 2010) 138.

349 "Dongfeng Motors 2012 Profit Beat Estimates Amid Decreased Sales," *Bloomberg News*, Mar 27, 2013.

350 "Volvo Said to Win China Approval to Begin Making Cars," *Bloomberg News*, March 19, 2013. Joe McDonald, "Volvo Set to Import 'Made in China' Cars To US," *Chicago Tribune/Associated Press*, April 23, 2015.

351 Jianxi Luo, Daniel Roos and John Moavenzadeh, "The Impact of Government Policies on Industrial Evolution: The Case of China's Automotive Industry," A revision of Jianxi Luo's Master Thesis in Technology and Policy, Massachusetts Institute of Technology, August 2006. p. 59. "GM Daewoo-Chery Copyright Suit Settled," *Asia Times Online*, November 22, 2005.

352 "Jaguar Land Rover And Chery Automobile Set Cornerstone For New Chinese Manufacturing Partnership," Jaguar Land Rover press release, November 18, 2012.

353 Jeremy Weber, "Chrysler and Chery 'Mutually Agree' to End Alliance," *Motor Authority* (online), December 8, 2008.

354 "Chery Automobile Drives an Industry Shift," *Wall Street Journal*, March 11, 2011, reprinted in *BizChinaNow.com*.

355 Yu Ning and Liang Dongmei, "Part II: Red Ink No Problem for Subsidized Chery Auto," Caixin online, January 13, 2011, http://english.caixin.cn/2011-01-13/100216509_2.html. Note: exchange rates used were 7.61 yuan per dollar in 2007, 6.95 in 2008, and 6.83 in 2009.

356 "European, American Car Designers Help Chinese Develop Own Style," *Automotive News Europe*, November 27, 2012.

357 Data from U.S. Department of Commerce.

358 "PRC Plans New Auto Export Rules," *Taipei Times* (Internet edition), January 2, 2007.

359 Import data from U.S. Department of Commerce, U.S. Trade Online database. Downloaded October 28, 2015.

360 Shasha Deng, "Boeing Delivers 1,000[th] Airplane to China," *Xinhuanet*, March 29, 2013.

361 Wen Wang, "Airbus Looks to Upstage Boeing with More Deliveries in China," *China Daily*, April 19, 2013.

362 The Chinese government is also attempting to boost its global competitiveness in defense aviation.

363 Commercial Aircraft Corporation of China, Ltd. (COMAC) website, http://english.comac.cc.

364 David Barboza, Christopher Drew and Steve Lohr, "G.E. to Share Jet Technology with China in New Joint Venture," *New York Times*, January 18, 2011, p. BI.

365 GE Aviation, "New C919 Orders Push Total LEAP Orders Past 4,300 Engines," GE Aviation press release, November 14, 2012.

366 Ryanair, "Ryanair and Comac (Commercial Aircraft Corp. of China) Sign C919 MOU in Paris," Ryanair news release, June 21, 2011.

367 *South China Morning Post*, January 19, 2011.

368 "GE's China Avionics Deal: A Q&A with Lorraine Bolsinger," *GE Reports*, January 19, 2011, at http://www.gereports.com/ges-china-avionics-deal-a-qa-with-lorraine-bolsinger.

369 David Barboza, Christopher Drew and Steve Lohr, "G.E. to Share Jet Technology with China," *op. cit.*

370 "Jet Sale Boosts China's Rivalry with Airbus, Boeing," *CNN International*, November 19, 2012.

371 Tiffany Lam, "Chinese Passenger Jet C919 Takes on Boeing and Airbus," *CNN GO*, November 17, 2010.

372 Boeing Corporation, *Current Market Outlook, 2011-2030*, September 2011.

373 "China's Aviation Industry Could Spring a Surprise: Boeing," *WantChinaTimes*, June 20, 2011.

374 Sharon Kahn, "Changing the Recipe for Chinese State-Owned Firms," *Chazen Global Insights*, June 6, 2013.

375 Sun Tzu *The Art of War*, Kindle Edition, October 5, 2012, p. 55..

376 United Nations Conference on Trade and Development, UNCTADSTAT database.

377 *China Statistical Yearbook*, 2013, Table 6-9. Uwe Bott, "The Coming Global Economic Ice Age?" *The Globalist*, August 12, 2013.

378 Richard D'aveni, "China's Economic Cold War on the United States," *U.S. News and World Report Blog*, October 20, 2012.

379 Dhruv Sarda, Michael Ding and Jeffrey Berry, "The Dragons are on the Move: Five Steps to Maximizing Value from Natural Resources M&A," Accenture special report, 2013, p. 4

380 Chris V. Nicholson, "Chinese Oil Company Gets $30 Billion Loan for Acquisitions," *The New York Times* (On-line edition), September 9, 2009.

381 Section 902 of the Foreign Relations Authorization Act, Fiscal Years 1990 and 1991 (P.L. 101-246; 22 U.S.C. 2151 note).

382 Interview by the author of a Vice President of the China Investment Corporation, December 14, 2010.

383 International Center for Settlement of Investment Disputes, "ICSID Database of Bilateral Investment Treaties," accessed September 3, 2013, https://icsid.worldbank.org/ICSID.

384 See Heritage Foundation, http://www.heritage.org/research/projects/china-global-investment-tracker-interactive-map. By the end of 2010, China reported that it had invested $8 billion in Australia, while the Heritage Foundation dataset indicated between 2005 and 2010, Australia received $34 billion in large direct investment projects.

385 Douglas Ferguson and Hans Hendrischke, "Demystifying Chinese Investment in Australia," KPMG and the University of Sidney Report, updated March 2013.

386 Eduardo Morcillo, "Buying "Below the Radar Assets, Chinese Outbound Investments, 2012-2015," *InterChina Insight*, February 15, 2013, p. 2.

387 Shujie Yao, Dylan Sutherland and Jian Chen, "China's Outward FDI and Resource-Seeking Strategy: A Case Study on Chinalco and Rio Tinto," *Asia-Pacific Journal of Accounting & Economics*, vol. 17, 2010, p. 322.

388 Shujie Yao and Dylan Sutherland, "Chinalco and Rio Tinto: The Long March for China's National Champions," The University of Nottingham, China Policy Institute, Briefing Series—Issue 51, July 2009.

389 "Rio Tinto Gets Deeper into China with Chinalco JV, *Forbes*, June 3, 2011, and "Rio Tinto, Chinalco Complete Setting Up Simandou JV," *China Daily*, April 26, 2012.

390 An entity that enjoys the benefits of ownership even though title may be in another name.

391 Thomas Anderson, "Activities of U.S. Affiliates of Foreign Multinational Enterprises in 2012," *Survey of Current Business*, November 2014. p. 6.

392 U.S. Bureau of Economic Analysis, "Foreign Direct Investment in the United States Tables," *Survey of Current Business*, September 2014. p. 30. Derrick T. Jenniges and James J. Fetzer, "Direct Investment Positions for 2014, Country and Industry Detail," *Survey of Current Business*, July 2015, p. 15.

393 Shirley A. Kan, "Long Beach: Proposed Lease by China Ocean Shipping Company (Cosco) at Former Naval Base," Congressional Research Service Report 97-476, August 11, 1999.

394 China Ocean Shipping Company Americas, Inc., "Pacific Maritime Services," http://www.coscoamericas.com/contents/157/220.html, accessed September 9, 2013.

395 Dick K. Nanto, James K. Jackson, and Wayne M. Morrison, "China and the CNOOC Bid for Unocal: Issues for Congress," Congressional Research Service Report RL33093, February 27, 2006.

396 Matthew Karnitschnig, Greg Hitt, and Bobby White, "Harsh Climate in Washington Ices 3Com Deal," *Wall Street Journal*, February 21, 2008, p. CI.

397 Reuters, "Huawei Backs Away from 3Leaf Acquisition," February 19, 2011.

398 Euan Rocha, "CNOOC closes $15.1 billion acquisition of Canada's Nexen," *Reuters*, February 25, 2013.

399 Ken Brown, "France Is Open to Selling Firms to China Buyers," *The Wall Street Journal*, April 28, 2013.

400 Françoise Nicolas, "Chinese Direct Investments in France: No French Exception, No Chinese Challenge," Chatham House IE Programme Paper IE PP 2010/02, January 2010.

401 Nora Chen, "Chinese Investors in Burgundy: Keep a Low Profile," *Jing Daily*, August 30, 2012 (Internet edition). Adam Lechmere, "Outrage over Gevrey Chambertin Purchase 'Storm in a Teacup,'" *Decanter.com*, August 29, 2012.

402 Technische Universität München, "Chinese Companies Investing in Technology Development through Acquisitions" News Release, Munich, April 11, 2013. "New Opportunities for German firms through Chinese Investments," *Research News*, April 11, 2013.

403 "Chinese Investments and Acquisitions in Switzerland," *SwissnexChina*, January 22, 2013.

404 Richard Weitz, "Superpower Symbiosis: The Russia-China Axis," *World Affairs*, November/December 2012.

405 Jane Perlezmay, "China and Russia Reach 30-Year Gas Deal," *The New York Times*, May 21, 2014, p. AI.

406 Brian Spegele, "China to Invest in Russian Fund," *The Wall Street Journal* (Internet edition), October 12, 2011.

407 Jeremy Clegg and Hinrich Voss, "Chinese Overseas Direct Investment in the European Union," Europe China Research and Advice Network, 2012.

408 Interviews by Andy Van Vleck in 2012 in Sweden.

409 Tania O'Conor, "Chinese Investment in Brazil: An Overview of Shifting Trends," *Inter-American Dialogue*, September 9, 2013.

410 "China Banks Get Full Banking Licenses in Singapore," *Xinhua*, October 9, 2012.

411 Tom McGregor, "Singapore Captivates Chinese Investors," *China Daily*, November 19, 2012.

412 Alex Oliver, "The Lowy Institute Poll 2013, Australia and the World," Lowy Institute for International Policy, June 24, 2013.

413 Australia Treasurer, "Australia's Foreign Investment Policy," 2013.

414 Peter Lee, "CITIC Pacific Hit by an Iron Bullet," *Asia Times*, July 23, 2011.

415 Gavin Lower and Andrew Critchlow, "Huawei Voices Dismay at Australia Network Exclusion," *Wall Street Journal (online version)*, March 26, 2012.

416 James K. Jackson, "The Committee on Foreign Investment in the United States (CFIUS)," Congressional Research Report RL33388, March 29, 2013, p. 3ff.

417 White House, Office of the Press Secretary, "Message to the Congress on the China National Aero-Technology Import and Export Corporation Divestiture of MAMCO Manufacturing, Incorporated," White House Message to the Congress, February 1, 1990.

418 U.S. Department of the Treasury, "CFIUS Reform: The Foreign Investment & National Security Act of 2007 (FINSA)," November 14, 2008.

419 John Lettieri, "Understanding the CFIUS Process," Organization for International Investment, c. 2012.

420 James K. Jackson, "The Committee on Foreign Investment in the United States (CFIUS)," op. cit., p. 9ff.

421 Wilson, Sonsini, Goodrich, & Rosati, "CFIUS and Chinese Investment: Lessons Learned from the First Half of 2013," *WSGR ALERT*, August 16, 2013. Michael Bathon, "Wanxiang Wins U.S. Approval to Buy Battery Maker A123," *Bloomberg*, Jan. 30, 2013.

422 Committee on Foreign Investment in The United States, "Annual Report to Congress," Report Period: CY2013, issued February 2015, Public/ Unclassified Version, p. 17.

423 "Chinese Exclusion Act (1882)," Harvard University Open Collections Program, Immigration to the United States, 1789-1930 Collection.

424 Economist Intelligence Unit, "A Brave New World, The Climate For Chinese M&A Abroad," A report from the Economist Intelligence Unit, 2010, p. 17.

425 Thilo Hanemann, "Chinese Investment: Europe vs. the United States," Rhodium Group Research Note, February 25, 2013.

426 Ding Qingfen, Li Jiabao, and Oswald Chen, "Ministry Predicts New Surge in ODI," *China Daily*, January 1, 2012.

427 Daniel H. Rosen and Thilo Hanemann, "An American Open Door? Maximizing the Benefits of Chinese Foreign Direct Investment," Special Report by the Center on U.S.-China Relations (Asia Society) and Kissinger

Institute on China and the United States (Woodrow Wilson International Center for Scholars), May 2011, p. 8.

428 International Monetary Fund, World Economic Outlook Database, updated April 2014.

429 Yukon Huang, "Realizing China's Sustainable Growth Rate," *Financial Times*, October 24, 2014.

430 "Overcapacity Troubles Chinese Economy, Reform Needed," *WantChinaTimes.com*, April 14, 2013.

431 Tracy Alloway, "Why China's Steel Mills Won't Cut Back Production," *Bloomberg Business*, November 24, 2015.

432 John Chan, "Chinese Premier Li Signals New Pro-Market Reforms before European Tour," *World Socialist Web Site*, May 25, 2013.

433 Keith Bradsher, "Chinese Solar Panel Giant Is Tainted by Bankruptcy," *The New York Times*, March 20, 2013. Wayne Ma and Emily Glazer, "Suntech Is Pushed into Chinese Bankruptcy Court," *The Wall Street Journal*, March 20, 2013.

434 Paul Midler, *Poorly Made in China* (Hoboken, NJ, John Wiley and Sons, updated 2011) 245 p.

435 "Understanding Permanent Establishments in China," *China Briefing Magazine*, May 2013.

436 Sheridan Prasso, "Why We Left Our Factories in China," *CNN Money*, June 29, 2011.

437 Ben Klayman, "Aston Martin Recalls 17,590 Cars Due To Counterfeit Material," *Reuters*, February 5, 2014.

438 Matthew Boesler, "Caterpillar Shares Are Falling after It Reveals a Big Accounting Problem at a Chinese Company It Acquired," *Business Insider*, January 22, 2013.

439 Clayton Christensen, *The Innovators Dilemma, When New Technologies Cause Great Firms to Fail* (Boston: Harvard Business Review Press, 1997), 253 p.

440 World Trade Organization, "Trade Policy Review China, Record of the Meeting Addendum, Replies by China to Written Questions," WTO report number WT/TPR/M/264/Add.1, August 22, 2012.

441 Sharon Kahn, "How GE Does Business in China," *Chazen Global Insights*, October 2, 2013.

442 Wouter Baan and Christopher Thomas, "How China Country Heads Are Coping," *McKinsey Quarterly* (Internet edition), October 2015.

443 "Foreign Firms in China, You're Still Welcome." *The Economist* (Internet edition), January 24, 2015.

444 CNBC, Squawk Box, "Uber CEO: Investing in China," April 26, 2016.

Printed in the United States
By Bookmasters